FOURTH EDITION

UNI 150
DESIGNING *your* MAJOR

EXPLORING *MAJORS* & *CAREERS*

ASU MAJOR & CAREER EXPLORATION

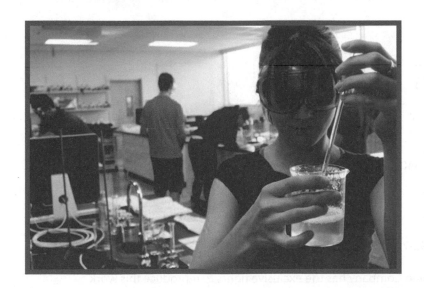

Kendall Hunt
publishing company

Cover image © ASU

Kendall Hunt
publishing company

www.kendallhunt.com
Send all inquiries to:
4050 Westmark Drive
Dubuque, IA 52004-1840

Copyright © 2016, 2017, 2018, 2019 by ASU: Major Career and Exploration

ISBN: 978-1-5249-8992-7

Published in the United States of America

CONTENTS

What Are My Interests?

Learning Objectives

- Recall the names of five classmates

- Understand and recall the expectations and goals for the course

- State and discuss at least two possible purposes of a career

- Identify between 5-10 of your interests

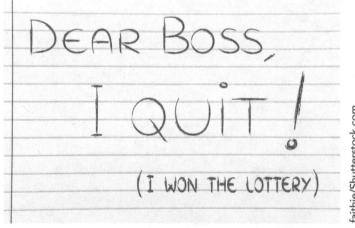

†Work, Life, And The Lottery

Have you noticed how many people dream of winning the lottery, assuming that doing so would instantly and automatically improve the quality of their lives? What would you do if you won the lottery? Let's say that you won enough money to support yourself (and your family, if that's in your picture) in grand style for the rest of your life.

Would you, as a wealthy person, include work in your future? If so, you just might be one of those few who have discovered a rather well-kept secret, but we're getting ahead of ourselves here! (You will have to read on to discover what that is.) If you're sure that you would never work if you didn't have to—why is that? Could it be that you view work as a drudge, an unpleasant activity made necessary perhaps because of original sin, a family or cultural work ethic, or just the basic need to keep bread on the table? Do you see work as a necessary evil that keeps you from what you would rather be doing?

It probably comes as no surprise that most people report that they would quit their jobs without a moment's hesitation should they hit the lottery big time.

Why would anyone freely elect to work, for that matter? There's only one reason, say most people—"to make a buck!" Actually, there are some very good reasons for working, even if you don't have to. Psychological research suggests there are at least five basic motivations for working:[1]

1. income
2. having something to do with our time and energy
3. a way to achieve identity and status
4. a way of having personal and professional relationships
5. a source of meaning in life.

Regardless of the motivations for work, most people still think their lives would be better if they didn't have to work. But consider this group of retirees. They all retired relatively young, in good health, and were financially secure with lots of disposable income. After a few years of travel, visiting, and leisure activities, they began to get restless. One by one, they got part-time jobs, began volunteering, and took up new hobbies. Conversations with them revealed that they missed the sense of structure, the camaraderie, and the sense of purpose and identity that work had given them. The one thing they did have that many of us lack was the choice regarding what to do with their time. Pretend that you were able to "retire" at your current age or that you won the lottery. How would you spend your time?

Imagining what you might do if you won the lottery is actually a productive way to expand your thinking on how to have a more interesting life. Common responses to that question are things like travel, pay off bills, permanently inhabit the beach, do absolutely nothing, and buy a new car/house/wardrobe. If traveling is your answer, think about this: Where would you go? What does traveling really mean to you? How long would you want to do it? And, what would you do when the "bloom" eventually wears off traveling? Or, if your vision involves paying off bills, rushing off to the shopping malls, or simply doing nothing—consider how those things would enhance the total quality of your life.

†From *Your Career Planner*, Eleventh Edition by Cheryl Bonner and Susan Musich. Copyright © 2017 by Kendall Hunt Publishing Company. Reprinted by permission.

Money, in itself, doesn't automatically produce a meaningful life (nor does a life of ease). While we're not advocating poverty here, we are aware that people whose lives have been full and interesting used their time, talents, and energies for work they cared passionately about. This may be what British playwright George Bernard Shaw (1856–1950) had in mind in reporting that he wanted to be totally used up when he died. He wanted to have no unused talents nor unfulfilled life/work desires left in reserve on his last day here. Perhaps Shaw, who needed almost 100 years of vigorous living to achieve his stated desire, was advocating for a fundamental principle of life vitality. Most of us really want to be engaged in things that are interesting and worthwhile!

When you have a vision for the life you really want, ask yourself, "Is there any way I might possibly achieve that without the aid of a big lottery win?" Many of us use money, or the lack of it, as an excuse to avoid going after what we truly want in life. In truth, you already have something more powerful than money. You have natural endowments, including your mind, your creativity, and life energy (maybe even your good looks). Our world could greatly benefit from the cumulative effect of a lot more people pursuing what they care deeply about. Why not be one of them? The next time you're inclined to buy a lottery ticket in hopes of becoming rich, consider instead meditating upon a vision of what a fully engaged and challenging life might be. Note how a career can influence your life in the following table.

A Few Things Your Career Will Dictate or Influence

- Esteem and self-worth
- Talents used and developed
- Interests that are expressed and energized
- Financial resources
- The nature of organizations with which you will associate
- Where you will live
- Lifestyle
- Health and vitality
- Longevity
- Activities you will perform
- Type of knowledge you will acquire

- Kinds of people with whom you will associate
- Time, energy, and resources for:
  - Leisure
  - Family
  - Personal growth
  - Professional growth
- Kinds and levels of responsibilities you will have
- What you will be learning
- Employment contract
- Your friends and associates
- The contributions you make

Defining Career

There are many ways to be engaged in things that are interesting and worthwhile. Paid work is just one of them. We spend a lot of time at work. Ideally, work shouldn't be a means to an end. We shouldn't just work so we have the money to live outside of work. Work, when it engages our unique combination of talents, interests, personality, and values, contributes to meaning and fulfillment. In fact, we believe that it is such an important aspect of our existence that this entire book is written to help you find the type of work that is the best fit for you. However, paid work is just one of the many life roles that we play that make up career.

Donald Super, a person who studied career development in America in the last half of the twentieth century, proposed the idea that a career is really made up of many different life roles.[2] People who are happy in their careers are those who are able to integrate those roles together. Super proposes that we play the following roles: child, student, worker, homemaker, spouse/partner, parent, citizen, and leisurite:

Child

Beginning at birth, this role is played until the death of our parents. Throughout childhood, we play this role for a majority of our time. As we reach adulthood, we may play this role less or more depending upon our family structure. Many people find themselves playing this role more as their parents' age and they need assistance with health care and financial decisions.

Student

Most Americans play this role through formal education from 1st until the 12th grade. The setting for the student role could include public, private, and even home schooling. After completing the formal training, the role is played on and off as individuals pursue advanced degrees, engage in noncredit courses related to work or other life areas or interests, or any other way in which we are involved in learning.

Worker

This refers to the paid work role. It could be a part-time job such as delivering papers or the full-time job of newspaper reporter. This is the role that we will concentrate on throughout this book.

Rawpixel.com/Shutterstock.com

Homemaker

At some point, most people will be responsible for a home, be it a house with the white picket fence, a downtown penthouse, or a college apartment that is shared with three roommates. In the beginning when a person establishes a residence separate from one's parents, this role addresses the various responsibilities of home operation, including decorating, bill paying, food preparation, and maintenance.

Spouse/Partner

This role centers on the building and maintaining of a satisfying long-term relationship with another person. Some people never play this role, others play it until death, while others play it intermittently.

Constantin Stanciu/Shutterstock.com

M. Stasy/Shutterstock.com

Parent

Like some of the other roles, not everyone will choose to play this role. This role involves the activities of raising children. It is a role that is played with the most effort during the child's early years. It begins to taper off as the child becomes more and more independent.

Citizen

Many people give back to their communities in some way. This role addresses the ways in which we participate in our communities. Some people are involved on school boards or other volunteer political offices; others belong to civic groups or seek involvement in local educational or religious communities.

Leisurite

Leisure time seems to be rare in today's society, but how we spend our leisure time can provide balance to the other life roles we play. A person who spends a lot of time with other people in the worker role may elect to spend leisure time alone in activities such as running or hiking. Leisure time also allows for the pursuit of other things that may not be found in the other roles, such as physical activity for a person with a sedentary job or gardening for a person who enjoys physical and aesthetic activities but has no way of integrating them into other life roles.

Super noted that we play these roles throughout our lifetimes. At some points, we may be playing all eight roles. The concept of life-role theory can be exciting. It tells us that career does not just have to be relegated to the 9-to-5 workday, but that career, like the strands of a rope, is the integration of all the roles we play.

When we talk about career, we mean all of it. Not just the paid worker role but the volunteer experiences, families, free-time activities, and more. Like the pieces of a puzzle, when they all fit together, they work to make a complete picture. Most people do not play all of the roles at once, and some do not even play all of the roles during their lifetimes. You may choose not to enter into a serious long-term relationship with another person, or you may choose not to have or adopt children. You may decide that you don't want to spend time in the citizen role. Some people choose not to work for pay so they are able to spend their time taking care of children and a house and participating in volunteer activities. Those people who are happy in the combination of life roles they have selected, according to Super, are those who have found a satisfying career.

This concept is incredibly freeing. People suddenly don't have to get all of their interests, abilities, values, and other needs met in one single occupation. Translated, this means the pressure is off to make one choice that is going to be the perfect decision for the rest of your life. Let's consider the following example. Jane was considering two occupations but was torn because one paid a lot of money (a value) while the other allowed a greater contribution to society (another value). Since these two values seemed to carry equal weight, there didn't seem to be a best answer other than to explore other occupations. When Jane considered the options based on the life-role theory, she decided to pursue the occupation that paid more money as her worker role, but began to volunteer in the community youth center as her citizen role. Jane found a job she really liked and was able to meet the one missing value through her volunteer activities.

What about you? Do you feel pressure to select the one right career that is going to be the be-all and end-all? Do you believe that you have the freedom to express yourself and find satisfaction in a variety of different roles? Our life roles allow us to explore career choices as well. A volunteer opportunity at a local vegetable co-op might pave the way for a career in horticulture. Saturdays at a homeless shelter might open the possibility of a career in psychology, social work, or even politics as you seek to find ways to alleviate poverty, not just help support those in this situation. How are you using your various life roles to explore careers and discover your passions?

A Personal Guide

But how do you discover what a deeply fulfilling life and career would consist of? How can you know what your unique interests and best potentials really are? How do you find a meaningful career? Clearly, these are perplexing questions for everyone. But don't give up; there is hope. A willingness to seriously address questions such as these is an important step in getting answers. Remember that career in terms of paid work may not be singularly satisfying. Use this book to guide you in your quest for greater self-understanding so that you can make a career choice that is best for you, but be aware that some of the deeper questions of life and meaning and purpose may not be found in getting a better job. Other books are available on these topics of spirituality, love, and personal acceptance. Dick Bolles writes that most of us move from "I need to find a job that I like" to "I need to find my purpose in life." He offers that these are deeper questions of the heart that are unique to each of us and probably won't be answered through a book such as this.

As we consider our lives, we are often quick to run to our families or friends to find the answers. We forget that we may actually be able to find the answers within ourselves. We come to this life equipped with a wise inner guide. Unfortunately, far too few of us ever consult with or pay attention to our own inner counsel. We're just too busy and preoccupied with the sights, sounds, and activities of the outer world. Devoting quiet time for self-reflection directed to important life and career questions can lead to "discernment." Discernment comes from the Latin word *discernere*, which means "to separate, to distinguish, to determine, to sort out."[3] Intuition is a human capacity, a form of intelligence accessible only in the vast reaches of our quiet minds. Accessing it involves asking the hard and specific questions of ourselves, tuning out the loud music and other outer-worldly distractions vying for our attention, and tuning into the quiet consultation of our inner guidance system.

Lifelong Career Decision-Making

Many people think of career choice as a simple act governed by the single-minded logic of getting a good job. If you're a college student or a re-careering adult, your career-selection logic might be to complete an academic program that leads to a top-paying job, regardless of what the job might be. Such a motivation involves this potentially dangerous assumption: When I get a job with a high salary, my life will fall into place.

There is far more to life than a high-salaried job. We have seen too many people whose single-minded focus on a high-paying job has brought them to the sobering realization that their jobs have come to control their lives. That might be OK if you love your job, but what if you don't? What if you find it doesn't utilize and develop your talents and/or engage your interests? What if it conflicts with your core values? What if you become a fast-track manager and then one day are stunned to realize that your kids are being brought up by their nanny because you've been too engaged in work? For reasons such as these, we urge you, regardless of your life stage, to give the process of creating your future serious attention.

Career/life decision-making is an ongoing and lifelong process because we're going to be faced with important life and work choices for as long as we're around. In a way, our lives are like books of many chapters. Your book of life has some past chapters and many more, we hope, in the future. Your career and life book probably has some overall general direction (a storyline) to it with major and minor themes emerging and fading. We write our books one chapter at a time. Here we are concerned about your future chapters, especially the next one.

Career and life decision-making involves work in two realms—the inner universe of self and the outer world of possibilities. Exploring the inner realm involves assessment and self-discovery, particularly in identifying and defining those interests, values, and skills you identify as important to your future. The outer universe of work requires that you learn about possibilities and options available and suited to your unique talents and attributes—now and in the future.

As you become involved in this process of writing the next career chapter of your life, you may feel restricted by any number of circumstances and conditions that appear to be limiting your options. If so, please bear this in mind: The work world is huge, multidimensional, and ever changing. We'll have more to say about overcoming your barriers later on, but for now keep this simple truth in mind: There are always more opportunities than any single individual, on his or her own, can possibly be aware of. So, whether or not you are currently more motivated by material success than inner values, here is your best strategy: Find a career direction that you could really enjoy and that would capitalize on your top strengths and personal assets.

Jobs and Careers

The term *career* is often misunderstood. Often you hear the terms *career* and *job* used interchangeably. We think of *job* as employment. It's what somebody is paying you to do. Jobs have traditionally been viewed as long-term positions for which we were hired, given titles, and provided an annual salary along with some associated benefits. Traditionally, jobs came with job descriptions. These defined what kinds of tasks and responsibilities you did and did not do (That's my job! That's not my job!). If we are to believe futurist thinkers such as William Bridges, author of *Job Shift*,[4] and Jeremy Rifkin, author of *The End of Work*,[5] jobs are disappearing! The concept of job came in with, and now may be going out with, the industrial era. We may need, therefore, to begin thinking of employment in a very different way. William Bridges advocates thinking of ourselves as contracting agents with expertise suited to particular kinds of work for hire.[6]

A *career* implies that you have prepared for and are building expertise and experience in a particular field, trade, or business endeavor. *Career* defines the general nature of work that you see yourself prepared (or preparing yourself) to perform. *Career* serves as a frame of reference for the kinds of work you will seek, qualify for, and accept. It is also the context in which you will continue to develop new skills and insights. Ben Affleck's career is acting; he's had a number of jobs making specific movies. An airline mechanic may master her trade (career) through a combination of training and supervised work experiences and obtain employment (jobs) with various airlines throughout her career.

Career And Self-Concept

From our earliest days, we get personality programming and career-image shaping messages from our families, cultures, and social environments. As we develop, we acquire an image of ourselves, a self-concept. Most of us are not even consciously aware that we possess one, but it's there, and it is very likely to be reflected in our behaviors and actions. The important point here is that we unconsciously seek jobs and pursue careers to match our inner self-image. For example, people who acquire self-images that are neat, well-organized, and good with numbers may seek careers as accountants or actuaries

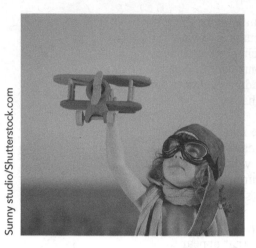

Sunny studio/Shutterstock.com

(these are the folks possessing statistical skills who do things like compute insurance rates and analyze how likely we are to have an accident if we own a small red sports car with a great big engine). Those who develop an intellectual's self-concept may pursue professions featuring rigorous mental concentration such as law, physics, or literary scholarship. Those who acquire a nurturer's self-view may track themselves toward career roles as social worker, nurse, or vocational rehabilitation therapist.

Unwitting career selection works well for some, but not for all. The problem is that our self-concept may evolve from an inaccurate understanding of our true nature. Some of us acquire self-limiting and handicapping concepts in the form of lack of self-confidence. From an early age, self-concepts begin developing in response to what we hear our parents and elders say about us, such as "Isn't she just the perfect little mother," or "He's just like his father" (when Father is a lawyer, or stone mason), or "He's going to be a super athlete," or "She's a mental wizard." When others make observations, either negative or positive, they influence the shaping of our youthful self-image.

A poor self-concept undermines your career development as well as your life satisfaction. Fortunately, we can change our self-concept over time and through conscious attention. By taking a more deliberate and systematic approach to determining your skills, personal traits, preferences, needs, and values, you can bring your self-image into line with your true abilities and desires. You can also greatly enhance your self-confidence by knowing what you are particularly good at and what you can achieve with your talents and abilities. The payoff for generating an accurate self-concept can be tremendously gratifying. This kind of self-knowledge can guide you through appropriate employment and career changes, make you more resilient in dealing with life's challenges, and guide you in finding a sense of security within yourself, even in difficult times.

The observations of others can provide a wealth of information when taken in the right context. When people blindly follow the ideas that others have for their lives without taking into account any potential cultural, personal, or other biases, they run the risk of following careers that are not well suited for them. However, the opinions of others can give you clues about your personality, temperament, strengths, and talents that you may not naturally realize. Take a minute to reflect on the feedback you have been given from those you respect. Think of observations or suggestions that they have made and write them in the space below. For example, reflect on things your family has noticed about you. Perhaps they think that you are a great cook, good with little kids, skilled with technology, a talented speaker, a loyal friend… all of these will provide you with insights into potential careers. Bosses, teachers, and friends also have given you feedback. Before you move on, take a minute to quickly jot down these observations.

Family:

_____

_____

_____

Teachers:

_____

_____

_____

Supervisors:

_____

_____

_____

Friends:

_____

_____

_____

Others:

_____

_____

_____

Positive Mental Imaging

Negative thinking undermines decision-making ability. Could you conceive of anyone performing successfully as a decision maker if his view of the world allowed him to see only mediocre and/or uninviting options? People able to see a future filled with interesting opportunities willingly invest in effective decision-making.

As you begin this decision-making process, we offer you a challenge. See if you can entertain a viewpoint that the future presents you with limitless possibility and that your opportunities now are greater than at any time in history. Try out the assumption that the future will present you with continual opportunities for such things as:

- discovering just how excellent you are capable of becoming;
- growing and developing in ways you've barely dared to dream about;
- making satisfying contributions;
- creating and operating your own business;
- working from your high-tech cottage on a mountaintop;
- becoming a cyberspace citizen of the world.

It may be worth noting here that there are many kinds of work that you would dislike and/or not perform very successfully. There are also many types of work that you would fully enjoy and in which you could thrive. The kind of work that fits us depends upon our uniqueness. We have different fingerprints and different interests. We are also uniquely talented. Fortunately, there are many different kinds of work available now, and there will be even more in the future.

Career Decision-Making

In spite of the critically important role that career plays in life, most people slip into careers and their associated lifestyles with very little forethought or preparation. In fact, most of us spend more time selecting new clothes or a new car than we do in deciding upon our careers. Based on years of experience in assisting career seekers and job hunters, career planning specialist Richard Bolles concludes that most people choose their occupation absentmindedly, and make career decisions in haphazard fashion—without awareness that there are real alternatives from which to choose.[7]

Making a decision is required whenever we are faced with more than one alternative or confronted with unsettling circumstances. Whether we rationally or intuitively settle these questions or reach our conclusions consciously or unconsciously, we have made our

Rawpixel.com/Shutterstock.com

decision. Many of us are afraid of decision-making. Actually, we're probably afraid of making a wrong choice or even one that's less than perfect. For these reasons, too many of us look for others to tell us what to do, while others of us master procrastination, and some of us even put off coming to a decision indefinitely.

Unfortunately, avoiding decisions does not result in eliminating risks or unwanted outcomes. At best, not making a decision results in keeping things the way they are, and at worst, we miss a window of opportunity to avoid an unpleasant result or set the stage for a good outcome. This is true even with everyday decisions. For example, if you stay at home on a Saturday evening because you can't decide whether to go to the movies, see a play, go bowling, or visit a friend, the result is the same as deciding to stay at home. Incidentally, staying at home by choice feels much better than staying at home out of default because you couldn't make up your mind.

In a more serious vein, what are the consequences to people in jobs they hate (or an academic program that does not suit them) when they do nothing to change? The result of indecision is predictable. They are, in effect, deciding to stay with an unsatisfactory situation. By not deciding, you forfeit the opportunity of achieving a better outcome.[8] In a sense, you give up your control of the situation. Your performance, self-confidence, and attitude could suffer as a result.[†]

<table>
<tr><td>

Holland's Basic Categories of Career Interests

- Realistic
- Investigative
- Artistic
- Social
- Enterprising
- Conventional

</td></tr>
</table>

*Exploring Your Interests

Interests are simply what a person likes to do. As interests are developed, they can become a passion. Research shows that students who choose a major that matches their interests are more likely to earn high grades and finish their degrees.[9] It is difficult to be gritty if you are not interested in what you are doing. After college, people are more satisfied with their jobs if it matches their interests. If you like your job, both your job performance and life satisfaction increase.

How do you learn about your interests? Interests are a result of many factors, including personality, family life, values, and interaction with the environment. Part of developing an interest is trying new things and sticking with them for a while to find out if they match your interests. Participating in extracurricular activities, volunteering, internships, and working part time while in college can help you to explore your interests. One barrier to discovering your interests is unrealistic expectations. Often students are expecting the perfect job; however, every job has enjoyable aspects and aspects you don't like.

Another way to explore your interests is through vocational interest assessments. By studying people who are satisfied with their careers, psychologists have been able to help people choose careers based on their interests. The U.S. Department of Labor has developed the O*Net Interest Profiler, which helps to identify your career interests.[10] The O*Net Interest Profiler is compatible with Holland's Theory of Vocational Personality. This is one of the most widely accepted approaches to vocational choice. According to the theory, there are six vocational personality types. These six types and their accompanying definitions are presented below. As you read through each description, think about your own interests.

Realistic

People with **realistic** interests like work activities that include practical, hands-on problems and solutions. They enjoy dealing with plants, animals, and real-world materials like wood, tools, and machinery. They enjoy outside work. Often people with realistic interests do not like occupations that mainly involve doing paperwork or working closely with others.

Investigative

People with **investigative** interests like work activities that have to do with ideas and thinking more than with physical activity. They like to search for facts and figure out problems mentally rather than to persuade or lead people.

Artistic

People with **artistic** interests like work activities that deal with the artistic side of things, such as forms, designs, and patterns. They like self-expression in their work. They prefer settings where work can be done without following a clear set of rules.

Social

People with **social** interests like work activities that assist others and promote learning and personal development. They prefer to communicate more than to work with objects, machines, or data. They like to teach, give advice, help, or otherwise be of service to people.

Enterprising

People with **enterprising** interests like work activities that have to do with starting up and carrying out projects, especially business ventures. They like persuading and leading people and making decisions. They like taking risks for profit. These people prefer action rather than thought.

Conventional

People with **conventional** interests like work activities that follow set procedures and routines. They prefer working with data and detail rather than with ideas. They prefer work in which there are precise standards rather than work in which you have to judge things by yourself. These people like working where the lines of authority are clear.

    According to Holland, most individuals can be described by one or more of these six personality types, frequently summarized as R-I-A-S-E-C (the first letter of each personality type). Additionally, the theory proposes that there are six corresponding work environments (or occupational groups), and that people seek out work environments that match their personality types. The better the match individuals make, the more satisfied they will be with their jobs.[11]

    Holland arranged these interests on a hexagon that shows the relationship of the interests to one another. He notes that most people are not just one type, but rather a combination of types. Types that are close to each other on the hexagon are likely to have interests in common. For example, a person who is social is likely to have some artistic interests and some enterprising interests. Interests on opposite points of the hexagon are very different. For example, artistic and conventional types are opposites. Artistic types prefer freedom to be creative; conventional types prefer structure and order. The figure that follows illustrates the relationship between interest areas.[12]

Interests and Lifestyle

Our occupational interests determine what we study and the kinds of occupations we choose. While study and work form the basis of our lifestyle, there are other important components. What we choose to do for fun and relaxation helps us to be refreshed and keeps life interesting. Another component of a balanced lifestyle is time spent with friends and family. It is important to choose work that allows you to have the resources and time to lead a balanced lifestyle with all of these components. A balanced lifestyle has been

> "The only way to do great work is to love what you do."
> Steve Jobs

> "Even if you're on the right track, you'll get run over if you just sit there."
> Will Rogers

> "Real success is finding your life work in work that you love."
> David McCullough

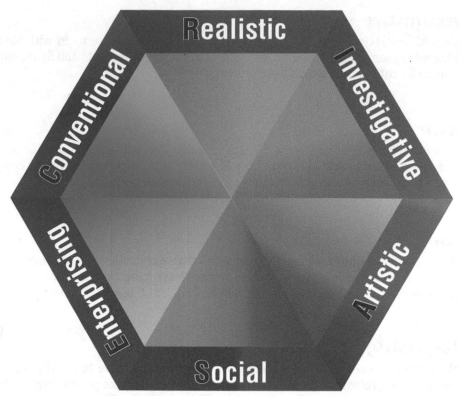

Figure 1.1 Relationships between interest areas.
© Kendall Hunt Publishing Company

described as a triangle with work and study forming the base, leisure and recreation forming one side, and kinship and friendship forming the other side.

Give some thought to the kind of lifestyle you prefer. Think about balancing your work, leisure, and social activities.

†Comparison of the Personality Types

	Realistic	Investigative	Artistic	Social	Enterprising	Conventional
Characteristics	Stable Physical Practical Frank Self-reliant	Analytical Independent Curious Intellectual Precise	Imaginative Idealistic Original Expressive Impulsive	Cooperative Understanding Helpful Tactful Sociable	Persuasive Domineering Energetic Ambitious Flirtatious	Conscientious Orderly Persistent Conforming Efficient
Likes	Outdoor work Mechanics Athletics Working with plants, tools, and animals	Abstract problems Science Investigation Unstructured situations Mind work	Ideas Self-expression Creativity Unstructured situations Working alone	People Attention Discussion Helping Socializing	Power People Status Persuading Managing	Order Detail work Organizing Structure Working with data
Dislikes	Theory Self-expression Working with people	Repetitive activities Close supervision Working with People	Structure Rules Physical work Details Repetitive activities	Physical work Working with tools Working outdoors Solitary activities	Systematic activities Precise work Concentrated intellectual work	Unsystematized activities Lack of structure Ambiguity
Preferred skills	Building Repairing Making and growing things Operating equipment	Problem solving Analytical reasoning Developing models and systems	Creating Visualizing Unstructured tasks Imagining Idea generating	Interpersonal activities Establishing rapport Communicating Helping	Leading Managing Persuading Motivating others	Detailed tasks Following directions precisely Repetitive tasks
	Realistic	Investigative	Artistic	Social	Enterprising	Conventional

(continued)

Realistic	Investigative	Artistic	Social	Enterprising	Conventional
Thomas Edison	Albert Einstein	Alex Haley	Helen Keller	Henry Ford	E. F. Hutton
The Wright Brothers	Sherlock Holmes	Ludwig von Beethoven	Carl Menninger	Winston Churchill	Dr. Watson (Sherlock Holmes' assistant)
Antonio Stradivari	Marie Curie	Michelangelo	Florence Nightingale	Martin Luther King, Jr.	
Johannes Gutenberg	Sigmund Freud	Luciano Pavarotti	Mother Theresa	Nelson Mandela	Noah Webster (dictionary)
Neil Armstrong	Charles Darwin	William Shakespeare	Mahatma Gandhi	Oprah Winfrey	Melvil Dewey (Dewey decimal system)
Amelia Earhart	Dr. Jonas Salk	Mikhail Baryshnikov	Coretta Scott King	Madeleine Albright	Carolus Linnaeus (botanist)
Arthur Ashe	Stephen Hawking	Emily Dickinson	Desmond Tutu	General George Patton	Miss Manners
Michael Jordan	Mark Zuckerberg	Frank Lloyd Wright	Mr. Rogers	Walt Disney	Charles Schwab
Phil Mickelson	Steve Wozniak	Maya Angelou	Lucy	Steve Jobs	Marcie
Willy Mays	Linus	Stevie Wonder		Mark Cuban	
Pele		Elton John		Bill Gates	
Peppermint Patty		Toni Morrison		Snoopy	
		Charles Shultz			
		J.K. Rowling			
		Schroder			

People who characterize the styles

¹From *Your Career Planner*, Eleventh Edition by Cheryl Bonner and Susan Musich. Copyright © 2017 by Kendall Hunt Publishing Company. Reprinted by permission.

ACTIVITY

*The Interest Profiler[13]

Place a checkmark next to the items in each list that you might **like to do**. Keep a positive attitude when thinking about your interests. You do not need to know how to do these activities or have the opportunity to do them to select items that you might like to do in the future. Also, be careful not to select an activity just because it is likely to produce higher income. You can earn higher income by increasing your skills and education in these areas. For example, if you would like to build a brick walkway, you could work in construction, or with more education, become a civil engineer. Just indicate what you would enjoy doing. Remember that this is not a test and that there are no right or wrong answers to the questions. The goal is for you to learn more about your personal career interests and related occupations.

When you are finished with each section, tally the number of checkmarks in each area. Sample job titles for each area of interest are included. Underline any jobs that appeal to you. You can also match your interests to over 900 occupations listed at O*Net Online (https://www.onetonline.org/find/descriptor/browse/Interests/). This site includes information on specific occupations, including work tasks; tools and technology; knowledge, skills, and abilities required; work activities and work context; level of education required; work styles; work values; and wages and employment information.

Realistic (R)

I would like to:

_____ Build kitchen cabinets

_____ Guard money in an armored car

___✓___ Operate a dairy farm

_____ Lay brick or tile

_____ Monitor a machine on an assembly line

_____ Repair household appliances

_____ Drive a taxi cab

_____ Install flooring in houses

___✓___ Raise fish in a fish hatchery

_____ Build a brick walkway

_____ Assemble electronic parts

_____ Drive a truck to deliver packages to offices and homes

_____ Paint houses

___✓___ Enforce fish and game laws

_____ Operate a grinding machine in a factory

_____ Work on an offshore oil-drilling rig

_____ Perform lawn care services

_____ Assemble products in a factory

___✓___ Catch fish as a member of a fishing crew

_____ Refinish furniture

_____ Fix a broken faucet

_____ Do cleaning or maintenance work

___✓___ Maintain the grounds of a park

_____ Operate a machine on a production line

_____ Spray trees to prevent the spread of harmful insects

_____ Test the quality of parts before shipment

_____ Operate a motorboat to carry passengers

_____ Repair and install locks

_____ Set up and operate machines to make products

_____ Put out forest fires

R = 5

Matching Job Titles for Realistic Interests[14]

Construction worker, building contractor, cook, landscaper, housekeeper, janitor, firefighter, hazardous materials removal worker, security guard, truck driver, automotive mechanic, cardiovascular technologist, civil engineer, commercial pilot, computer support specialist, plumber, police officer, chemical engineer, fish and game warden, surveyor, archaeologist, athletic trainer, dentist, veterinarian

Investigative (I)

I would like to:

_✓_ Study space travel

_✓_ Make a map of the bottom of an ocean

_____ Study the history of past civilizations

_✓_ Study animal behavior

_____ Develop a new medicine

_✓_ Plan a research study

_✓_ Study ways to reduce water pollution

_____ Develop a new medical treatment or procedure

_____ Determine the infection rate of a new disease

_____ Study rocks and minerals

_____ Diagnose and treat sick animals

_____ Study the personalities of world leaders

_____ Conduct chemical experiments

_✓_ Conduct biological research

_____ Study the population growth of a city

_✓_ Study whales and other types of marine life

_____ Investigate crimes

_✓_ Study the movement of planets

_____ Examine blood samples using a microscope

_____ Investigate the cause of a fire

_____ Study the structure of the human body

_____ Develop psychological profiles of criminals

_____ Develop a way to better predict the weather

_✓_ Work in a biology lab

_____ Invent a replacement for sugar

_____ Study genetics

_____ Study the governments of different countries

_✓_ Do research on plants or animals

_____ Do laboratory tests to identify diseases

_____ Study weather conditions

I = 10

Matching Job Titles for Investigative Interests

Electronic engineering technician, emergency medical technician, fire investigator, paralegal, police detective, engineer (aerospace, biomedical, chemical, electrical, computer, environmental, or industrial), chemist, computer systems analyst, geoscientist, market research analyst, anesthesiologist, biochemist, biophysicist, clinical psychologist, dietician, physician, microbiologist, pharmacist, psychiatrist, surgeon, veterinarian, science teacher, college professor

Artistic (A)

I would like to:

_____ Conduct a symphony orchestra

_____ Write stories or articles for magazines

_____ Direct a play

_____ Create dance routines for a show

_____ Write books or plays

_____ Play a musical instrument

(Continued)

_____	Perform comedy routines in front of an audience	_____	Audition singers and musicians for a musical show
_____	Perform as an extra in movies, plays, or television shows	✓	Design sets for plays
_____	Write reviews of books or plays	_____	Announce a radio show
_____	Compose or arrange music	_____	Write scripts for movies or television shows
_____	Act in a movie	_____	Write a song
_____	Dance in a Broadway show	_____	Perform jazz or tap dance
✓	Draw pictures	_____	Direct a movie
_____	Sing professionally	_____	Sing in a band
_____	Perform stunts for a movie or television show	✓	Design artwork for magazines
_____	Create special effects for movies	_____	Edit movies
_____	Conduct a musical choir	_____	Pose for a photographer
_____	Act in a play		
✓	Paint sets for plays		

$$A = 4$$

Matching Job Titles for Artistic Interests

Model, actor, fine artist, floral designer, singer, tile setter, architectural drafter, architect, dancer, fashion designer, film and video editor, hairdresser, makeup artist, museum technician, music composer, photographer, self-enrichment education teacher, art director, broadcast news analyst, choreographer, editor, graphic designer, landscape architect, creative writer, public relations specialist, teacher (of art, drama, or music)

Social (S)

I would like to:

✓	Teach an individual an exercise routine	_____	Perform rehabilitation therapy
_____	Perform nursing duties in a hospital	_____	Do volunteer work at a nonprofit organization
_____	Give CPR to someone who has stopped breathing	_____	Help elderly people with their daily activities
_____	Help people with personal or emotional problems	_____	Teach children how to play sports
✓	Teach children how to read	_____	Help disabled people improve their daily living skills
_____	Work with mentally disabled children		
✓	Teach an elementary school class	_____	Teach sign language to people with hearing disabilities
_____	Give career guidance to people		
✓	Supervise the activities of children at a camp	_____	Help people who have problems with drugs or alcohol
_____	Help people with family-related problems	_____	Help conduct a group therapy session
		_____	Help families care for ill relatives

_____ Provide massage therapy to people

_____ Plan exercises for disabled patients

_____ Counsel people who have a life-threatening illness

_____ Teach disabled people work and living skills

_____ Organize activities at a recreational facility

_____ Take care of children at a day care center

_____ Organize field trips for disabled people

_____ Assist doctors in treating patients

_____ Work with juveniles on probation

_____ Provide physical therapy to people recovering from injuries

_____ Teach a high school class

$$S =$$

Matching Job Titles for Social Interests

Host, hostess, bartender, lifeguard, food server, child care worker, home health aide, occupational therapist, occupational therapist aide, personal and home care aide, physical therapist, physical therapist aide, veterinary assistant, dental hygienist, fitness trainer, medical assistant, nanny, teacher (preschool, kindergarten, elementary, middle, or high school), registered nurse, respiratory therapist, self-enrichment education teacher, tour guide, mediator, educational administrator, health educator, park naturalist, probation officer, recreation worker, chiropractor, clergy, counseling psychologist, social worker, substance abuse counselor, physician assistant, speech and language pathologist

Enterprising (E)

I would like to:

_____ Buy and sell stocks and bonds

_____ Manage a retail store

_____ Sell telephone and other communication equipment

_____ Operate a beauty salon or barber shop

_____ Sell merchandise over the telephone

_____ Run a stand that sells newspapers and magazines

_____ Give a presentation about a product you are selling

_____ Buy and sell land

_____ Sell compact discs at a music store

_____ Run a toy store

_____ Manage the operations of a hotel

_____ Sell houses

_____ Sell candy and popcorn at sports events

_____ Manage a supermarket

_____ Manage a department within a large company

_____ Sell a soft drink product line to stores and restaurants

_____ Sell refreshments at a movie theater

_____ Sell hair-care products to stores and salons

_____ Start your own business

_____ Negotiate business contracts

_____ Represent a client in a lawsuit

_____ Negotiate contracts for professional athletes

_____ Be responsible for the operation of a company

_____ Market a new line of clothing

_____ Sell newspaper advertisements

_____ Sell merchandise at a department store

_____ Sell automobiles

_____ Manage a clothing store

_____ Sell restaurant franchises to individuals

_____ Sell computer equipment to a store

$$E =$$

(Continued)

Matching Job Titles for Enterprising Interests

Cashier, food worker, customer service representative, sales worker, supervisor, gaming dealer, inspector, retail sales clerk, chef, food service manager, operations manager, real estate broker, realtor, sheriff, wholesale or retail buyer, advertiser, appraiser, construction manager, criminal investigator, financial manager, insurance sales agent, meeting and convention planner, personal financial advisor, sales engineer, judge, lawyer, business or political science teacher, educational administrator, librarian, medical health manager, treasurer, controller

Conventional (C)

I would like to:

_____ Develop a spreadsheet using computer software

_____ Proofread records or forms

_____ Use a computer program to generate customer bills

_____ Schedule conferences for an organization

_____ Keep accounts payable/receivable for an office

_____ Load computer software into a large computer network

_____ Transfer funds between banks using a computer

_____ Organize and schedule office meetings

_____ Use a word processor to edit and format documents

_____ Operate a calculator

_____ Direct or transfer phone calls for a large organization

_____ Perform office filing tasks

_____ Compute and record statistical and other numerical data

_____ Generate the monthly payroll checks for an office

_____ Take notes during a meeting

_____ Keep shipping and receiving records

_____ Calculate the wages of employees

_____ Assist senior-level accountants in performing bookkeeping tasks

_____ Type labels for envelopes and packages

_____ Inventory supplies using a handheld computer

_____ Develop an office filing system

_____ Keep records of financial transactions for an organization

_____ Record information from customers applying for charge accounts

_____ Photocopy letters and reports

_____ Record rent payments

_____ Enter information into a database

_____ Keep inventory records

_____ Maintain employee records

_____ Stamp, sort, and distribute mail for an organization

_____ Handle customers' bank transactions

C =

Matching Job Titles for Conventional Interests

Cashier, cook, janitor, landscaping worker, resort desk clerk, medical records technician, medical secretary, bookkeeping and accounting clerk, dental assistant, drafter, loan officer, paralegal, pharmacy technician, purchasing agent, accountant, auditor, budget analyst, city and regional planner, computer security specialist, cost estimator, credit analyst, database administrator, environmental compliance inspector, financial analyst, geophysical data technician, librarian, proofreader, computer science teacher, pharmacist, statistician, treasurer

Summing Up Your Results

Put the number of checkmarks from each section of the Interest Profiler on the lines that follow:

_____ Realistic   _____ Social

_____ Investigative   _____ Enterprising

_____ Artistic   _____ Conventional

What are your top three areas of interest? (Realistic, Investigative, Artistic, Social, Enterprising, Conventional?)

1. _____

2. _____

3. _____

REFLECTION

List your top three areas of interest from the Interest Profiler above (realistic, investigative, social, enterprising, or conventional). Go to https://www.onetonline.org/find/descriptor/browse/Interests/ and click on your highest interests to find matching careers. List one matching career and briefly describe the education required, salary, and projected growth for the career. Here is an easy outline:

My top three interests on the Interest Profiler are . . .

One career that matches my interests is . . .

The education required is . . .

The median salary is . . .

Interests and Lifestyle

Our occupational interests determine what we study and the kinds of occupations we choose. While study and work form the basis of our lifestyle, there are other important components. What we choose to do for fun and relaxation helps us to be refreshed and keeps life interesting. Another component of a balanced lifestyle is time spent with friends and family. It is important to choose work that allows you to have the resources and time to lead a balanced lifestyle with all of these components. A balanced lifestyle has been described as a triangle with work and study forming the base, leisure and recreation forming one side, and kinship and friendship forming the other side.

Give some thought to the kind of lifestyle you prefer. Think about balancing your work, leisure, and social activities.

In seeking to accomplish lifetime goals, sometimes people are not successful because they place too much emphasis on work, study, leisure, or social life. How would you balance work, study, leisure, and social life to achieve your lifetime goals?

Interests

Test what you have learned by selecting the correct answers to the following questions.

1. Realistic people are likely to choose a career in

    a. construction or engineering.
    b. accounting or real estate.
    c. financial investments or banking.

2. Investigative people are likely to choose a career in

    a. art or music.
    b. teaching or social work.
    c. science or laboratory work.

3. Enterprising people are likely to choose a career in

    a. computer programming or accounting.
    b. business management or government.
    c. health care or social services.

4. Conventional people are likely to choose a career in

    a. health care or social services.
    b. financial investments or banking.
    c. manufacturing or transportation.

5. Social types generally

    a. enjoy working with tools and machines.
    b. are humanistic and idealistic.
    c. have skills in selling and communication.

Notes*

1. U.S. Department of Labor, "O*Net Interest Profiler," available at http://onetcenter.org

2. U.S. Department of Labor, "O*Net Interest Profiler User's Guide," available at http://onetcenter.org

3. John L. Holland, *Making Vocational Choices: A Theory of Vocational Personalities and Work Environments* (2nd Ed.), (Englewood Cliffs, NJ: Prentice-Hall, 1985).

4. U.S. Department of Labor, "O*Net Interest Profiler User's Guide."

5. Adapted from U.S. Department of Labor, "O*Net Interest Profiler."

6. Job titles in this section from http://www.onetonline.org/find/descriptor/browse/Interests/

What is plagiarism?

- Stealing or passing off someone else's words, ideas, and pictures as your own.
- Using someone else's work without crediting them (i.e. citations).
- Fraud committed against another person or against you (**self**-plagiarism).
- Presenting information as new, when it is actually from an existing source.

What are <u>some</u> examples of plagiarism?

- Submitting someone else's work as your own.
- Copying words, ideas, and pictures without giving proper credit to the original author or artist (i.e. citations).
- Failing to add quotation marks to information that is quoted.
- Providing incorrect info about the source of words, ideas, pictures, or quotations.
- Copying the sentence structure of another source without properly citing the work.
- Copying words or ideas from a source without changing the ideas and meaning into your own words and ideas.
- **Using your own, previously written, assignments** in a different class (self-plagiarism).

Why can't I use my own assignments again, for a different class?

- This is considered self-plagiarism. You can use some of the same ideas or rephrase your comments, but you have to cite yourself. Turning in complete assignments that you've previously submitted is academic dishonesty and you will face consequences.

What are <u>some</u> of the potential consequences if I plagiarize or self-plagiarize at ASU?

- You could lose points on your assignment
- You could fail your class
- You can get an XE grade for the class, failing for academic dishonesty
- You could lose your scholarships
- You could be expelled from school

Where can I find resources that help me properly cite material that I use in my assignments?

- The ASU Library - http://libguides.asu.edu/content.php?pid=122697&sid=1054432
- Citation reference manuals – available online and in hard copy
- Attend an ASU event - https://asuevents.asu.edu/writing-effectively-avoiding-plagiarism-1
- APA and MLA Handouts - http://omeka.lib.asu.edu/items/show/58

References:

Bretag, T. & Mahmud, S. (2009). Self-plagiarism or appropriate textual re-use? *Journal of Academic Ethics, (7)*193–205. Retrieved from http://www.springerlink.com.ezproxy1.lib.asu.edu/content/256280445158v940/

Publication Manual of the American Psychological Association. (6th ed.). (2010). Washington, DC: American Psychological Association.

Developed by ASU Major and Career Exploration

You have been chosen as a marketing consultant for the College of _____ (e.g., Mary Lou Fulton Teachers College, Herberger Institute, W.P. Carey School of Business, Ira A. Fulton School of Engineering). You will work with your team to create a <u>3 minute presentation and pamphlet</u> for this college. The purpose of this presentation is to EDUCATE and possibly RECRUIT someone into this college. With that being said you should focus on what would make an individual student a good "fit" for this program. The specific guidelines for both the presentation and the pamphlet are provided blow.

Purpose

- To gather information about colleges and majors at ASU
- To introduce you and your peers to the colleges
- To work in a group on a project
- To present information in a visual form

Guidelines for Presentation

Basic Info - Points will be deducted if you do not comply with the basic requirements

- Must be 3 minutes in length.
- Must be uploaded to Blackboard (under Discussions) as a PPT day before your presentation.

Must include the Following:

- What majors are offered in this college/school?

- What are the matriculation requirements?

- What are some of the interesting classes offered in this college?

- What kind of certificate programs does the college offer?

- What is the salary of three growing careers that a student could pursue within this college?

- Who do students contact for more information?

Should also include <u>at least two of the following:</u>

- Current Student Perspectives (why they chose the major, classes, professors, etc.)

- What kinds of careers can you go into with a major in X?

- What might be some unexpected careers?

- How does a major in X help prepare students for the obvious careers? (e.g. ANS for veterinarian, CPE for computer engineer) and the not-so-obvious ones (e.g. Physics for lawyer, history for business manager) If the college offers many degrees, discuss careers for majors that are representative of the college.

- What is the faculty student ratio?

Guidelines for Pamphlet

Please see https://templates.office.com/en-us/Brochures for free downloadable brochure templates

Basic Info
- Must be an easy to read handout (max. 1 page front & back) for your classmates to have as a resource
- You will need 1 copy to turn into your instructor.

Grade

This assignment is worth 10 points. All members of the group will earn the same grade, with adjustments made for students who do not put forth the same effort as their peers. See the grading rubric for details on how your presentation and pamphlet will be evaluated.

In order to earn any points for this assignment, you MUST turn in a self- and group evaluation (see the form) the day your group presents.

All presentations must be completed and presented in class, where all class members will view them.

Team Members

Name	Email	Phone Number

Grading Rubric

College:

Members of group	Evaluation form turned in?
1.	
2.	
3.	
4.	

	Yes	No
Presentation turned in on time		
Provided a class handout/brochure		
Basic Info		
Majors offered		
Matriculation requirements		
Faculty-student ratio		
Contact for more info		
Topics (3 addressed)		
Student Perspectives		
Special opportunities		
Advising procedures		
What to expect after graduation		
Careers		
Expectations of students in the college		
Presentation / Aesthetics		
Info is presented in a clear, organized fashion		
Info is presented in a creative or appealing fashion		

Grade: _____ points out of 10   **Comments:**

Self and Group Evaluation of College Presentation

Your Name (please print):

What College did your group present on?

Who is in your presentation group? (please print):

Briefly describe your experience working with your presentation group:

1. How did the group decide what to do?

2. What was the experience of working with this group like for you?

3. How did the group resolve any conflicts or handle setbacks?

4. Do you feel all members of the group participated equally?

5. How would you evaluate your own contribution?

How would you define the word "successful"?

†Holland Code Occupational Interests Chart

Scan down the list of occupations corresponding to the primary letter in your three-letter Holland code and circle those occupations you find interesting. Then go on to the occupation groups corresponding to the second and third letters of your Holland code and circle any of these occupations that interest you.

_____

_____

_____

_____

_____

Personality Types and Occupational Characteristics

Occupational Groups (Realistic)

Occupational Group	Occupation	Holland Code
	Access Coordinator, Cable TV	REI
	Airbrush Artist	RCA
	Animal Trainer	RES
	Architectural Drafter	RCI
	Auto Mechanic	RCI
	Biomedical Equipment Technician	RIE
	Cable TV Line Technician	REC
	Commercial Airline Pilot	ERI
	Computer Technician	RIC
REALISTIC	Dispensing Optician	
	Emergency Medical Technician	RSI
	Electronic Technician	RIS
	Estimator	RCE
	Firefighter	RES
"Hands-On" Technically Oriented	Fish and Game Warden	RES
	Helicopter Pilot	RIC
	Historical Restoration Specialist	RIC
	Home Inspector	RCI
	Industrial Arts Teacher	REI
	Landscape Gardener	RIS
	Locksmith	REC
	Merchant Mariner	REA
	MRI Technologist	RIC
	National Park Ranger	REI
	Nuclear Medicine Technologist	RIS
	Piano Tuner	RCS

†From *Your Career Planner*, Eleventh Edition by Cheryl Bonner and Susan Musich. Copyright © 2017 by Kendall Hunt Publishing Company. Reprinted by permission.

	Prosthetic Technician	RSE
	Quality Control Inspector	RSC
	Radiographer	RIS
	Robotic Machine Operator	RSE
	Ship's Crew	RCI
	Solar-Energy-System Installer	RCI
	Sound Mixer	RCS
	State Highway Police Officer	RSE
	Tool Designer	RIS
	Ultrasound Technologist	RSI

Evolving Careers

Bionic limb technician
Robotic technician
Mechanics for new engines (solar, hydrogen, ion)
Space vehicle pilot
Holographic imagery technician
Communication satellite television

Occupational Groups (Investigative)

Occupational Group	Occupation	Holland Code
	Actuary	ISE
	Aeronautical Engineer	IRS
	Anthropologist	IRE
	Astronomer	IRA
	Astrophysicist	IAR
	Biologist	IAR
	Biomedical Engineer	IRE
INVESTIGATIVE	Chemist	IRE
	Computer Science Faculty Member	IRC
	Criminologist	IRC
Abstract Problem Solving	Dentist	ISR
	Economist	IAS
	Exercise Physiologist	ISR
Science Oriented	Geologist	IRE
	Internal Auditor	ICR
	Laser Technician	IRE
	Market-Research Analyst	ISC
	Mathematician	IER
	Mechanical Engineer	IRS
	Medical Researcher	IAR
	Meteorologist	IRS
	Museum Curator	IRS
	Optometrist	ISE
	Pharmacist	IES
	Physician	ISR

	Physicist	IAR
	Psychiatrist	ISA
	Research Dietician	ISR
	Research Psychologist	IAE
	Science and Technology Writer	IAE
	Statistician	IRE
	Systems Analyst	IER
	Translator	ISC
	Veterinarian	IRS

Evolving Careers
Global economist
Genetic engineer
Artificial intelligence engineer
Ecology scientist
Information architect
New product researcher

Occupational Groups (Artistic)

Occupational Group	Occupation	Holland Code
	Actor/Actress	AES
	Advertising Manager	AES
	Architect	AIR
	Art Teacher	ASE
	Book Editor	AES
	Cartoonist	AES
	Columnist/Commentator	AES
	Commercial Designer	AER
ARTISTIC	Copywriter	AIS
	Dancer	AER
	Drama Teacher	ASE
Idea Creators	English Teacher	ASE
	Entertainer	AES
Artistic and Self-Expressive	Exhibit Designer	ASE
	Fashion Artist	AER
	Graphic Designer	AER
	Illustrator (traditional and digital)	AER
	Landscape Architect	AIR
	Lawyer—Trial Counsel	AER
	Musician, Instrumental	ARC
	Music Teacher	AES
	Newswriter	AEI
	Paintings Restorer	ASR
	Pastry Chef	ASE
	Photojournalist	AEC
	Promotions Manager	AEI

	Prose Writer	AIE
	Public Relations Manager	ASE
	Reporter	ASI
	Sculptor	AER
	Set Designer	AES
	Stage Technician	ARS
	Technical Illustrator	ARI
	Website Designer	AIC
Evolving Careers		

Creative director
Actors, seniors and multilingual
Web graphics production artist
Presentation graphics consultant
Cross-cultural writer

Occupational Groups (Social)

Occupational Group	Occupation	Holland Code
	Air-Traffic-Control Specialist, Tower	SER
	Athletic Trainer	SRE
	Athletic Coach	SEI
	Clinical Psychologist	SIA
	Corrections Officer	SER
	Counselor	SAE
	Elementary Teacher	SAE
SOCIAL	Employee Relations Specialist	SEA
	Equal Opportunity Officer	SRI
	Faculty Member, College/University	SEI
People/Plant/ Animal Helpers Nurturing	Health Care Administrator	SER
	High School Teacher	SAE
	Interpreter, Deaf	SCE
	Librarian	SAI
	Minister, Priest, Rabbi	SEA
	Music Therapist	SAE
	Nurse	SIA
	Occupational Development Consultant	SRE
	Occupational Therapist	SEI
	Organization Learning Specialist	SEI
	Passenger Service Representative	SEI
	Park Naturalist	SER
	Personal Coach	SEI
	Personnel Recruiter	SIA
	Physical Education Instructor	SCE
	Physical Therapist	SIE

	Occupation	Holland Code
	Probation and Parole Officer	SIE
	Professional Athlete	
	Respiratory Therapist	SRC
	School Counselor	SIR
	Social Worker, Psychiatric	SEA
	Special Agent, Customs	SEC
	Speech Pathologist	SRI
	Teacher, Learning Disabled	SAI
	Vocational Rehabilitation	SER
	Counselor	SEC

Evolving Careers

Accelerated learning consultant
Actualization psychologist
Cultural diversity consultant
Conflict resolution mediator
Age 60+ career/relationship counselor/coach
Corporate ethics consultant

Occupational Groups (Enterprising)

Occupational Group	Occupation	Holland Code
	Airport Manager	ESR
	Budget Officer	ESI
	Business Manager	ESC
	Camp Director	ESA
	Chef	ESR
	College Administrator	ESC
	Criminal Lawyer	ESA
	Day Care Center Director	ESC
ENTERPRISING	Federal Government Executive	EIC
	Flight Attendant	ESA
People Influencers Power/Status/ Prestige Oriented	Food Services Director	EIS
	Fundraising Director	ESA
	Golf Club Manager	ECS
	Head Waiter/Waitress	ESA
	HMO Manager	ECI
	Hospital Administrator	ESC
	Hotel/Motel Manager	ESR
	Judge	EIA
	Lobbyist	ESA
	Media Marketing Director	ESR
	Merchandise Manager	ESR
	Military Officer	ECR
	Museum Director	ESR

	National Park Manager	ESR
	Newscaster	ESI
	Organizational Development Consultant	EIA
	Research and Development Director	ERI
	Real Estate Agent	ESR
	Sales Manager	ESA
	Salesperson, Clothing	EAS
	Sales Representative, Sporting Goods	ESA
	School Principal	ESI
	Securities Trader	ECS
	Tax Attorney	ESI
	Travel Agent	ECS
	Umpire/Referee	ESR
	Urban Planner	ESI

Evolving Careers

High-technology sales
Global trade attorney
Medical research center manager
Multimedia project manager
Coach for entrepreneurs

Occupational Groups (Conventional)

Occupational Group	Occupation	Holland Code
	Abstractor	CSI
	Account Manager	CSI
	Accountant	CSI
	Budget Analyst	CER
	Bursar	CEI
	Caseworker	CSE
	Central-Office Repairer	CRE
CONVENTIONAL	Computer Security Specialist	CIS
	Computer Programmers	CIA
	Congressional-District	CES
	Aide	CSE
	Court Clerk	CIE
	Cost Accountant	CSE
	Customer Service Representative	CEI
Orderly and Efficient	Customs Inspector	CIA
	Editorial Assistant	CIA
	Financial Analyst	CES
Data and Detail Oriented	Fire Inspector	CSE
	Insurance Underwriter	CSE
	Legal Secretary	CSE
	Library Assistant	CSR
	Loan Review Analyst	CIR

Medical Records	CES	
Technician	CRS	
Medical Secretary	CIS	
Mortgage Loan Processor	CRE	
Paralegal Assistant	CSI	
Payroll Clerk	CES	
Proofreader		
Quality Control	CES	
Coordinator	CSE	
Reservation Agent	CES	
Secretary	CSE	
Tax Preparer	CSE	
Title Examiner		
Tourist Information Assistant	CES	
Word Processing Supervisor		

Evolving Careers

Information system security expert
Robotic programmer
Office information system manager
Electronic information specialist
Space telemetering analyst

*Major Motivation

Think about a major you've chosen or are considering and answer the following questions:

1. Why are you considering this major? What led or caused you to become interested in this choice? Why or why not?

> I am considering this major because I am very interested in sustainability & climate change. I became interesed in this when I lived overseas because it showed me sustainable practices & cultures.

2. Would you say that your interest in this major is motivated primarily by intrinsic factors—i.e., factors "inside" of you, such as your personal abilities, interests, needs, and values? Or is your interest in the career motivated more heavily by extrinsic factors—i.e., factors "outside" of you, such as starting salary or meeting the expectations of parents?

> I believe my interest in this is strongly intristic factors. I am doing it because I really love the subject. Not for a salary.

What life roles are you engaging in currently (i.e., child, student, worker, parent, partner, homemaker, citizen, leisurite)?

_____

_____

_____

What do you enjoy about these roles?

_____

_____

_____

How can you use these roles as places to gather information that would be helpful in making a career decision?

_____

_____

_____

Think about the life roles you anticipate playing (child, student, worker, parent, partner, homemaker, citizen, leisurite). How do you think these roles will blend together to help you create a satisfying career/life?

_____

_____

_____

Your Career/Life Decisions Of The Past

A career/life decision is one that has had a significant effect on your career and your life. In the spaces provided, list several of the most significant career/life choices you have made so far in your life. Examples include: early childhood memories (changing training wheels on bike, joining a youth choir, etc.), first work experience, summer job, selection of high school courses, decision to attend college, first job, job change, getting married, having children, leaving home, moving, joining the service.

Start by listing the earliest decision you can recall and then record each subsequent major career/life choice in chronological order to the present time. Enter your decisions to the right of the numbers below, leaving the line to the left blank for now.

My Career/Life-Shaping Decisions of the Past and How I Made Them

_____ 1. _____
_____ 2. _____
_____ 3. _____
_____ 4. _____
_____ 5. _____
_____ 6. _____
_____ 7. _____
_____ 8. _____
_____ 9. _____
_____ 10. _____

Fill in the lines to the left of each decision above with the appropriate letter(s) from the following list:

- **A.** Took the safest way.
- **B.** Took the easiest way.
- **C.** Let someone else decide for me.
- **D.** Did what I thought others expected me to do.
- **E.** Did what I had been taught that I should do.
- **F.** Did the first thing that came to my mind.
- **G.** Did nothing.
- **H.** Chose what I felt was intuitively right.
- **I.** Consciously weighed all of the alternatives available and then chose the best one.
- **J.** Used some other approach. _____
  _____

1. What did you learn about the way you have made your career/life decisions in the past?
   _____
   _____
   _____

2. What effects have your past career/life choices had on your life? How do the outcomes of these decisions affect you now?

_____
_____
_____

3. Based what you learned about your past career/life decision-making style and the effect of these choices on your life, what changes would you like to make?

_____
_____
_____

What Types of Research Will Help Me Make an Informed Decision about My Major and Career?

Learning Objectives

- Interpret your Kuder results and understand how it relates to your self-assessment of interests

- Identify several majors and/or career possibilities using the Kuder results.

- Use the Degree Search tool and Kuder results to find specific information about majors.

- Learn information about colleges and majors at ASU from other students' presentations.

†The Bureau of Labor Statistics

Understanding the current nature of work is important.

Perhaps two of the most misused factors in selecting a career are the concepts of workplace trends and occupational projections.

Ignored, quoted out of context, or taken as indisputable facts, the misuse of these factors have resulted in poor career choices for many people.

It is important to be informed. Armed with reliable information, a person can make a great decision about their future.

Sources of good information come from organizations with little to no agendas such as political leanings, interest in causes, or funding from sources which could benefit from certain findings. Start with the BLS.

The BLS is a traditionally nonpartisan government agency under the DOL. According to http://www.bls.gov/bls/infohome.htm, their mission is as follows:"The Bureau of Labor Statistics of the U.S. Department of Labor is the principal Federal agency responsible for measuring labor market activity, working conditions, and price changes in the economy. Its mission is to collect, analyze, and disseminate essential economic information to support public and private decision-making. As an independent statistical agency, BLS serves its diverse user communities by providing products and services that are objective, timely, accurate, and relevant."

The Bureau of Labor Statistics has provided essential economic information to support public and private decision-making since 1884. Yet, even this organization shares this caveat as part of their projections:

The BLS projections are focused on long-term structural trends of the economy and do not try to anticipate future business cycle activity. To meet this objective, specific assumptions are made about the labor force, macroeconomy, industry employment, and occupational employment. Critical to the production of these projections is the assumption of full employment for the economy in the projected year. Thus, the projections are not intended to be a forecast of what the future will be, but instead are a description of what would be expected to happen under these specific assumptions and circumstances. When these assumptions are not realized, actual values will differ from projections. Users of these data should not assume that the difference between projected changes in the labor force and in employment implies a labor shortage or surplus. The BLS projections assume labor market equilibrium, that is, one in which labor supply meets labor demand except for some level of frictional unemployment. In addition, the employment and labor force measures use different definitional and statistical concepts. For example, employment is a count of jobs, and one person may hold more than one job. Labor force is a count of people, and a person is counted only once regardless of how many jobs he or she holds.[10]

http://www.bls.gov/news.release/pdf/ecopro.pdf

This technical, legal sounding language essentially says: there are factors we simply cannot control.

Predictions based on solid research and data are to be considered as one of many factors. Successful career decision makers do not look once, but maintain an awareness of the future of a chosen industry or occupation. Economists remind us that changesd to industries are the result of many elements, some foreseeable, some suspected, and some which will catch the industry completely unaware. New inventions can revolutionize an industry—decimating one part and strengthening another, war or civil unrest in a country can impact the availability of materials essential to the industry, social and political interests can impact funding and consumer behavior.

†From *Your Career Planner*, Eleventh Edition by Cheryl Bonner and Susan Musich. Copyright © 2017 by Kendall Hunt Publishing Company. Reprinted by permission.

Attitudes About Work

How do you view the marketplace? How do you view work? For some, the uncertainties of the economy provoke anxiety. These stress levels may undoubtedly be elevated by decades of conditioning to seek job security and avoid risk. Pursuing a personal passion may well be the best antidote to "newage" stress.

In this regard, passion is directly related to energy and inversely related to stress. Unremitting stress robs us of energy, enthusiasm, and hope. These, conversely, are just the ingredients that our personal passions generate. Both stress and passion involve the imagination in anticipation of the future. Personal energy becomes directed, concentrated, and action-focused when we visualize ourselves achieving interesting goals. We motivate ourselves from the inside out—a highly self-empowering process. Stress, on the other hand, involves preoccupation with frightening possibilities, draining away energy into deceptive fantasies—a self-victimizing activity.

How do you measure your own attitudes about work? Are you stressed as you consider your skills against the backdrop of the external market factors, or do you view these market factors as being able to provide you with new opportunities (see figure below)?

Decades ago, an author named Studs Terkel wrote a book that told the stories of real people in real jobs. This book, designed to chronicle the lives of everyday Americans, became a snapshot of the culture of the day. In the opening words of his introduction, Turkel writes:

This book, being about work, is, by its very nature, about violence—to the spirit as well as to the body. It is about ulcers as well as accidents, about shouting matches as well as fistfights, about nervous breakdowns as well as kicking the dog around. It is, above all (or beneath all), about daily humiliations. To survive the day is triumph enough for the walking wounded among the great many of us.[11]

Wow! Not sure you can get more depressing than this. One might wonder if Mr. Terkel had it rough in the workplace. His bio says he graduated from acclaimed schools and held interesting jobs. He also came of age during very rough points in the American experience. How did this influence his view of career? Or did he simply find out that work was hard from the countless interviews with average citizens?

Terkel writes more in his introduction:

It is about a search, too, for daily meaning as well as daily bread, for recognition as well as cash, for astonishment rather than torpor; in short, for a sort of life rather than a Monday through Friday sort of dying. Perhaps immortality, too, is part of the quest. To be remembered was the wish, spoken and unspoken, of the heroes and heroines of this book.[12]

Up to this point, how do you define work? Is it a job for survival, a paycheck, a means to an end? Or is work something that is fulfilling and enjoyable? Think about how you define paid work and your own perspectives. What did you think about work before? How might your thinking change as you read this book and go through these exercises? Before you go on, write some of your own thoughts here.

My current thoughts on work:

PAUSE

Writing Your Story

Your career is about YOU. Throughout this book, you will have the opportunity to gather information about you and the world of work. You will be taking a few assessments. These assessments are not designed to tell what you should be doing with your life, but to help you develop a language that you can use to explore your opportunities. The assessments should not put you in a box. They are intended to help you think outside of the box and open up your choices. In each chapter in the early part of the book, you will be able to gain an understanding of a different aspect of yourself. It is important that you remember that each chapter and the assessments in these chapters will give you information on a specific area and will help you understand how you might fit in with these areas. The assessments included in each chapter will take a measurement of how you respond to a specific set of questions on a specific day. Take this into consideration as you develop your career profile. If the results of one assessment seem out of step with all of the others, you may want to consider how you were feeling on the day you took the assessment. If you were feeling stressed out by the

PAUSE

> What gives you meaning? What are you doing when you feel most alive? If you are in the stage of early adulthood, this might be a tough question to answer. Limited life experiences may not have yielded a lot of thought on this subject. Later in this book you will have the chance to do some accomplishment exercises. These exercises will allow you to think through the things, perhaps maybe even small things that will give you clues about the places where you will find energy. Before you go on, write some of your own thoughts to this here. Reflect on something you did recently that really energized you. Write a few sentences about that experience.
>
> **My current thoughts on work and an experience that energized me:**

people around you, you may have selected answers that reflected a greater-than-usual desire to work alone. If tasks were stressing you out, this may have had an influence on your responses as well. The assessments are used to begin your self-discovery and not end it.

Many of the activities in the book are designed to get you to think deeper. Use them as a jumping-off point for your career exploration. What you will get out of the self-discovery sections depends on what you put into them. Take these exercises and assessments seriously, but think of them as getting you started in the process of being able to articulate your career dreams and goals.

During your self-exploration, expand your world. If some of the assessments are pointing in a specific direction, try it out. Use the citizen and leisurite roles to do some volunteering or take on a new hobby. You are probably thinking that you'd love to, but you don't have the time. Think of how you can incorporate these activities with things you already do. Get your friends to volunteer with you. Play basketball with the kids at the shelter instead of the guys at the gym. Take an accountant to lunch to learn more about the accounting profession. It is true that there are some skill and interest areas that are easier to try on than others, so you may need to be creative. Bounce ideas off others and get their input on how you can try out some of the ideas that will be presented in this book.

If you do engage in volunteer or other experiences as you are working through this book, by the time you get to the final chapters on job searching, not only will you know what you want to do but you will also have gained tangible experiences that you can write about on your resume and talk to employers about in an interview.

Beginning the Journey

If you are reading this book for a class, there is a good chance that you took the course because you were looking for some direction in your career decision. We are sure this book and your class will help. But as you begin, it is important that you relax. Let's get a few things straight before we move any further. Number 1: If Donald Super is correct (and we believe he is), then career is about a lot more than what we do for paid work. If you are looking for that total be-all, life is wonderful, total fulfillment sense from a job, and then perhaps you might want to manage those expectations. Some people have jobs that are pretty good most of the time. They are a good fit. They make sense for them. We hope that this will be you. But if you think that the job is going to be the only thing that will satisfy you—or you feel that you need to find a job that will satisfy 40 hours a week, 52 weeks a year—then perhaps it is time to take the pressure off. Paid work can be wonderful! It creates necessary structure for lives, income, and, in many cases, meaning and purpose as it uses our skills and passions. But, paid work does not do this always or completely. Sometimes, just sometimes, work is hard. Bosses are not encouraging, clients are demanding, the hours are long, and the pay is low.

But a career, when taken to mean the totality of all of the roles that we play, allows us to use many skills, explore many passions, and have multiple experiences that result in meaning and satisfaction. As you are working through the activities in this book that will lead to increased self-discovery and new knowledge about yourself and work, remember that it doesn't need to all happen in the arena of paid work. If you discover that you love being with little kids but don't really want to be a teacher, recognize that you can do some volunteering on the weekends that will enable you to act on this passion. Be creative!

So relax. Take the pressure off. In the coming weeks, you will undertake a journey of self-discovery that will enable you to write your own story, taking into consideration opportunities outside of paid work as well as paid work. You will find that you will see some naturally recurring patterns in your own life that will shape your story. As you enjoy the self-discovery and learning about all of the opportunities available to you, you will begin to see some patterns emerging. Patterns will help you shape and define your story. It may be a bit frustrating at times. It may even be a bit strange to be doing all of this self-focus in the beginning. But it is important. As you take the time to discover your interests, skills, abilities, values, thinking style, and decision-making style, you will uncover career opportunities that are a good fit for you. Enjoy the journey!

*Once you have completed a thorough self-assessment, you may still have several majors to consider. At this point, it is important to do some research on the outlook for a selected career in the future and the pay you would receive. Sometimes students are disappointed after graduation when they find there are few job opportunities in their chosen career field. Sometimes students graduate and cannot find jobs with the salary they had hoped to earn. It is important to think about the opportunities you will have in the future. If you have several options for a career you would enjoy, you may want to consider seriously the career that has the best outlook and pay.

© Maryna Pleshkun/Shutterstock.com

According to the Bureau of Labor Statistics, fields with the best outlook include health care, computers, and the new "green jobs" related to preserving the environment. The top-paying careers all require math skills and include the science, engineering, computer science, health care, and business fields. Only 4% of college graduates choose the engineering and computer science fields. Since there are fewer students in these majors, the salaries are higher. If you have a talent or interest in math, you can develop this skill and use it in high-paying careers.

Some Majors with the Highest Earnings for Bachelor's Degrees 2017*[5]

Notice that the majors with the highest earnings require math, science, and/or business.

College Major	Beginning Median Salary	Mid-Career Median Salary
Petroleum Engineering	96,700	172,000
Actuarial Science	60,800	119,000
Chemical Engineering	69,800	119,000
Computer Science & Engineering	71,200	116,000
Nuclear Engineering	68,500	116,000
Electrical and Computer Engineering	68,100	114,000
Aeronautical Engineering	63,000	113,000
Physics & Mathematics	56,200	111,000
Government	49,600	105,000
Biomedical Engineering	62,700	104,000
Physician Assistant Studies	85,200	103,000
Finance & Real Estate	59,500	101,000
Economics	53,900	100,000

*Includes bachelor's degrees only. Excludes medicine, law, and careers requiring advanced degrees.

Other Common Majors and Earnings*[6]

Major		
Accounting and Finance	52,800	86,400
Business and Marketing	45,800	85,300
Advertising	41,400	79,800
Geology	44,800	79,800
Architecture	45,100	79,300
Biological Sciences	42,900	79,200
Fashion Design	41,400	77,700
History and Political Science	44,500	76,000
Entrepreneurship	48,000	74,600
English Literature	41,100	74,300
Foreign Languages	42,500	74,200
Business Administration	46,100	72,400
Communication	42,100	72,300
Forestry	41,500	67,400
Multimedia & Web Design	42,300	66,500
Film, Video & Media Studies	39,600	66,300
Music Performance	39,900	65,000
Criminal Justice	39,000	63,900
Art History	40,800	63,300
Hotel & Restaurant Management	50,500	62,700
Art & Design	39,500	62,600
Liberal Arts	39,100	62,300
Psychology	38,300	62,100
Secondary Education	40,200	61,400
Humanities	40,900	57,200
Elementary Education	34,700	48,900

* Includes bachelor's degrees only. Excludes medicine, law, and careers requiring advanced degrees.

© Anson0618/Shutterstock.com

Most Meaningful College Majors*[7]

Money is often not the most important consideration in choosing a major. These careers were determined to be the most meaningful with the potential for changing the world.

College Major	Beginning Salary	Mid-Career Median Salary
Medical Laboratory Science	47,900	61,500
Pastoral Ministry	32,800	36,300
Physical Therapy	60,000	86,600
Practical Nursing	45,300	58,100
Physician Assistant Studies	85,200	103,000
Diagnostic Medical Sonography	57,700	71,100
Exercise Physiology	38,400	60,300
Nursing	57,500	74,100
Respiratory Therapy	46,200	62,900
Therapeutic Recreation	35,200	47,700
Community Health Education	37,200	55,200
Dietetics	44,300	60,500
Dental Hygiene	65,400	74,900
Environmental Health & Safety	51,200	89,800
Foods and Nutrition	40,900	58,700
Health	35,700	60,700
Social Work	33,800	46,700
Child Development	32,000	42,500

*Based on an extensive survey by Payscale.com asking college graduates with a bachelor's degree, "Does your work make the world a better place to live?"

"We act as though comfort and luxury were the chief requirements of life, when all that we need to make us really happy is something to be enthusiastic about."
Charles Kingsley

"Only passions, great passions, can elevate the soul to great things."
Denis Diderot

Every career counselor can tell stories about students who ask, "What is the career that makes the most money? That's the career I want!" However, if you choose a career based on money alone, you might find it difficult and uninteresting for a lifetime of work. You might even find yourself retraining later in life for a job that you really enjoy. Remember that the first step is to figure out who you are and what you like. Then look at career outlook and opportunity. If you find your passion in a career that is in demand and pays well, you will probably be very happy with your career choice. If you find your passion in a career that offers few jobs and does not pay well, you will have to use your ingenuity to find a job and make a living. Many students happily make this informed choice and find a way to make it work.

© iQoncept/Shutterstock.com

© Iculig/Shutterstock.com

Mark Twain said, "The secret of success is making your vocation your vacation." Find what you like to do. Better yet, find your passion. If you can find your passion, it is easy to invest the time and effort necessary to be successful.

How do you know when you have found your passion? You have found your passion when you are doing an activity and you do not notice that the time is passing. The great painter Picasso often talked about how quickly time passed while he was painting. He said, "When I work, I relax; doing nothing or entertaining visitors makes me tired." Whether you are an artist, an athlete, a scientist, or a business entrepreneur, passion provides the energy needed to be successful. It helps you to grow and create. When you are using your talents to grow and create, you can find meaning and happiness in your life. Finding your passion can help you to be grittier too.

Psychologist Martin Seligman has written a book entitled *Authentic Happiness,* in which he writes about three types of work orientation: a job, a career, and a calling.[1] A job is what you do for the paycheck at the end of the week. Many college students have jobs to earn money for college. A career has deeper personal meaning. It involves achievement, prestige, and power. A calling is defined as "a passionate commitment to work for its own sake."[2] When you have found your calling, the job itself is the reward. He notes that people who have found their calling are consistently happier than those who have a job or even

(Continued)

a career. One of the ways that you know you have found your calling is when you are in the state of "flow." The state of "flow" is defined as "complete absorption in an activity whose challenges mesh perfectly with your abilities."[3] People who experience "flow" are happier and more productive. They do not spend their days looking forward to Friday. Understanding your personal strengths is the beginning step to finding your calling.

Seligman adds that any job can become a calling if you use your personal strengths to do the best possible job. He cited a study of hospital cleaners. Although some viewed their job as drudgery, others viewed the job as a calling. They believed that they helped patients get better by working efficiently and anticipating the needs of doctors and nurses. They rearranged furniture and decorated walls to help patients feel better. They found their calling by applying their personal talents to their jobs. As a result, their jobs became a calling.

Sometimes we wait around for passion to find us. That probably won't happen. The first step in finding your passion is to know yourself. Then find an occupation in which you can use your talents. You may be able to find your passion by looking at your present job and finding a creative way to do it based on your special talents. It has been said that there are no dead-end jobs, just people who cannot see the possibilities. Begin your search for passion by looking at your personal strengths and how you can apply them in the job market. If the job that you have now is not your passion, see what you can learn from it and then use your skills to find a career where you are more likely to find your passion.

> "Success is not the key to happiness; happiness is the key to success. If you love what you are doing, you will be successful."
>
> Anonymous

College Success 1

The College Success 1 website is continually updated with supplementary material for each chapter including Word documents of the journal entries, classroom activities, handouts, videos, links to related materials, and much more. See http://www.collegesuccess1.com/.

© Lyudmyla Kharlamova/ Shutterstock.com

Notes

1. Judith Provost and Scott Anchors, eds., *Applications of the Myers-Briggs Type Indicator In Higher Education* (Palo Alto, CA: Consulting Psychologists Press, 1991), 51.

2. Ibid., 49.

3. Otto Kroeger and Janet Thuesen, *Type Talk: The 16 Personality Types That Determine How We Live, Love and Work* (New York: Dell, 1989), 204.

4. Ibid.

5. Payscale, "College Salary Report 2016–17," from http://www.payscale.com/college-salary-report, accessed July 2017.

6. Ibid.

7. Ibid.

8. Martin Seligman, Authentic Happiness (Free Press, 2002).

9. Martin Seligman, as reported by Geoffrey Cowley, "The Science of Happiness," *Newsweek*, September 16, 2002, 49.

10. Ibid.

Developments Affecting Future Careers

Jobs of the future will continue to be influenced by changes in our society and economy. These new developments will affect the job market for the future:[4]

We are evolving into a service, technology, and information society. Fewer people are working in agriculture and manufacturing. Futurists note that we are moving toward a service economy based on high technology, rapid communications, biotechnology for use in agriculture and medicine, health care, and sales of merchandise.[5] Service areas with increasing numbers of jobs include health care and social assistance; professional, scientific, and technical services; education services; accommodation and food services; government; retail trade; transportation and warehousing; finance and insurance; arts, entertainment, and recreation; wholesale trade; real estate, rental, and leasing; and information management.

There will be an increased need for education. Constant change in society and innovation in technology will require lifelong learning on the job. Education will take place in a variety of forms: community college courses, training on the job, private training sessions, and learning on your own. Those who do not keep up with the new technology will find that their skills quickly become obsolete. Those who do keep up will find their skills in demand. Higher education is linked to greater earnings and increased employment opportunities.

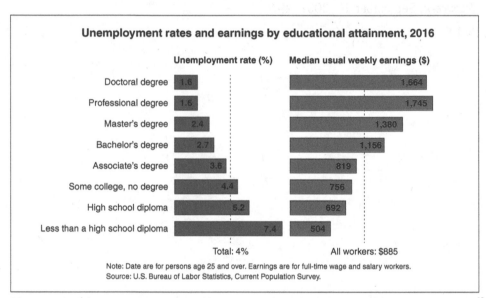

Figure 2.1 Education Pays, Unemployment rate and median weekly earnings, 2014.[15]

There will be increased opportunities for Stem (science, technology, engineering, and math) jobs. These jobs will grow 17% by 2020. These occupations jobs include many of the highest paying jobs.

Beware of job outsourcing. To reduce costs and improve profits, many jobs in technology, manufacturing, and service are being outsourced to countries such as India, China, and Taiwan, where well-educated, English-speaking workers are being used to do these jobs. For example, programmers in India can produce software at only 10% of the cost of these services in the United States. Jobs that are currently being outsources include accounting, payroll clerks, customer service, data entry, assembly line workers, industrial engineering, machine operators, computer-assisted design (CAD) technicians, purchasing managers, textile workers, software developers, and technical support. Jobs that are most likely to be outsourced are[6]

- Repetitive jobs, such as accounting,
- Well-defined jobs, such as customer service,
- Small manageable projects, such as software development,
- Jobs in which proximity to the customer is not important, such as technical support.

Jobs that are least likely to be outsourced include

- Jobs with ambiguity, such as top management jobs,
- Unpredictable jobs, such as troubleshooters,
- Jobs that require understanding of the culture, such as marketing,
- Joss that require close proximity to the customer, such as auto repair,
- Jobs requiring a high degree of innovation and creativity, such as product design,
- Jobs in entertainment, music, art, and design.

To protect yourself from outsourcing,

- Strive to be the best in the field.
- Be creative and innovative.
- Avoid repetitive jobs that do not require proximity to the customer.
- Choose a career where the demand is so high that it won't matter if some are outsourced.
- Consider a job in the skilled trades: carpenters, plumbers, electricians, hair stylists, construction workers, auto mechanics, and dental hygienists will always be in demand.

Globalization is changing the job market. Multinational corporations will locate their companies based on the availability of workers and the cost of labor. This trend will reduce the cost of goods and services but will change the nature of the job market. While this trend has resulted in outsourcing, there are increasing numbers of jobs in the United States requiring workers who speak different languages and understand how to do business in other countries.

Nontraditional jobs are increasing. Unlike traditional workers, nontraditional workers do not have full-time, year-round jobs with health and retirement benefits. Employers are moving toward using nontraditional workers, including multiple job holders, contingent and part-time workers, independent contractors, and temporary workers. Nearly four out of five employers use nontraditional workers to help them become more efficient, prevent layoffs, and access workers with special skills. There are advantages and disadvantages to this arrangement. Nontraditional workers have no benefits and risk unemployment. However, this arrangement can provide workers with a flexible work schedule in which they work during some periods and pursue other interests or gain new skills when not working.

© Mathias Rosenthal/Shutterstock.com

© VLADGRIN/Shutterstock.com

Automation will continue to reduce repetitive jobs in every industry. Increasingly sophisticated robots will be used to decrease the cost of goods and services. Engineers and technicians will be needed to design and maintain these robots.

There is a mismatch between workers and available jobs. It is often difficult for companies to fill jobs requiring highly skilled technical and scientific workers. These workers are often hired in other countries and use technology to work remotely.

More companies will use teleworking. Teleworking involves using smart phones to do some work at home. Currently, about 40% of workers use their smart phones to do some work at home. As a result, there will be increased flexibility of work hours and more people will work remotely using smart devices. There will be increased demand for application designers and designers for smart devices.

E-commerce is changing the way we do business. E-commerce is the purchasing of goods, services, and information over the Internet. More people are using e-commerce because of convenience, selection, cost savings, and ease of shopping. Online sales are a growing part of the market, increasing 10–20% a year for the past several years. By 2017, the web will account for 10% of retail sales, and approximately 43% of sales are influenced by online research.[7] There are more career opportunities in related fields such as computer graphics, web design, online marketing, and package delivery services.

Business will increase virtual collaboration. Workers are increasingly using Skype and other collaboration software to work with others.

New media literacy will become an essential skill for most new jobs. Workers who do not keep up with new media will quickly find their skills obsolete.

Career Trends for 2020

The good news is that over 20 million new jobs will be created by 2020, which represents a 14% annual growth rate. Approximately 60% of the competitive, high-demand, and high-paying jobs will require at least a bachelor's degree. Majors most in demand include accounting, engineering, computer science, business, and economics. However, most college students are majoring in history, education, and social science, which are lower in demand. Here are some specific areas where there will be increasing demand in the future.[8]

Data analysis. Companies are increasingly using data for market research. Opportunities exist for those who can find and analyze data.

Mental health. After being neglected for a long time, people are beginning to understand the importance of mental health for safety and the enjoyment of life. Current health-care insurance includes mental health coverage that will result in increased demand for services.

Technology-related jobs will continue to increase. Information and technology workers are now the largest group of workers in the United States. The Bureau of Labor Statistics reports that two million technology-related jobs will be created by 2018. Jobs in computer systems design and related services are expected to increase by 34% by 2018.[9]

Careers in **information technology** include the design, development, and support of computers, software, hardware, and networks. Some newer jobs in this area include animation for video games, film, videos, setting up websites, and Internet security. Jobs that will grow faster than the average include computer network administrators, data communications analysts, web developers, and App designers. Some new fields include data loss prevention, online security, and risk management. Computer science degrees are especially marketable when combined with traditional majors such as finance, accounting, or marketing. [10]

Radiation and laser technologies will provide new technical careers in the future. It has been said that lasers will be as important to the 21st century as electricity was for the 20th century. New uses for lasers are being found in medicine, energy, industry, computers, communications, entertainment, and outer space. The use of lasers is creating new jobs and causing others to become obsolete. For example, many welders are being replaced by laser technicians, who have significantly higher earnings. New jobs will open for people who purchase, install, and maintain lasers.

Careers in fiber optics and telecommunications are among the top new emerging fields in the 21st century. Fiber optics are thin glass fibers that transmit light. This new technology may soon make copper wire obsolete. One of the most important uses of fiber optics is to speed up delivery of data over the Internet and to improve telecommunications. It is also widely used in medical instruments, including laser surgery.

Artificial intelligence has interesting possibilities for the future. It enables computers to recognize patterns, improve from experience, make inferences, and approximate human thought. Artificial intelligence will be increasingly used in robots and smart machines. Two recent examples are IPhone's Siri, which uses voice recognition software to search the Internet, and Google's development of the self-driving car.

Research. There will be high demand for people with advanced degrees in engineering, chemistry, math, biology, biotechnology, and other sciences who will be the innovators in technology, medicine, and manufacturing.

Biology. Future historians may describe the 21st century as the biology century because of all the developments in this area. One of the most important developments is the Human Genome Project, which has identified the genes in human DNA, the carrier of genetic material. This research has resulted in new careers in biotechnology and biomedical technology.

Biotechnology will become increasingly important as a way to combat disease, develop new surgical procedures and devices, increase food production, reduce pollution, improve recycling, and provide new tools for law enforcement. Biotechnology includes genomic profiling, biomedical engineering, new pharmaceuticals, genetic engineering, and DNA identification. In the future, biotechnology may be used to find cures for diabetes, arthritis, Alzheimer's disease, and heart disease.

The field of **biomedical engineering,** which involves developing and testing health-care innovations, is expected to grow by 72% by 2018.[11] Biomedical technology is the field in which bionic implants are being developed for the human body. Scientists are working on the development of artificial limbs and organs including eyes, ears, hearts, and kidneys. A promising new development in this field is brain and computer interfaces. Scientists recently implanted a computer chip into the brain of a quadriplegic, enabling him to control a computer and television with his mind.[12] Biotechnology also develops new diagnostic test equipment and surgical tools.

Veterinary medicine. The demand for veterinarians is expected to increase by 35% because of the demand for pet products and health. However, it is interesting to note that there will be 35 times as many jobs for nurses as for veterinarians.[13]

Health-care occupations will add the most new jobs between 2012 and 2022 and registered nurses will see the most job growth.[14] This trend is being driven by an aging

© zhang kan/Shutterstock.com

population, increased longevity, health-care reform, and new developments in the pharmaceutical and medical fields. Demand will be especially high for dentists, nurses, physician specialists, optometrists, physical therapists, audiologists, pharmacists, athletic trainers, and elder-care providers. Because of increasing health-care costs, many of the jobs done by doctors, nurses, dentists, or physical therapists are now being done by physician's assistants, dental assistants, physical therapy aides, and home health aides. Health-care workers will increasingly use technology to do their work. For example, a new occupation is nursing informatics, which combines traditional nursing skills with computer and information science. Health care will be continually connected to technology such as in the biomedical engineering field.

Environmental science. There will be increased demand for limited resources requiring new technology to conserve water, control pollution, manage global warming, and produce food.

Green jobs are occupations dealing with the efficient use of energy, finding renewable sources of energy, and preserving the environment.

As fossil fuels are depleted, the world is facing a major transformation in how energy is generated and used. Sustainability, wind turbines, solar panels, farmer's markets, biofuels, and wind energy are just some of the ways to transition to a post-fossil fuel world. Jobs in this field include engineers who design new technology, consultants to audit energy needs, and technicians who install and maintain systems. Here are some titles of green jobs: environmental lawyer, environmental technician, sustainability consultant, sustainability project director, green architect, green building project manager, marine biologist, environmental technician, energy efficiency specialist, organic farmer, compliance manager, product engineer, wind energy engineer, and solar engineer.

Finance. Money management has become increasingly complex and important requiring professionals who understand finance, investments, and taxes.

Business. Today's business managers need to understand increased competition, the global economy, and must stay up-to-date with the latest forms of communication and social media. The median salaries in this category range from 70,000 to 80,000 and beyond making this occupation a good choice for those interested in higher incomes. Jobs with fast growth include market research analysts, marketing specialists, personal financial advisers, and health-care managers.

Entrepreneurship and small business. An important trend for the new millennium is the increase in entrepreneurship, which means starting your own business. Small

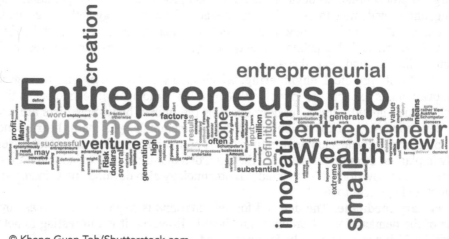
© Kheng Guan Toh/Shutterstock.com

businesses that can find innovative ways of meeting customer needs will be in demand for the future. A growing number of entrepreneurs operate their small businesses from home, taking advantage of telecommuting and the Internet to communicate with customers. While being an entrepreneur has some risks involved, there are many benefits, such as flexible scheduling, being your own boss, taking charge of your destiny, and greater potential for future income if your company is successful. You won't have to worry about being outsourced either.

Teaching. As the current generation of Baby Boomers retires, there will be increased jobs for educators who will serve the children of the New Millennial generation.

The effect of terrorism and the need for security. Fear of terrorism has changed attitudes that will affect career trends for years to come. Terrorist attacks have created an atmosphere of uncertainty that has had a negative effect on the economy and has increased unemployment. People are choosing to stay in the safety of their homes, offices, cars, and gated communities. Since people are spending more time at home, they spend more money making their homes comfortable. As a result, construction, home remodeling, and sales of entertainment systems are increasing.

Another result of terrorism is the shift toward occupations that provide value to society and in which people can search for personal satisfaction. More people volunteer their time to help others and are considering careers in education, social work, and medical occupations. When people are forced to relocate because of unemployment, they are considering moving to smaller towns that have a sense of community and a feeling of safety.

As the world population continues to grow, there is continued conflict over resources and ideologies and an increased need for security and safety. Law enforcement, intelligence, forensics, international relations, foreign affairs, and security administration careers will be in demand.

Careers with a Good Outlook for the Future

Jobs That Will Always Be in Demand[25]	2016 Best Jobs Rankings[26]	Top 10 Jobs for the Next Decade and Beyond[27]
Teachers	App Developer	Computer Programmer
Lawyers	Nurse Practitioner	Day Care Provider
Engineers	Information Security Analyst	Elder Care Specialist
Doctors	Computer Systems Analyst	Employment Specialist
Law Enforcement	Physical Therapist	Environmental Engineer
Accountants	Market Research Analyst	Home Health Aide
Food Preparers and Servers	Medical Sonographer	Management Consultant
	Dental Hygienist	Networking Specialist
	Operations Research Analyst	Physician's Assistant
	Health Services Manager	Social Services Coordinator

REFLECTION

Do a quick review of the developments affecting future careers and career trends for 2020. Write one paragraph about how any of these trends might affect your future.

Top Jobs for the Future[15]

Based on current career trends, here are some jobs that should be in high demand for the next 10 years.

Field of Employment	Job Titles
Business	Marketing Manager, Security and Financial Service, Internet Marketing Specialist, Advertising Executive, Buyer, Sales Person, Real Estate Agent, Business Development Manager, Marketing Researcher, Recruiter
Education	Teacher, Teacher's Aide, Adult Education Instructor, Math and Science Teacher
Entertainment	Dancer, Producer, Director, Actor, Content Creator, Musician, Artist, Commercial Artist, Writer, Technical Writer, Newspaper Reporter, News Anchor Person
Health	Emergency Medical Technician, Surgeon, Chiropractor, Dental Hygienist, Registered Nurse, Medical Assistant, Therapist, Respiratory Therapist, Home Health Aide, Primary Care Physician, Medical Lab Technician, Radiology Technician, Physical Therapist, Dental Assistant, Nurse's Aide
Information Technology	Computer Systems Analyst, Computer Engineer, Web Specialist, Network Support Technician, Java Programmer, Information Technology Manager, Web Developer, Database Administrator, Network Engineer
Law/Law Enforcement	Correction Officer, Law Officer, Anti-Terrorist Specialist, Security Guard, Tax/Estate Attorney, Intellectual Property Attorney
Services	Veterinarian, Social Worker, Hair Stylist, Telephone Repair Technician, Aircraft Mechanic, Guidance Counselor, Occupational Therapist, Child Care Assistant, Baker, Landscape Architect, Pest Controller, Chef, Caterer, Food Server
Sports	Athlete, Coach, Umpire, Physical Trainer
Technology	Electrical Engineer, Biological Scientist, Electronic Technician, CAD Operator, Product Designer, Sales Engineer, Applications Engineer, Product Marketing Engineer, Technical Support Manager, Product Development Manager
Trades	Carpenter, Plumber, Electrician
Travel/Transportation	Package Delivery Person, Flight Attendant, Hotel/Restaurant Manager, Taxi Driver, Chauffeur, Driver

QUIZ

Career Trends of the Future

Test what you have learned by selecting the correct answers to the following questions:

1. Students in Generation Z are
   a. limited by technology.
   b. more likely to have a lifetime career.
   c. more likely to appreciate ethnic diversity.

2. Use of the Internet will result in
   a. increased e-commerce.
   b. increased use of conventional stores.
   c. decreased mail delivery.

3. The largest group of workers in the United States is in
   a. manufacturing.
   b. information technology.
   c. agriculture.

4. Jobs unlikely to be outsourced include
   a. jobs that require close proximity to the customer.
   b. computer programming jobs.
   c. customer service jobs.

5. Future historians will describe the 21st century as the
   a. art and entertainment century.
   b. biology century.
   c. industrial development century.

Work Skills for the 21st Century

Because of rapid changes in technology, college students of today may be preparing for jobs that do not exist right now. After graduation, many college students find employment that is not even related to their college majors. One researcher found that 48 percent of college graduates find employment in fields not related to their college majors.[16] More important than one's college major are the general skills learned in college that prepare students for the future.

To define skills needed in the future workplace, the U.S. Secretary of Labor created the Secretary's Commission on Achieving Necessary Skills (SCANS). Based on interviews with employers and educators, the members of the commission outlined foundation skills and workplace competencies needed to succeed in the workplace in the 21st century.[17] The following skills apply to all occupations in all fields and will help you to become a successful employee, regardless of your major. As you read through these skills, think about your competency in these areas.

Foundation Skills

Basic Skills

- Reading
- Writing
- Basic arithmetic
- Higher-level mathematics
- Listening
- Speaking

© iQoncept/Shutterstock.com

Thinking Skills

- Creative thinking
- Decision making
- Problem solving
- Mental visualization
- Knowing how to learn
- Reasoning

Personal Qualities

- Responsibility
- Self-esteem
- Sociability
- Self-management
- Integrity/honesty

© VLADGRIN/Shutterstock.com

Workplace Competencies

The following are some workplace competencies required to be successful in all well-paying jobs. The successful employee:

- can manage resources such as time, money, materials, and human resources;
- has good interpersonal skills and can participate as a member of a team, teach others, serve clients and customers, exercise leadership, negotiate workable solutions, and work with diverse individuals;
- can learn new information on the job and use computers to acquire, organize, analyze, and communicate information;
- works within the system, monitors and corrects performance, and improves the system as needed;
- uses technology to produce the desired results.

Because the workplace is changing, these skills may be more important than the background acquired through a college major. Work to develop these skills and you will be prepared for whatever lies ahead.

How to Research Your Career

After you have assessed your personality, interests, values, and talents, the next step is to learn about the world of work. If you can match your personal strengths to the world of work, you can find work that is interesting and you can excel in it. To learn about the world of work, you will need to research possible careers. This includes reading career descriptions and investigating career outlooks, salaries, and educational requirements.

Career Descriptions

The career description tells you about the nature of the work, working conditions, employment, training, qualifications, advancement, job outlook, earnings, and related occupations. The two best sources of job descriptions are the *Occupational Outlook Handbook* and *Occupational Outlook Quarterly*. The *Handbook*, published by the Bureau of Labor Statistics, is like an encyclopedia of careers. You can search alphabetically by career or by career cluster.

The *Occupational Outlook Quarterly* is a periodical with up-to-date articles on new and emerging occupations, training opportunities, salary trends, and new studies from the Bureau of Labor Statistics. You can find these resources in a public or school library, at a college career center, or on the *College Success Website* at http://www.collegesuccess1.com/Links9Career.htm.

© iQoncept/Shutterstock.com

Career Outlook

It is especially important to know about the career outlook of an occupation you are considering. Career outlook includes salary and availability of employment. How much does the occupation pay? Will the occupation exist in the future, and will there be employment opportunities? Of course, you will want to prepare yourself for careers that pay well and have future employment opportunities.

You can find information about career outlooks in the sources listed above, current periodicals, and materials from the Bureau of Labor Statistics. The following table, for example, lists the fastest-growing occupations, occupations with the highest salaries, and occupations with the largest job growth. Information from the Bureau of Labor Statistics is also available online.

Employment Projections 2008–2018[18]

10 Fastest-Growing Occupations	10 Industries with the Largest Wage and Salary Employment Growth	10 Occupations with the Largest Numerical Job Growth
Biomedical engineers	Management, scientific, technical	Registered nurses
Network systems and data communications analysts	Physicians	Home health aides
Home health aides	Computer systems design and related	Customer service representatives
Personal and home care aides	General merchandise stores	Food preparation workers
Financial examiners	Employment services	Personal and home care aides
Medical scientists	Local government	Retail salespersons
Physician assistants	Home health care services	Office clerks
Skin care specialists	Services for elderly and disabled	Accountants and auditors
Biochemists and biophysicists	Nursing care facilities	Nursing aides, orderlies
Athletic trainers	Full-service restaurants	Postsecondary teachers

There are many print and online resources to assist with your career research. Each one will serve one or many purposes. This section lists a few suggested resources but there are many excellent resources available to you for free through your campus or public library.*

†Occupational Outlook Handbook (OOH)

This site is accessed at https://www.bls.gov/ooh/

The OOH will allow you to conduct general research on careers from a few different perspectives. It is updated approximately every two years by the Bureau of Labor Statistics. The "Search Handbook" box allows users to input an occupation then view the profile. The profile typically includes information on the types of things a worker in this occupation will do, the work environment, required education or training, pay, job outlook, and suggested similar occupations. State and area data is provided for further exploration.

Occupation Groups

The Occupation Groups section will allow for exploration of a variety of occupations based on industry categorization. Each group provides a quick snap shot of occupations including a brief job summary, required education for entry-level employment, and median pay. It also includes a link to more in-depth information on the occupation if it is covered by the OOH.

Criteria

This section allows for a search based on median pay, entry-level education, types of on-the-job training, projected number of new jobs and projected growth rate. In 2017, this search reviewed 575 jobs. While there are many more job titles, this general research allows for information gathering that can be applied to other occupations. For example, predicted growth in many areas of the medical field may indicate similar growth for other related medical occupations. If you are looking for a high paying job with a higher than average projected growth rate, this is a good place to start your search.

†From *Your Career Planner*, Eleventh Edition by Cheryl Bonner and Susan Musich. Copyright © 2017 by Kendall Hunt Publishing Company. Reprinted by permission.

Featured Occupations

The OOH periodically selects occupations to profile. These are not necessarily high growth jobs, high paying jobs, or even in high demand. The featured occupation may suggest something you have not considered. If you are interested, take the time to do a deeper dive into the information by clicking on the "view profile" link.

Other Areas for Research

It will also allow you to browse occupations by highest paying, fastest growing, and most new jobs. It is important to note that all of these are general factors and may not allow for differences in geographic area, type of industry, or even required skills.

one photo/Shutterstock.com

Fastest growing is based on the current number of people in the field and projected growth. An industry such as Wind Turbine Technician with only 4400 jobs in 2014 will see a 108% growth in the next 10 years. However, this will only amount to an additional 4800 new jobs for a total of 9200 jobs.

Compare this to Personal Care Aids. The growth rate is only 26% but this occupation is expected to go from 1,768,400 jobs in 2014 to 2,226,600 jobs in 2024. This is an addition of 458,000 jobs.

Factors such as new technology, changing market conditions, or governmental policy can all alter job growth. Because of this, it is important to consider many factors when considering a career.

O*NET

The site typically used for career research is https://www.onetonline.org/.

This tool is sponsored by the U.S. Department of Labor, Employment and Training Administration. It is a recent addition to career research tools and replaces the Dictionary of Occupational Titles. Information on occupations is updated on an ongoing basis.

The O*NET allows for the search of a specific occupation or allows the user to browse for occupations based on skills and related occupations.

Once you view the occupation, you will find information on how this occupation meets 35 skills. These skills are basic skills such as reading, writing, math, and so on. They are also cross-functional skills such "quality control analysis" that exist in other occupations.

Forty-one Generalized Work Activities are provided including functions such as "interacting with computers" and "organizing."

The interests are grouped according to occupational types.

The work styles over 16 style characteristics that connect to values. These are similar to the values you identified during your self-discovery.

Work context is covered by 57 physical and social factors.

The final section is "Job Zones" that indicate the required levels of training and education.

Ikeskinen/Shutterstock.com

Professional Associations

You will find that both the Occupational Outlook Handbook and the O*NET reference professional associations. Professional associations exist to support the careers of those related to a specific industry and advance the overall profession.

Many associations include educational resources and discounts for students. These associations are not only excellent tools for the purposes of information gathering but also for establishing relationships with professionals in a field as a part of your networking efforts.

To find a professional association related to your field, you may perform a basic internet search. In addition, there are many sites offering lists of associations. The careeronestop is a website sponsored by the U.S. Department of Labor. As of the printing of this book, the site could be found at https://www.careeronestop.org/.

To help you find a specific organization, there is a page in their Business Center dedicated to finding professional associations. It can be found at https://www.careeronestop.org/businesscenter/professionalassociations/find-professional-associations.aspx.

Social Media and the Internet

Most companies will use a branded website as the main page for all related information. This is the place to start when researching companies for internship or job application, prior to interviews, or to stay current on industry-related initiatives. For example, selecting a dozen or so tech companies to follow will provide you with hiring patterns, job growth, product changes, and new developments.

pramot/Shutterstock.com

Many companies use various forms of social media as a part of their marketing strategies. Because social media is rapidly changing, you will want to use the ones that are currently popular with a mainstream audience. Twitter, Facebook, and LinkedIn are currently the sites most companies will use to share information.

Digital media such as newspapers and magazines offer insights into companies. Use respected sources to read about the latest executive level hiring, layoffs and expansions, and other "newsworthy" information.

KNOWLEDGE IS POWER!

Maksim Kabakou/Shutterstock.com

Other Areas

Do not neglect good old fashioned library research. Your local librarian can offer you a variety of resources to help you learn about careers, industries, and companies. While libraries may have less print resources on their shelves, most subscribe to online tools that will provide the insights you need to make a good career decision. Be sure to also take the time to visit a career center on your college campus or a special section of the library for additional resources related to your career interests.

In this day of seemingly unlimited access to information, job seekers are expected to have substantial knowledge of an employer prior to the interview. Career seekers have access to insights and information that will help them make educated decisions. Those considering more education can be informed consumers of training and higher education programs.

Take the time to do your research as you determine your best choices for today and the future.[†]

ASU Colleges Presentations – Peer Evaluation Form

Use this form to evaluate the group presentations. You do not need to evaluate your own group. These evaluations will be used in determining the final score for each group. After you've evaluated all groups, rank them in order here:

Overall Best Presentation: 1.   2.   3.

Group #1:
On a scale of 1 (poor) to 5 (excellent) assess the group in the following areas,

The group was well-prepared.	1	2	3	4	5
The presentation was informative.	1	2	3	4	5
The group was engaging.	1	2	3	4	5

List two things you learned about this college.

1.   2.

Based on what you learned today, would you consider declaring a major in this college? Why or why not?

Group #2:
On a scale of 1 (poor) to 5 (excellent) assess the group in the following areas,

The group was well-prepared.	1	2	3	4	5
The presentation was informative.	1	2	3	4	5
The group was engaging.	1	2	3	4	5

List two things you learned about this college.

1.   2.

Based on what you learned today, would you consider declaring a major in this college? Why or why not?

Group #3:
On a scale of 1 (poor) to 5 (excellent) assess the group in the following areas,

The group was well-prepared.	1	2	3	4	5
The presentation was informative.	1	2	3	4	5
The group was engaging.	1	2	3	4	5

List two things you learned about this college.

1.   2.

Based on what you learned today, would you consider declaring a major in this college? Why or why not?

Group #4:

On a scale of 1 (poor) to 5 (excellent) assess the group in the following areas,

The group was well-prepared.	1	2	3	4	5
The presentation was informative.	1	2	3	4	5
The group was engaging.	1	2	3	4	5

List two things you learned about this college.

1.   2.

Based on what you learned today, would you consider declaring a major in this college? Why or why not?

Group #5:

On a scale of 1 (poor) to 5 (excellent) assess the group in the following areas,

The group was well-prepared.	1	2	3	4	5
The presentation was informative.	1	2	3	4	5
The group was engaging.	1	2	3	4	5

List two things you learned about this college.

1.   2.

Based on what you learned today, would you consider declaring a major in this college? Why or why not?

Group #6:

On a scale of 1 (poor) to 5 (excellent) assess the group in the following areas,

The group was well-prepared.	1	2	3	4	5
The presentation was informative.	1	2	3	4	5
The group was engaging.	1	2	3	4	5

List two things you learned about this college.

1.   2.

Based on what you learned today, would you consider declaring a major in this college? Why or why not?

Group #7:
On a scale of 1 (poor) to 5 (excellent) assess the group in the following areas,

The group was well-prepared.	1	2	3	4	5
The presentation was informative.	1	2	3	4	5
The group was engaging.	1	2	3	4	5

List two things you learned about this college.

1.   2.

Based on what you learned today, would you consider declaring a major in this college? Why or why not?

Academic Integrity Scenarios

Your roommate asks you to send your paper to her in an email. She just wants some ideas so that she can write her paper. What is the concern here? ** ROLE PLAY

You are unable to attend class because you need to complete another assignment due on the same day. If you go to class the assignment will be late. However, if you don't make it to class, you will lose participation points for that day making you fall below the "receive credit for class line." In order to avoid failing and submitting a late assignment, you ask your close friend who is also in the same class to sign your name for you on the attendance sheet. **ROLE PLAY

When looking at your reflection assignment, you see a passage that summarizes exactly your viewpoint on the specified subject. You write down this passage in your reflection but you do not cite where the passage came from.

You and a classmate work very closely on an assignment, sharing various viewpoints, of which are found in both papers upon submission. Neither of you cited the other in the ideas and thoughts that were submitted.

For a volunteering assignment, you are expected to participate in four hours of direct service. You only participated in two hours of service, but you submitted four hours in order to meet the requirements of the assignment.

The professor for your chemistry course does not share powerpoint lectures on blackboard or through email. Thinking you are being helpful to your fellow classmates, you decide to post the lectures and your notes on a note taking website. You do not consult with the professor prior to posting your notes or the lecture powerpoints.

†Uncovering Your Hidden Values

1. This exercise requires you to imagine that you have just been given a gift of one million dollars with only one stipulation: You must use the million only for yourself.

   a. List under Column A some of the possible ways you would like to use your gift. What would you want to do, have, or be? Some examples are provided to help start you thinking about this exercise.

Column A	Column B
Uses	Possible Values
Examples:	
1. Invest in stocks and bonds	1. Financial security, challenge/risk taking
2. Reserve season tickets to symphony, theater, and dance performances	2. Aesthetics, pleasure
3. Set aside funds for continuing education	3. Intellect, personal development, job security
4. Start a small business	4. Independence, risk taking, achievement
Uses	*Possible Values*
Your Selections:	

   b. Having determined how you would use your million dollars, assess what values are represented by your choices. In our first example, for instance, investing in stocks and bonds represents the value of financial security to those who invest in safe, low-yield securities. But to those who prefer more chancy, high-return investments, it represents the value of risk taking. Analyze each of your million-dollar choices for the value(s) they represent to you and list those values in Column B. Refer to the list of Life Values from Application 7-B for possible values words.

†From *Your Career Planner*, Eleventh Edition by Cheryl Bonner and Susan Musich. Copyright © 2017 by Kendall Hunt Publishing Company. Reprinted by permission.

2. You are the recipient of yet another million-dollar gift, this time with a different stipulation: This gift is to be used only for the good of others.

a. Ask yourself what needs doing in your family, neighborhood, country, and the world. How could you best contribute? List the ways you would make a contribution under Column A. Refer to the examples below in Column A to stimulate your thinking.

Column A	Column B
Uses	*Possible Values*
Examples:	
1. Create an institute for peace studies	1. Ethical living, freedom, spirituality
2. Reform the educational system	2. Intellect, personal development, and freedom
3. Establish parenting classes for young parents	3. Affection, family, and emotional strength
4. Implement a neighborhood watch in my community	4. Service, personal safety
Uses	*Possible Values*
Your Selections:	

b. Again analyze your list of choices in Column A for the value(s) that each represents and place them (the values) in Column B.

Work Values Assessment

1. Read the definitions of the work values listed in four categories (a through d) below. Rate each work value according to its degree of importance to you. Use the following scale in assigning your ratings:

   1 = unimportant in my choice of career

   2 = somewhat important in my choice of career

   3 = very important in my choice of career

Place the number corresponding to your rating in the blank to the left of each work value.

   a. *Workplace Conditions.* Characteristics of the workplace environment.

   _____ *Safety/Security*—a work environment free from physical danger or personal harassment.

   _____ *Pleasant Setting*—an aesthetically pleasing and comfortable work setting.

   _____ *Caring Coworkers*—working with people who get along and cooperate with one another.

   _____ *Respectful Supervision*—having understanding supervisors who respect your wants and needs.

   _____ *Competition*—a work setting where outdoing your coworkers or exceeding your own or the company's standards is important.

   _____ *Fast-Paced Work*—working rapidly to meet time or performance deadlines.

   _____ *Variety/Change*—performing many different work tasks.

   _____ *Travel*—work where travel is an integral part of the routine.

   _____ *Inside Work*—working inside a building, usually in an office setting.

   _____ *Outside Work*—working outdoors exposed to the elements.

   _____ *Both Inside and Outside Work*—striking a balance between both inside and outside work.

   _____ *Working Alone*—doing assignments by yourself involving minimal contact with coworkers or the public.

   _____ *Working on a Team*—carrying out work responsibilities as an integral part of a group of coworkers.

   b. *Workplace Outcomes.* The purpose(s) that work serves in your life.

   _____ *Being Competent*—striving to excel at the work that you do.

   _____ *Using Abilities*—utilizing the competencies you possess to their maximum.

   _____ *Making Things*—using your hands to produce or repair concrete, tangible things.

   _____ *Problem-Solving*—figuring out how something should be done.

   _____ *Developing New Ideas*—improving upon the ways things have been done or coming up with new ways of doing them.

   _____ *Precise Work*—performing work that meets exacting standards.

   _____ *Mental Challenge*—performing demanding tasks that challenge your intellect.

   _____ *Social Contribution*—seeking to improve the human condition.

_____ *Influencing Others*—affecting others in ways designed to change attitudes or opinions or motivating them to take action.

_____ *Supervising/Directing Others*—being in a position to oversee and/or take responsibility for the work of others.

_____ *Aesthetic Contribution*—performing work that contributes to making the world a more beautiful place.

_____ *Spiritual Fulfillment*—doing work that contributes to the religious or spiritual fulfillment of yourself or others.

c. *Workplace Rewards.* The rewards you expect from your work.

_____ *High Salary*—choosing an occupation where the rate of compensation is in the top third (33%) for all occupations.

_____ *Good Benefits*—having healthcare, disability insurance, etc. as part of your compensation package.

_____ *Equitable Pay*—being compensated at a rate that is commensurate with the amount and quality of work you do.

_____ *Opportunity for Advancement*—having a good chance to advance into positions of increasing authority and responsibility.

_____ *Job Availability and Security*—working in an occupational field where you have a good opportunity to obtain and maintain a job.

_____ *Recognition/Prestige*—being perceived by others as doing important work or being an expert in your field of endeavor.

d. *Personal/Family Considerations.* Attempting to balance work and personal life.

_____ *Time Flexibility*—arranging your own work hours or working according to your own schedule.

_____ *Job Sharing*—being able to share the duties and responsibilities of a job with another person or other people.

_____ *Autonomy*—having discretion in how you complete or perform your job tasks.

_____ *Self-Employment*—being employed by and working for yourself.

_____ *Ethical/Moral Standards*—being free to act in accordance with a set of standards regarding what is the right or fair thing to do.

_____ *Regular Hours*—working a regular work schedule that allows you time for yourself and/or your family.

_____ *Easy Commute*—living close to where you work.

_____ *Acceptance*—being accepted for what you can contribute although your lifestyle may differ from those of your coworkers.

2. List below your three or four most important work values in each of the four categories. Add any others that are important but were not covered above.

Workplace Conditions

_____

_____

_____

Workplace Rewards

_____

_____

_____

_____

_____

_____

Workplace Outcomes

_____

_____

_____

Personal/Family Considerations

_____

_____

_____

_____

_____

_____

3. Select your 10 most important values from those you have listed in number 2.

_____

_____

_____

_____

_____

_____

_____

_____

_____

_____

_____

The Core of Your Values

1. List below your top five to ten values from each of the values from the previous exercises.

Life Values Assessment	Uncovering Your Hidden Values		Work Values
	Million/Self	Million/Others	

2. Combine the values in the four columns above in order to come up with your top five values. Pay particular attention to those values that appear in more than one column.

3. Place your top five values in the following box.

My Top Five Prioritized Values

_____ 1. _____

_____ 2. _____

_____ 3. _____

_____ 4. _____

_____ 5. _____

Use this space to record your research on your careers. This is a page you will return to often and expand upon as you progress through the book. Make additional copies of the page as needed.

Occupation Research

Occupational Title		**Alternate Titles or Related Occupations**	
Brief Description		Five things a person in this occupation does	1 2 3 4 5
Required Skills and Abilities		Personality traits and Characteristics	
Education (Minimum required, desired certifications)		Places where training is provided and length of training	
Compensation (Salary, hourly pay, benefits)		Average hours per day spent working and additional work requirements (overtime, travel, schedule)	

Job Outlook		Typical Employers	
Things I LIKE About This Job		Things I DISLIKE About This Job	

Occupational Title		Alternate Titles or Related Occupations	
Brief Description		Five things a person in this occupation does	1 2 3 4 5
Required Skills and Abilities		Personality traits and Characteristics	
Education (Minimum required, desired certifications)		Places where training is provided and length of training	
Compensation (Salary, hourly pay, benefits)		Average hours per day spent working and additional work requirements (overtime, travel, schedule)	

Job Outlook		Typical Employers	
Things I LIKE About This Job		Things I DISLIKE About This Job	

Title	Meets My Interests	Meets My Skills or Potential	Meets My Values	Insights Gained from Career Research	Insights Gained from Informational Interviews	Personal Notes and Next Steps	Current Rating	Final Rating
Pet Food Taster	VERY HIGH: Passionate about food and healthy animals.	MODERATE: Very detailed, note taking, high sensory ability	HIGH: Competitive field, money is fair but not great. Need to move for promotions	Not a lot of information available	Hard to find someone but did talk to a wine taster. Another career to consider	Call a Pet Food manufacturer to learn more, do a larger search.	As of 10/4 I am still considering this as a choice. 4 on a scale of 1 to 5.	

Title	Meets My Interests	Meets My Skills or Potential	Meets My Values	Insights Gained from Career Research	Insights Gained from Informational Interviews	Personal Notes and Next Steps	Current Rating	Final Rating

Developing and Assessing Your Career Alternatives Create Your List

1. List your 10 occupations on the chart.

2. Research the careers you are considering. Write a brief summary of the career alternative on the chart in the second Column. Note the O*NET code if available under the first column.

Career Alternative	Brief Description	Compatibility Ratings 1–5 scale (low–high)						My Evaluation
		A	B	C	D			
O*NET # (if available)	From Internet, Information Interview, O*Net, OOH	Transferable Skills	Personality Style	Needs, Wants, Values	Employment Outlook	Cumulative Score	Overall Suitability	What I like most and least
EXAMPLE: Athletic Trainers: 29-9091.00	Evaluate and advise individuals to assist recovery from or avoid athletic-related injuries or illnesses, or maintain peak physical fitness. May provide first aid or emergency care.	4	3	5	2	14	#5	Excellent match for my values and thinking style. Will enable me to use most of my best skills and to stay connected to athletics, which I love. Bright job outlook. Not sure about I want to do that much education.

Career Alternative	Brief Description	Compatibility Ratings 1–5 scale (low–high)						My Evaluation
		A	B	C	D			
O*NET # (if available)	From Internet, Information Interview, O*Net, OOH	Transferable Skills	Personality Style	Needs, Wants, Values	Employment Outlook	Cumulative Score	Overall Suitability	What I like most and least

Career Alternative	Brief Description	Compatibility Ratings 1–5 scale (low–high)						My Evaluation
		A	B	C	D			
		Transferable Skills	Personality Style	Needs, Wants, Values	Employment Outlook	Cumulative Score	Overall Suitability	
O*NET # (if available)	From Internet, Information Interview, O*Net, OOH							What I like most and least

Career Alternative	Brief Description	Compatibility Ratings 1–5 scale (low–high)						My Evaluation
		A	B	C	D			
O*NET # (if available)	From Internet, Information Interview, O*Net, OOH	Transferable Skills	Personality Style	Needs, Wants, Values	Employment Outlook	Cumulative Score	Overall Suitability	What I like most and least

Career Alternative	Brief Description	Compatibility Ratings 1–5 scale (low–high)						My Evaluation
		A	B	C	D			
		Transferable Skills	Personality Style	Needs, Wants, Values	Employment Outlook	Cumulative Score	Overall Suitability	
O*NET # (if available)	From Internet, Information Interview, O*Net, OOH							What I like most and least

Career Alternative	Brief Description	Compatibility Ratings 1–5 scale (low–high)						My Evaluation
		A	B	C	D			
O*NET # (if available)	From Internet, Information Interview, O*Net, OOH	Transferable Skills	Personality Style	Needs, Wants, Values	Employment Outlook	Cumulative Score	Overall Suitability	What I like most and least

College 101 Video

1) I agree with what she says about waiting. I thought I new what I wanted to do when I first got here but ended up changing my major multiple times.

What Are the Benefits of an Informational Interview?

Learning Objectives

- Name three Career Center and/or online resources useful for researching careers

- Research two careers of interest and identify important details about the careers and how you can investigate them further

- Describe the purpose of and benefits from conducting an informational interview.

- Practice skills to conduct an effective informational interview, then conduct one with a person working in a career that interests you

*Informational Interviewing

The informational interview is an informal conversation useful for finding career information, exploring your career, building your network, or possibly finding future employment. It is not a job interview and the purpose is not to find employment. It is a way to find more personal information about a career you may be considering and to see if you are a good fit for this occupation.

The informational interview differs from the traditional interview in that you are in control and can ask questions about daily job tasks and how they relate to your interests. It is a great way to build your self-confidence and prepare you for an actual job interview. To obtain an informational interview, check your LinkedIn contacts to see if anyone you know is employed in the industry. Ask your friends, family, and employers if they can recommend someone for the interview. You can also work with your college Career Services to see if they have contacts for informational interviews. They often have contacts with college alumni who are willing to speak with students. You can visit websites to identify individuals you would like to interview. Most professionals enjoy helping others who have an interest in their field.

Regard the informational interview as a business appointment and dress the way others dress in this occupation. Make a short appointment (generally 15–30 minutes), state that the purpose of the appointment is to gain career information and advice, and show up on time. You can suggest that the person meet you for coffee (and be sure to pay the bill yourself). Be prepared with a list of questions to ask and to take some brief notes on the information. To begin the interview, give a brief 30 second overview of your career goals and reasons for contacting this person. Remember that the focus of the interview is to find career information. It is best not to ask for a job at this time. If there is a job available and you are a good fit for the job, he or she will likely tell you about it.

It is important to thank the interviewee and then follow up a thank you note or email. Ask the person if he or she is on LinkedIn and if you can request a link online. Bring your resume and hand it to the person at the end of the interview. Do not begin the interview with the resume since you want the focus on career information rather than on yourself.

Here is a sample phone call asking for an informational interview:

Hello. My name is _____ and I am a student at _____University. I found your name at your company website. (Or _____ gave me your name and suggested that I contact you.) Although I am not currently looking for a job, I am interested in the field of _____ and would like to learn more about this occupation. Would it be possible to schedule 15–30 minutes of your time to ask a few questions and get your advice on how to enter this field?

© 2013, Shutterstock, Inc.

*From *College & Career Success*, Eighth Edition by Marsha Fralick. Copyright © 2018 by Kendall Hunt Publishing Company. Reprinted by permissions.

†A Time Line For an Informational Interview

Initiating the Meeting

Asking for a time to meet someone for an informational interview can be a little intimidating. Take the time to think about what you are going to say before you initiate a contact.

Any contact should include your name, how you know the person or how you were referred, the reason you are reaching out, a suggested way to connect, and your contact information.

You may want to consider creating a script using the following examples:

Hello. My name is Cody and I am currently in my second semester at Regional State College. The staff at the Career Center suggested that you would be a good resource for me as I am trying to decide between two career options. My options are currently accounting or marketing. As an accountant, I would appreciate any insights you can provide about your field. Would you be available any evening next week for a fifteen to twenty minute phone call? Please contact me at Cody0348@regionalstate.edu. Thank you for considering my request.

Mrs. Alan,

You may remember me from a few years ago when I was a student at Peachy High School. I initially began studying to become a teacher. As I approach my senior year, I am having second thoughts. I am taking a career planning course this semester and I have an assignment to do an informational interview with someone on my list of career options. One of the directions I am considering is to go to graduate school and eventually become a guidance counselor. I have read a lot about this career path and think it might be a good direction for me. I have some questions I would like to ask you about your role as a guidance counselor. Could we meet after school on a day in the next few weeks? You can reach me at 555.555.5555.

Thank you for any help you can offer. It will great to see you again.

Sincerely,

Erin Chawla

Day of Meeting

Be sure **to** show up or call at set time. Respect the person and the time they have set aside. Come prepared with your questions. If you see that you are running out of time, be respectful. Ask for a few more minutes or permission to find another time to meet again. You may suggest that you send your questions by email for them to answer but do not send more than a few questions. Be selective.

After the Meeting

Show your appreciation for the time that was invested in helping you with your career. Send an electronic or print thank-you note. If your connection gave you additional people to contact, then be sure to keep your connection in the loop. As you move forward with your career choice, send updates. You never know how this person could have an impact on your career in the future or where your paths will cross.

†From *Your Career Planner*, Eleventh Edition by Cheryl Bonner and Susan Musich. Copyright © 2017 by Kendall Hunt Publishing Company. Reprinted by permission.

SAMPLE THANK YOU EMAIL/COVER LETTER
Informational Interview

TO: Marissa Watkins, Director <Marissa.watkins@idia.org>
FROM: Kaitlyn Manning <kmanning@gmail.com>
DATE: November 9, 2017
SUBJECT: Thank you for meeting with me today

Dear Marissa,

Thank you for taking so much time to share with me the extensive and impressive educational exchange programs sponsored by the International Development Institute of America. I was both surprised and impressed by how much IDIA's office has grown over the last two years. I was also fascinated to hear the details about your career path. It confirms many of my own career interests and plans moving forward.

Also, thank you for sharing with me the names of other professionals in your career field and similar organizations. I have already reached out to Jeff Banner, and will let you know how that meeting goes.

Again, I'm grateful for your time and generosity. I look forward to staying connected and will send you a LinkedIn invitation to connect later today.

All the best,

Kaitlyn Manning
kmanning@gmail.com
234.543.1234
www.linkedin.com/kaitlynmanning

Networking through Informational Interviews

Networking is an effective job search strategy of making connections with individuals and groups of people who can help you to build relationships that can lead to job offers or help you with your career success. Research indicates that more than 80% of all job seekers find their jobs through some kind of networking strategy.

Informational interviews are excellent ways to develop your network and leverage professionals to support your job search.

Networking contacts should include people you know professionally, socially, and personally.

Potential Networking Contacts		
Professional contacts	**Social contacts**	**Personal contacts**
• Members of professional organizations and associations • Contacts from informational meetings, conferences, trade shows, etc. • Coworkers and former coworkers • Former employers • Chamber of Commerce	• Current/former classmates • Alumni • Acquaintances (sports, clubs, social activities, etc.) • Business people (bank manager, insurance agent, etc.) • Professionals (doctor, lawyer, dentist, etc.) • Religious groups (clergy, members) • Sports clubs	• Friends • Relatives • Neighbors (current and past)

How to Leverage your Network to Support your Job Search

Inform them of your job search and ask if they can suggest others who might be of assistance. Keep in mind that upon accepting a job offer, contact those in your network who assisted you and/or are referring you to others. Be sure to thank them and offer to help them in the future.

20 Strategies to Grow and Maximize Your Network

1. Use every opportunity to make contacts. Sometimes contacts come from the most unlikely places or people.
2. Choose members based on information not position. Most networking is for information and referrals so consider what your information needs are, not the position of the individual.
3. Be specific about what you want from the people you contact and make reasonable and appropriate requests.
4. Follow up when you receive information, advice, or a referral. Let the person know the result of the contact you made or advice you received from them. They will be more likely to help you in the future.
5. Help others. Networking is a two-way street. Others will be more likely to assist you and more individuals will seek you out when you have a reputation for providing information and advice willingly.

6. Get to know the right people. Our brand/reputation is influenced as much by who we know as by our past work. Get to know the key people in your field or the influential people in your organization.
7. Identify your social strengths and weaknesses and develop strategies for improving your effectiveness. If you are better in "one-on-one" situations take advantage of them. If you have difficulty in formal situations, such as conferences or meetings, find ways to improve your skills in these settings.
8. Protect those in your network. Don't refer people who may reflect poorly on you.
9. Don't be afraid to ask for information. Ask for what you need. Most people want to help others and it makes them feel good about themselves.
10. Say thank you. Show appreciation to those who help you.
11. Volunteer to assist in organizing special events and meetings for a group at your academic institution.

20 Strategies to Grow and Maximize Your Network	
12. Attend welcoming programs for groups of interest. 13. Offer to lead a job support program for other students in your career field. 14. Join LinkedIn and invite participants in this program. 15. Identify and connect with participants of local affiliate groups. 16. Attend career service presentations on topics related to your career. 17. Contact alumni in your area (or U.S. at large) who work in your career field.	18. If you are an international student or student with international interests, ask an embassy for a listing of local organizations (for-profit and nonprofit) that are involved with your country of interest or home country, then research and contact them for meetings. 19. Set up one information meeting each week. 20. Search LinkedIn to find 10–20 people who currently work in your field and then "cold-call" them for a meeting.

Tips to Make a Good First Impression with a New Networking Contact

- Talk about your talent, not your title
- Listen, then share
- Speak slowly and clearly—in an assertive voice
- Be specific, reasonable, appropriate with requests
- Follow up and send a "thank-you" note/email within 24 hours

Networking through LinkedIn, Facebook, and Twitter

Chances are you are already using social media for personal and, possibly, professional reasons. You may have a Facebook page or Twitter account. You may even have a LinkedIn profile. As you think about these three social media giants, consider the networking power available to you. Learning a few strategies and techniques can move a stalled search into a powerful one. Below are some tips to help you build, nurture and grow your networking power through these three social media.

LinkedIn

If you haven't already set up a profile on LinkedIn, now is the time to take that step. You will find a plethora of resources and tools available to you to network effectively with professionals in your career field and organizations of interest.

Take time to explore the many Discussion Groups available to you. Try to avoid joining groups that only focus on job postings, and instead focus on groups that actively discuss topics in your career field. As you develop a comfort level with the conversations, be sure to comment on others' posts, contribute resources/links to articles, or pose questions to the group.

You will also want to identify thought leaders in your career field. "Follow" them, try to connect formally as LinkedIn connections, and contribute to conversations they are involved in.

Find companies and organizations that are of interest to you. Recent research shows that more than 90% of employers have an active presence and recruit on LinkedIn. Most of these organizations have a company page where you can learn about what they do and what topics are most relevant to their needs.

Search for alumni in your career field or organizations of interest by visiting the university or college page (search using the institution's name) and click on "Alumni."

Be sure to contribute content with your Groups, on your status page, and with your interactions with organizations. By contributing to professional conversations, you are developing your brand as a leading edge professional.

Tips for Your LinkedIn Profile
• Develop a profile using key words, skills, and achievements that shares more than what you would on your resume. Take a half hour every month to update your profile and keep it fresh. • Upload samples of projects or links to blogs/articles/research relevant to your career interests. • Add skills to the Skills section. • Add a clear photo/headshot that has you looking into the camera and smiling. • Ask professors, mentors, current/former employers and colleagues for recommendations. Try to have one to two recommendations for each position included on your profile. • Remember to include school activities and volunteer work.

Facebook

Although you may already use Facebook for social reasons, there are many professional reasons to be involved with Facebook. If you choose to only use Facebook for personal reasons, be sure to visit the Facebook settings to ensure maximum privacy.

Should you choose to use Facebook for your job search and professional networking, you may need to overhaul your Facebook profile or set up a separate one altogether.

You can build your Facebook network by finding company pages, organizations of interest, alumni groups and other professional groups. Be sure to "like" their page and request to join their group. Once you are accepted in the group, engage in professional discussions with other members.

Twitter

Twitter is an excellent way to learn about industries, identify and follow thought-leaders, stay in-the-know with organizations, and build your professional brand. You will need to create your Twitter "handle" or username, which you should try to keep professionally using your own name or relevant career key words. Add your photo (can be the same headshot you use for LinkedIn).

You will want to add a professional profile that explains your career background, skills, major achievements, and a brief notation that you are seeking career opportunities. Cross-link your profile by adding a link to your LinkedIn profile.

Be sure to follow thought-leaders, companies, recruiters and others of professional interest, with the hope that they will also follow you. Send out tweets daily or twice a day with career-related information to share. You can use Hootsuite to organize and schedule tweets so you can plan this activity weekly or monthly without having to remember to get on Twitter every day.

Mastering Business Protocol/Culture and Etiquette

Business culture section adapted from © 2017 Passport Career, LLC, www.Passport Career.com.

Almost everything you do in your job search will have some aspect of culture tied to it. Whether it is the way you greet somebody in a meeting or how you write your resume. Culture, protocol, and etiquette are intrinsically linked to the job search. Your ability to master the nuances of the business culture will serve you well in your job search and throughout your career.

Learning and applying the business culture is critical to making a strong first impression as well as demonstrating professional behavior to your peers and potential employers.

Let's take a look at some of the U.S.-specific business etiquette that you will need to know.

Greetings and introductions

Protocol for introductions is important. Such issues you should take note or include exchange of business cards, handshakes, gestures, hierarchy of introductions, and monikers including "Dr.," "Professor," or "Ms.," along with many other introductory nuances. Small talk is common and often important to develop business relationships. However, you often avoid small talk related to family, health, and other personal matters as well as politics and religion.

You will find that many people will introduce themselves by first name, and if they do so, then you may call them by their first name. University settings often have a more formal protocol, however, and frequently professors prefer to be addressed by their title of "Dr." or "Professor." You will need to carefully observe your situation to see how people present themselves and then follow suit.

You should feel comfortable presenting yourself by your first name. Keep in mind that people may have a difficult time pronouncing your name (both first and last) if it is not a common name in the United States. If this is the case, then be sure to help them learn your first name by creating a way to help them learn your name.

Time

It is extremely important to be on time for interviews, networking events, and other job search activities. People are very time-conscious and being late may create a poor professional image. On the same note, you don't want to arrive too early and appear too enthusiastic or anxious. The rule of thumb is to arrive about 5–10 minutes before the beginning of a meeting.

Communication style

Nonverbal communication is powerful. Master the nuances of eye contact, good posture, appropriate gestures and head nods, personal space, facial expressions, touching others on the arms, demonstration of listening, and use and placement of arms, hands, and body.

In the United States, it is important to learn appropriate eye contact. You should always look the person in the eye for a few seconds, then it is okay to look away before looking at them in the eye again. Do not "stare a person down" by continually looking at them without looking away. You look for a few seconds, then look away, then look at them in the eye again, then look away. If you don't look the person in the eye, then they may think you have something to hide, or that you are insecure, or that you are not to be trusted. If you are uncomfortable looking at others in the eye, then practice at home in a mirror or practice with friends, as this is important in the U.S. culture.

Your posture should be straight with no hunched-over shoulders. Stand up or sit up straight with shoulders back. Women should cross their legs at the ankle when sitting, and not at the knee. Men should sit with both feet on the floor, legs closer together.

Handshakes are very important as well. Handshakes should involve a firm grip from both men and women. It is important to practice your handshake with friends and get feedback from them as to whether your grip is too strong or too weak or limp. Make sure it is a confident handshake that is firm—not too hard or too soft—with both men and women.

As for personal space, most people are comfortable with a distance of about an arm's length between you and them.

Avoid putting your hands on your hips when talking or crossing your arms. Leave your arms comfortably at your side, or resting on a table, or hands-only crossed in front of you.

Verbal communication, assertiveness, and self-reliance include language/dialects, "small talk," greetings, asking questions, self-promotion, directness, and speaking one's mind. It also includes an accurate representation of skill level, how to present yourself in interviews, and how to appropriately network with both nationals and expats. In addition, verbal communication can help you to take responsibility for planning your job search and making career decisions by asking for help when needed.

Americans are direct with their communication, for the most part. If you ask a question, such as directions to an organization, you will get a direct answer, such as how to get there or they will let you know that they don't know how to get there. However, sometimes there are subtle differences in the culture with regard to direct communication. Americans will not always tell you that they don't like something, such as your resume or your communication style. Americans consider this to be disrespectful, and instead will be complimentary even if they don't like something.

In interviews, you will be asked direct questions, such as questions about your strengths and weaknesses, and are expected to provide an honest reply. These types of questions need to be carefully considered as you want to respond, but don't want to be so honest that you are presenting yourself in a negative way. See the section on interviews for further guidance in this area.

Workplace norms and time

Workplace norms in the United States include equality among women and men. Although this is the spoken and written practice, there are many "unwritten" rules in many organizations where women face challenges in competing with men for senior-level positions. That said, in most cases, women find there are many opportunities that they may not find available to them in other countries.

Age issues can become apparent in many areas across the country. There is a lot of age discrimination against people who are older. However, there are certain markets where age can be a benefit—especially for consulting positions, where experience is highly regarded. Washington, DC is an example of an area where age can sometimes work in your favor.

The work situation is often informal, with staff addressing management by their first names. This is not always the case, and you should observe the situation to see how others address others.

Opportunities for promotion are available and in many cases offered to those who prove their value to the organization.

Salaries are often negotiated, even when an employer says that they don't have any room in the budget to negotiate it. Many times you can negotiate aspects of the compensation package, such as time off, work hours, flexible work arrangements, and other aspects of the job.

Gender and Age in Business

Gender and age relate to and affect the following: applying for jobs, getting hired, networking, interviewing, and the ability to be effective in a job. Keep in mind that age and gender play key roles in many societies and cannot be dismissed regardless of your opinion about the subject. Now is not the time to push your own agenda on this topic. This does not mean, however, that you need to succumb to harassment if you are female. It does mean, though, that you need to be aware of the issues and respectfully address them, as needed.

*Following is a list of potential interview questions that you can use to keep the conversation going. You probably won't have time to ask all these questions, so choose the ones most that are most personally relevant.

1. What is your job title? What other job titles are commonly used for this position?

2. How did you get this position? What was your career path from entry-level to the position you now have?

3. What are your key job responsibilities? What is the typical day like for you?

4. What skills and education are needed for this job?

5. What are the most valuable courses that you took to prepare you for this job?

6. What are employers looking for (skills, education, personal qualities)?

7. What certificates or degrees are required for this job?

8. What kinds of internships or work experiences are desirable? Are internships available?

9. How does a person obtain this type of employment? How is the job advertised? Is the job market competitive? How can I meet the competition?

10. What are some entry-level positions in this company?

11. What important words should I include on my resume or cover letter?

12. What are the opportunities for advancement?

13. What are some personal characteristics that lead to success on this job?

14. What do you find most satisfying about your job?

15. What are the best and worst things about working in this job? What do you like about your job? Dislike?

16. What stresses you out about your job? What is the most difficult part of your job?

17. What are some of the most important challenges facing your industry today? How will it change in the next 10 years?

18. What is the salary range? What is the potential for advancement?

19. If you were still a college student, what would it be helpful to know about your current job and how to find employment in your field?

20. Can you suggest other sources or persons who could be valuable sources of information for me?

It is always easier to get where you are going if you have a road map or a plan. To start the journey, it is helpful to know about yourself, including your personality, interests, talents, and values. Once you have this picture, you will need to know about the world of work and job trends that will affect your future employment opportunities. Next, you will need to make decisions about which road to follow. Then, you will need to plan your education to reach your destination. Finally, you will need some job-seeking skills such a writing a resume and cover letter, using social media to market yourself online, and preparing for a successful interview.*

Three Minute Paper

*An important part of professional development is asking, giving, and receiving feedback. The "three minute paper" is a chance for you to provide feedback on our course and an opportunity for me to make changes or answer any questions. Thank you for completing this **anonymous feedback** on our course as it helps improve our curriculum and my teaching.*

- What is the most important information learned in class so far?

- What unanswered question or needs do you still have?

- What teaching/learning strategies are most helpful in class so far?

- What specific recommendations can you give to enhance the learning in class?

Developed by ASU Major and Career Exploration

Handshake Scavenger Hunt Activity – UNI 150

Find the following information from Handshake,

1. Using an appropriate keyword, find a job or internship that interests you in Handshake and post the keyword and internship below.

2. Where can you find information on career fairs?

3. How do you schedule an appointment in Handshake?

4. What are the appointment types available in Handshake?

5. What are some sections you can find on your profile?

6. How can I select career interests?

Handshake Scavenger Hunt – Answer Key

1. Using an appropriate keyword, find a job or internship that interests you in Handshake. (Answer: click on the job tab, enter a keyword such as marketing along with the city/state to find a unique posting)

2. Where can you find information on career fairs? (Answer: Events tab → Fair search)

3. How do you schedule an appointment in Handshake? (Answer: Career Center Tab → Appointments → Schedule a New Appointment)

4. What are the appointment types available in Handshake? (Answer: Resume/Cover Letter Review, Explore, Build, Prepare, National Service/Peace Corps Prep)

5. What are some sections you can find on your profile? (Answer: Education, Work experience, Bio, Skills, Organizations/Extracurriculars, Documents, Course, Projects, Social Links, Personal Information, Projects)

6. How can I select career interests? (Answer: Click on your Name → Career interests)

Assignment - Career Research

Name _____   Occupation #1_____

Please thoroughly complete each question using information from online resources discussed in class. For each question, please state three pieces of information.

Do not copy word-for-word from ANY source, please put it in your own words to avoid plagiarism concerns

1. Nature of Work (What you do):

2. Working Conditions (Where and how you do the work):

3. Educational and Certification Requirements:

4. Employment and Job Outlook (Are people needed NOW in this field)/ Earnings, Salary Range:

5. ASU majors that will prepare you for this career:

6. Classes offered at ASU that could give you a "taste" for this career path:

7. Contact information for someone currently working in this field: (E-mail, phone number)

8. Sources of Additional Information (websites, books, referral sources):

9. Identify, explain and describe how this occupation matches your interests? List specific examples of interests and hobbies that you have.

10. Given that a career is not likely to fit all of our interests and fulfill all of our needs, what are your interests and needs that would not be met by this career? Explain your answer. (None is not an accepointsable answer.)

11. How did you first hear about this career? What were the sources of your information (e.g., TV, movies, magazines, someone you knew, etc.? How accurate do you think are these information and portrayals?

Name _____   Occupation #2_____

Please thoroughly complete each question. For each question, please state three pieces of information.

Do not copy word-for-word from ANY source, please put it in your own words to avoid plagiarism concerns

1. Nature of Work (What you do):

2. Working Conditions (Where and how you do the work):

3. Educational and Certification Requirements:

4. Employment and Job Outlook (Are people needed NOW in this field)/ Earnings, Salary Range:

5. ASU majors that will prepare you for this career:

6. Classes offered at ASU that could give you a "taste" for this career path:

7. Contact information for someone currently working in this field: (E-mail, phone number)

8. Sources of Additional Information (websites, books, referral sources):

9. Identify, explain and describe how this occupation matches your interests? List specific examples of interests and hobbies that you have.

10. Given that a career is not likely to fit all of our interests and fulfill all of our needs, what are your interests and needs that would not be met by this career? Explain your answer. (None is not an accepointsable answer.)

11. How did you first hear about this career? What were the sources of your information (e.g., TV, movies, magazines, someone you knew, etc.? How accurate do you think are these information and portrayals?

Why Is Diversity Important in the Workplace?

Learning Objectives

- Increase cultural self-awareness and understanding of diversity in the workplace

- List all the aspects of diversity in the ADRESSING model.

- Describe 2 examples of power, privilege, and oppression in academic and professional choices and decision making.

**Diversity

Learning about and from Human Differences

This chapter clarifies what "diversity" really means and demonstrates how experiencing diversity can deepen learning, promote critical and creative thinking, and contribute to your personal and professional development. Strategies are provided for overcoming cultural barriers and biases that block the development of rewarding relationships with diverse people and learning from others whose cultural backgrounds differ from our own. Simply stated, we learn more from people that are different from us than we do from people similar to us. There's more diversity among college students today than at any other time in history. This chapter will help you capitalize on this learning opportunity.

Gain greater appreciation of human differences and develop skills for making the most of diversity in college and beyond.

REFLECTION

Complete the following sentence:
When I hear the word *diversity*, the first thing that comes to my mind is . . .

What Is Diversity?

Literally translated, the word "diversity" derives from the Latin root *diversus*, meaning "various" or "variety." Thus, human diversity refers to the variety that exists in humanity (the human species). The relationship between humanity and diversity may be compared to the relationship between sunlight and the variety of colors that make up the visual spectrum. Similar to how sunlight passing through a prism disperses into the *variety* of colors that comprise the visual spectrum, the human species on planet earth is dispersed into a variety of different groups that comprise the human spectrum (humanity). Figure 4.1 illustrates this metaphorical relationship between diversity and humanity.

As depicted in the above figure, human diversity is manifested in a multiplicity of ways, including differences in physical features, national origins, cultural backgrounds, and sexual orientations. Some dimensions of diversity are easily detectable, others are very subtle, and some are invisible.

REFLECTION

Look at the diversity spectrum in Figure 4.1 and look over the list of groups that make up the spectrum. Do you notice any groups missing from the list that should be added, either because they have distinctive backgrounds or because they've been targets of prejudice and discrimination?

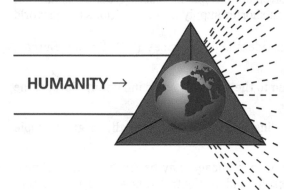

SPECTRUM
of
DIVERSITY

Gender (male-female)
Age (stage of life)
Race (e.g., White, Black, Asian)
Ethnicity (e.g., Native American, Hispanic, Irish, German)
Socioeconomic status (job status/income)
National *citizenship* (citizen of U.S. or another country)
Native (first-learned) *language*
National *origin* (nation of birth)
National *region* (e.g., raised in north/south)
Generation (historical period when people are born and live)
Political ideology (e.g., liberal/conservative)
Religious/spiritual beliefs (e.g., Christian/Buddhist/Muslim)
Family status (e.g., single-parent/two-parent family)
Marital status (single/married)
Parental status (with/without children)
Sexual orientation (heterosexual/homosexual/bisexual)
Physical ability/disability (e.g., able to hear/deaf)
Mental ability/disability (e.g., mentally able/challenged)
Learning ability/disability (e.g., absence/presence of dyslexia)
Mental health/illness (e.g., absence/presence of depression)

"We are all brothers and sisters. Each face in the rainbow of color that populates our world is precious and special. Each adds to the rich treasure of humanity."
—Morris Dees, civil rights leader and cofounder of the Southern Poverty Law Center

HUMANITY →

_ _ _ _ _ _ _ = dimension of diversity

*This list represents some of the major dimensions of human diversity; it does not constitute a complete list of all possible forms of human diversity. Also, disagreement exists about certain dimensions of diversity (e.g., whether certain groups should be considered races or ethnic groups).

Figure 4.1 Humanity and Diversity

Diversity includes discussion of equal rights and social justice for minority groups, but it's a broader concept that involves much more than political issues. In a national survey of American voters, the vast majority of respondents agreed that diversity is more than just "political correctness" (National Survey of Women Voters, 1998). Diversity is also an *educational* issue—an integral element of a college education that contributes to the learning, personal development, and career preparation of *all* students. It enhances the quality of the college experience by bringing multiple perspectives and alternative approaches to *what* is being learned (the content) and *how* it's being learned (the process).

> Ethnic and cultural diversity is an integral, natural, and normal component of educational experiences for all students."
> —National Council for Social Studies

Note

Diversity is a human issue that embraces and benefits all people; it's not a code word for "some" people. Although one major goal of diversity is to promote appreciation and equitable treatment of particular groups of people who've experienced discrimination, it's also a learning experience that strengthens the quality of a college education, career preparation, and leadership potential.

What Is Racial Diversity?

A *racial group (race)* is a group of people who share distinctive physical traits, such as skin color or facial characteristics. The variation in skin color we now see among humans is largely due to biological adaptations that have evolved over thousands of years among groups of humans who migrated to different climatic regions of the world. Currently, the most widely accepted explanation of the geographic origin of modern humans is the "Out of Africa" theory. Genetic studies and fossil evidence indicate that all Homo sapiens inhabited Africa 150,000–250,000 years ago; over time, some migrated from Africa to other parts of the world (Mendez, et al., 2013; Meredith, 2011; Reid & Hetherington, 2010). Darker skin tones developed among humans who inhabited and reproduced in hotter geographical regions nearer the equator (e.g., Africans). Their darker skin color helped them adapt and survive by providing them with better protection from the potentially damaging effects of intense sunlight (Bridgeman, 2003). In contrast, lighter skin tones developed over time among humans inhabiting colder climates that were farther from the equator (e.g., Scandinavia). Their lighter skin color enabled them to absorb greater amounts of vitamin D supplied by sunlight, which was in shorter supply in those regions of the world (Jablonksi & Chaplin, 2002).

Currently, the U.S. Census Bureau has identified five races (U.S. Census Bureau, 2013b):

White: a person whose lineage may be traced to the original people inhabiting Europe, the Middle East, or North Africa.

Black or African American: a person whose lineage may be traced to the original people inhabiting Africa.

American Indian or Alaska Native: a person whose lineage may be traced to the original people inhabiting North and South America (including Central America), and who continue to maintain their tribal affiliation or attachment.

Asian: a person whose lineage may be traced to the original people inhabiting the Far East, Southeast Asia, or the Indian subcontinent, including: Cambodia, China, India, Japan, Korea, Malaysia, Pakistan, the Philippine Islands, Thailand, and Vietnam.

Native Hawaiian or Other Pacific Islander: a person whose lineage may be traced to the original people inhabiting Hawaii, Guam, Samoa, or other Pacific islands.

It's important to keep in mind that racial categories are not based on scientific evidence; they merely represent group classifications constructed by society (Anderson & Fienberg, 2000). No identifiable set of genes distinguishes one race from another; in fact, there continues to be disagreement among scholars about what groups of people constitute a human race or whether distinctive races actually exist (Wheelright, 2005). In other words, you can't do a blood test or some type of internal genetic test to determine a person's race. Humans have simply decided to categorize themselves into races on the basis of certain external differences in their physical appearance, particularly the color of their outer layer of skin. The U.S. Census Bureau could have decided to divide people into "racial" categories based on other physical characteristics, such as eye color (blue, brown, and green), hair color (brown, black, blonde, or red), or body length (tall, short, or mid-sized).

AUTHOR'S EXPERIENCE

My father stood approximately six feet tall and had straight, light brown hair. His skin color was that of a Western European with a very slight suntan. My mother was from Alabama; she was dark in skin color with high cheekbones and had long curly black hair. In fact, if you didn't know that my father was of African American descent, you would not have thought he was black.

All of my life I've thought of myself as African American and all people who know me have thought of me as African American. I've lived half of a century with that as my racial identity. Several years ago, I carefully reviewed records of births and deaths in my family history and discovered that I had less than 50% African lineage. Biologically, I am no longer black; socially and emotionally, I still am. Clearly, my "race" has been socially constructed, not biologically determined.

—*Aaron Thompson*

While humans may display diversity in the color or tone of their external layer of skin, the reality is that all members of the human species are remarkably similar at an internal biological level. More than 98% of the genes of all humans are exactly the same, regardless of what their particular race may be (Bronfenbrenner, 2005). This large amount of genetic overlap accounts for our distinctively "human" appearance, which clearly distinguishes us from all other living species. All humans have internal organs that are similar in structure and function, and despite variations in the color of our outer layer of skin, when it's cut, all humans bleed in the same color.

AUTHOR'S EXPERIENCE

I was sitting in a coffee shop in the Chicago O'Hare airport while proofreading my first draft of this chapter. I looked up from my work for a second and saw what appeared to be a white girl about 18 years of age. As I lowered my head to return to work, I did a double-take and looked at her again because something about her seemed different or unusual. When I looked more closely at her the second time, I noticed that although she had white skin, the features of her face and hair appeared to be those of an African American. After a couple of seconds of puzzlement, I figured it out: she was an *albino* African American. That satisfied my curiosity for the moment, but then I began to wonder: Would it still be accurate to say she was "black" even though her skin was not black? Would her hair and facial features be sufficient for her to be considered or classified as black? If yes, then what would be the "race" of someone who had black skin tone, but did not have the typical hair and facial features characteristic of black people? Is skin color the defining feature of being African American or are other features equally important?

I was unable to answer these questions, but found it amusing that all of these thoughts were crossing my mind while I was working on a chapter dealing with diversity. On the plane ride home, I thought again about that albino African American girl and realized that she was a perfect example of how classifying people into "races" isn't based on objective, scientific evidence, but on subjective, socially constructed categories.

—Joe Cuseo

Categorizing people into distinct racial or ethnic groups is becoming even more difficult because members of different ethnic and racial groups are increasingly forming cross-ethnic and interracial families. By 2050, the number of Americans who identify themselves as being of two or more races is projected to more than triple, growing from 7.5 million to 26.7 million (U.S. Census Bureau, 2013a).

REFLECTION

What race(s) do you consider yourself to be?

Would you say you identify strongly with your racial identity, or are you rarely conscious of it? Why?

What Is Cultural Diversity?

"Culture" may be defined as a distinctive pattern of beliefs and values learned by a group of people who share the same social heritage and traditions. In short, culture is the whole way in which a group of people has learned to live (Peoples & Bailey, 2011); it includes their style of speaking (language), fashion, food, art and music, as well as their beliefs and values. Box 4.1 contains a summary of key components of culture that a group may share.

REFLECTION

Look at the components of culture cited in the previous list. Add another aspect of culture to the list that you think is important or influential. Explain why you think this is an important element of culture.

Box 4.1

Key Components of Culture

Language: How members of the culture communicate through written or spoken words; their particular dialect; and their distinctive style of nonverbal communication (body language).

Space: How cultural members arrange themselves with respect to social–spatial distance (e.g., how closely they stand next to each other when having a conversation).

Time: How the culture conceives of, divides, and uses time (e.g., the speed or pace at which they conduct business).

Aesthetics: How cultural members appreciate and express artistic beauty and creativity (e.g., their style of visual art, culinary art, music, theater, literature, and dance).

Family: The culture's attitudes and habits with respect to interacting with family members (e.g., customary styles of parenting their children and caring for their elderly).

Economics: How the culture meets its members' material needs, and its customary ways of acquiring and distributing wealth (e.g., general level of wealth and gap between the very rich and very poor).

Gender Roles: The culture's expectations for "appropriate" male and female behavior (e.g., whether or not women are able to hold the same leadership positions as men).

Politics: How decision-making power is exercised in the culture (e.g., democratically or autocratically).

Science and Technology: The culture's attitude toward and use of science or technology (e.g., the degree to which the culture is technologically "advanced").

Philosophy: The culture's ideas or views on wisdom, goodness, truth, and social values (e.g., whether they place greater value on individual competition or collective collaboration).

Spirituality and Religion: Cultural beliefs about a supreme being and an afterlife (e.g., its predominant faith-based views and belief systems about the supernatural).

I was watching a basketball game between the Los Angeles Lakers and Los Angeles Clippers when a short scuffle broke out between the Lakers' Paul Gasol—who is Spanish—and the Clippers' Chris Paul—who is African American. After the scuffle ended, Gasol tried to show Paul there were no hard feelings by patting him on the head. Instead of interpreting Gasol's head pat as a peace-making gesture, Paul took it as a putdown and returned the favor by slapping (rather than patting) Paul in the head.

This whole misunderstanding stemmed from a basic difference in nonverbal communication between the two cultures. Patting someone on the head in European cultures is a friendly gesture; European soccer players often do it to an opposing player to express no ill will after a foul or collision. However, this same nonverbal message meant something very different to Chris Paul—an African American raised in urban America.

—Joe Cuseo

What Is an Ethnic Group?

A group of people who share the same culture is referred to as an *ethnic group*. Thus, "culture" refers to *what* an ethnic group shares in common (e.g., language and traditions) and "ethnic group" refers to the *people* who share the same culture that's been *learned* through common social experiences. Members of the same racial group—whose shared physical characteristics have been *inherited*—may be members of different ethnic groups. For instance, white Americans belong to the same racial group, but differ in terms of their ethnic group (e.g., French, German, Irish) and Asian Americans belong to the same racial group, but are members of different ethnic groups (e.g., Japanese, Chinese, Korean).

Currently, the major cultural (ethnic) groups in the United States include:

- Native Americans (American Indians)
  - Cherokee, Navaho, Hopi, Alaskan natives, Blackfoot, etc.
- European Americans (Whites)
  - Descendents from Western Europe (e.g., United Kingdom, Ireland, Netherlands), Eastern Europe (e.g., Hungary, Romania, Bulgaria), Southern Europe (e.g., Italy, Greece, Portugal), and Northern Europe or Scandinavia (e.g., Denmark, Sweden, Norway)
- African Americans (Blacks)
  - Americans whose cultural roots lie in the continent of Africa (e.g., Ethiopia, Kenya, Nigeria) and the Caribbean Islands (e.g., Bahamas, Cuba, Jamaica)
- Hispanic Americans (Latinos)
  - Americans with cultural roots in Mexico, Puerto Rico, Central America (e.g., El Salvador, Guatemala, Nicaragua), and South America (e.g., Brazil, Columbia, Venezuela)
- Asian Americans
  - Americans whose cultural roots lie in East Asia (e.g., Japan, China, Korea), Southeast Asia (e.g., Vietnam, Thailand, Cambodia), and South Asia (e.g., India, Pakistan, Bangladesh)
- Middle Eastern Americans
  - Americans with cultural roots in Iraq, Iran, Israel, etc.

Culture is a distinctive pattern of beliefs and values that develops among a group of people who share the same social heritage and traditions.

REFLECTION

What ethnic group(s) are you a member of, or do you identify with? What would you say are the key cultural values shared by your ethnic group(s)?

> "I'm the only person from my race in class."
> —Hispanic student commenting on why he felt uncomfortable in his class on race, ethnicity, and gender

European Americans are still the majority ethnic group in the United States; they account for more than 50% of the American population. Native Americans, African Americans, Hispanic Americans, and Asian Americans are considered to be *minority* ethnic groups because each of these groups represents less than 50% of the American population (U.S. Census Bureau, 2015).

As with racial grouping, classifying humans into different ethnic groups can be very arbitrary and subject to debate. Currently, the U.S. Census Bureau classifies Hispanics as an ethnic group rather than a race. However, among Americans who checked "some other race" in the 2000 Census, 97% were Hispanic. This finding suggests that Hispanic Americans consider themselves to be a racial group, probably because that's how they're perceived and treated by non-Hispanics (Cianciatto, 2005). It's noteworthy that the American media used the term "racial profiling" (rather than ethnic profiling) to describe Arizona's controversial 2010 law that allowed police to target Hispanics who "look" like illegal aliens from Mexico, Central America, and South America. Once again, this illustrates how race and ethnicity are subjective, socially constructed concepts that reflect how people perceive and treat different social groups, which, in turn, affects how members of these groups perceive themselves.

The Relationship between Diversity and Humanity

As previously noted, diversity represents variations on the same theme: being human. Thus, humanity and diversity are interdependent, complementary concepts. To understand human diversity is to understand both our differences and *similarities*. Diversity appreciation includes appreciating both the unique perspectives of different cultural groups as well as universal aspects of the human experience that are common to all groups—whatever their particular cultural background happens to be. Members of all racial and ethnic groups live in communities, develop personal relationships, have emotional needs, and undergo life experiences that affect their self-esteem and personal identity. Humans of all races and ethnicities experience similar emotions and reveal those emotions with similar facial expressions (see Figure 4.2).

Other characteristics that anthropologists have found to be shared by all humans in every corner of the world include: storytelling, poetry, adornment of the body, dance, music, decoration with artifacts, families, socialization of children by elders, a sense of right and wrong, supernatural beliefs, and mourning of the dead (Pinker, 2000). Although different cultural groups may express these shared experiences in different ways, they are universal experiences common to all human cultures.

REFLECTION

In addition to those already mentioned, can you think of another important human experience that is universal—that is experienced by all humans?

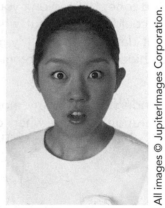

Figure 4.2

All images © JupiterImages Corporation.

You may have heard the question: "We're all human, aren't we?" The answer to this important question is "yes and no." Yes, we are all the same, but not in the same way. A good metaphor for understanding this apparent contradiction is to visualize humanity as a quilt in which we're all united by the common thread of humanity—the universal bond of being human (much like the quilt below). The different patches comprising the quilt represent diversity—the distinctive or unique cultures that comprise our shared humanity. The quilt metaphor acknowledges the identity and beauty of all cultures. It differs from the old American "melting pot" metaphor, which viewed cultural differences as something to be melted down and eliminated. It also differs from the old "salad bowl" metaphor that depicted America as a hodgepodge or mishmash of cultures thrown together without any common connection. In contrast, the quilt metaphor suggests that the unique cultures of different human groups should be preserved, recognized, and valued; at the same time, these cultural differences join together to form a seamless, unified whole. This blending of diversity and unity is captured in the Latin expression *E pluribus unum* ("Out of many, one")—the motto of the United States—which you'll find printed on all its currency.

© steven r. hendricks/Shutterstock.com

Note

When we appreciate diversity in the context of humanity, we capitalize on the variety and versatility of human differences while preserving the collective strength and synergy of human unity.

AUTHOR'S EXPERIENCE

When I was 12 years old and living in New York City, I returned from school one Friday and my mother asked me if anything interesting happened at school that day. I told her that the teacher went around the room asking students what they had for dinner the night before. At that moment, my mother became a bit concerned and nervously asked me: "What did you tell the teacher?" I said: "I told her and the rest of the class that I had pasta last night because my family always eats pasta on Thursdays and Sundays." My mother exploded and fired back the following question at me in a very agitated tone, "Why didn't you tell her we had steak or roast beef?" For a moment, I was stunned and couldn't figure out what I'd done wrong or why I should have lied about eating pasta. Then it dawned on me: My mom was embarrassed about being Italian American. She wanted me to hide our family's ethnic background and make it sound like we were very "American."

As I grew older, I understood why my mother felt the way she did. She grew up in America's "melting pot" generation—a time when different American ethnic groups were expected to melt down and melt away their ethnicity. They were not to celebrate their diversity; they were to eliminate it.

—Joe Cuseo

What Is Individuality?

It's important to keep in mind that there are individual differences among members of any racial or ethnic group that are greater than the average difference between groups. Said in another way, there's more variability (individuality) within groups than between groups. For example, among members of the same racial group, individual differences in their physical attributes (e.g., height and weight) and psychological characteristics (e.g., temperament and personality) are greater than any average difference that may exist between their racial group and other racial groups (Caplan & Caplan, 2008).

Note

While it's valuable to learn about differences between different human groups, there are substantial individual differences among people within the same racial or ethnic group that should neither be ignored nor overlooked. Don't assume that individuals with the same racial or ethnic characteristics share the same personal characteristics.

As you proceed through your college experience, keep the following key distinctions in mind:

- Humanity. All humans are members of the *same group*—the human species.
- Diversity. All humans are members of *different groups*—such as, different racial and ethnic groups.
- Individuality. Each human is a *unique individual* who differs from all other members of any group to which he or she may belong.

> I realize that I'm black, but I like to be viewed as a person, and this is everybody's wish."
> —Michael Jordan, Hall of Fame basketball player

> Every human is, at the same time, like all other humans, like some humans, and like no other human."
> —Clyde Kluckholn, American anthropologist

Major Forms or Types of Diversity in Today's World

Ethnic and Racial Diversity

America is rapidly becoming a more racially and ethnically diverse nation. Minorities now account for almost 37% of the total population—an all-time high; in 2011, for the first time in U.S. history, racial and ethnic minorities made up more than half (50.4%) of all children born in America (Nhan, 2012). By the middle of the 21st century, minority groups are expected to comprise 57% of the American population and more than 60% of the nation's children will be members of minority groups (U.S. Census Bureau, 2015).

More specifically, by 2050 the American population is projected to be more than 29% Hispanic (up from 15% in 2008), 15% Black (up from 13% in 2008), 9.6% Asian (up from 5.3% in 2008), and 2% Native Americans (up from 1.6% in 2008). The Native Hawaiian and Pacific Islander population is expected to more than double between 2008 and 2050. During this same timeframe, the percentage of white Americans will decline from 66% (2008) to 46% (2050). As a result of these demographic trends, today's ethnic and racial minorities will become the "new majority" of Americans by the middle of the 21st century (U.S. Census Bureau, 2015) (see Figure 4.3).

The growing racial and ethnic diversity of America's population is reflected in the growing diversity of students enrolled in its colleges and universities. In 1960, whites made up almost 95% of the total college population; in 2010, that percentage had decreased to 61.5%. Between 1976 and 2010, the percentage of ethnic minority students in higher education increased from 17% to 40% (National Center for Education Statistics, 2011). This rise in ethnic and racial diversity on American campuses is particularly noteworthy when viewed in light of the historical treatment of minority groups in the United States. In the early 19th century, education was not a right, but a privilege available only to those

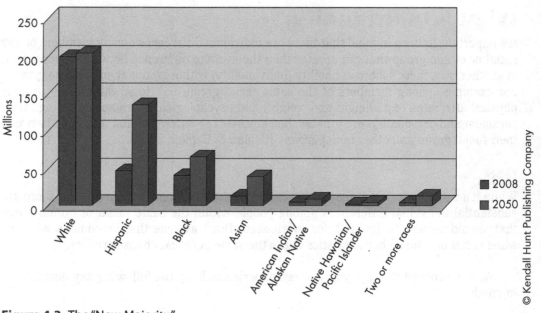

Figure 4.3 The "New Majority"

who could afford to attend private schools, which was experienced largely by Protestants of European descent (Luhman, 2007).

REFLECTION

1. What diverse groups do you see represented on your campus?

2. Are there groups on campus you didn't expect to see or to see in such large numbers?

3. Are there groups on campus you expected to see but don't see or, see in smaller numbers than you expected?

> Being born in the elite in the U.S. gives you a constellation of privileges that very few people in the world have ever experienced. Being born poor in the U.S. gives you disadvantages unlike anything in Western Europe, Japan and Canada."
>
> —David I. Levine, economist and social mobility researcher

Socioeconomic Diversity

Human diversity also exists among groups of people in terms of their socioeconomic status (SES), which is determined by their level of education, level of income, and the occupational prestige of the jobs they hold. Groups are stratified (divided) into lower, middle, or upper classes, and groups occupying lower social strata have less economic resources and social privileges (Feagin & Feagin, 2007).

Young adults from high-income families are more than seven times likely to have earned a college degree and hold a prestigious job than those from low-income families (Olson, 2007). Sharp discrepancies also exist in income level among different racial, ethnic, and gender groups. In 2012, the median income for non-Hispanic white households was $57,009, compared to $39,005 for Hispanics and $33,321 for African Americans (DeNavas-Walt, Proctor, & Smith, 2013). From 2005 to 2009, household wealth fell by 66% for Hispanics, 53% for blacks, and 16% for whites, largely due to the housing and mortgage collapse—which had a more damaging effect on lower-income families (Kochlar, Fry, & Taylor, 2011).

Despite its overall wealth, the United States is one of the most impoverished of all developed countries in the world (Shah, 2008). The poverty rate in the United States is almost twice the rate of other economically developed countries around the world (Gould & Wething, 2013). In 2012, more than 16% of the American population, and almost 20% of American children, lived below the poverty line ($23,050 yearly income for a family of four) (U.S. Census Bureau, 2013b).

REFLECTION

What do you think is the factor that's most responsible for poverty in:

a) the United States?

b) the world?

International Diversity

If it were possible to reduce the world's population to a village of precisely 100 people, with all existing human ratios remaining about the same, the demographics of this world village would look something like this:

61 would be Asians; 13 would be Africans; 12 would be Europeans; 9 would be Latin
    Americans; and 5 would be North Americans (citizens of the United States and
    Canada)
50 would be male, 50 would be female
75 would be non-white; 25 white
67 would be non-Christian; 33 would be Christian
80 would live in substandard housing
16 would be unable to read or write
50 would be malnourished and 1 would be dying of starvation
33 would be without access to a safe water supply
39 would lack access to modern sanitation
24 would have no electricity (and of the 76 who have electricity, most would only use it
    for light at night)
8 people would have access to the Internet
1 would have a college education
1 would have HIV
2 would be near birth; 1 near death
5 would control 32% of the entire world's wealth; all 5 would be U.S. citizens
48 would live on less than $2 a day
20 would live on less than $1 a day (Family Care Foundation, 2015).

In this world village, English would not be the most common language spoken; it would be third, following Chinese and Spanish (Lewis, Paul, & Fennig, 2014).

The need for American college students to develop an appreciation of international diversity is highlighted by a study conducted by an anthropologist who went "undercover" to pose as a student in a university residence hall. She found that the biggest complaint international students had about American students was their lack of knowledge of other countries and the misconceptions they held about people from different nations (Nathan, 2005). When you take the time to learn about other countries and the cultures of people who inhabit them, you move beyond being just a citizen of your own nation, you become *cosmopolitan*—a citizen of the world.

Generational Diversity

Humans are also diverse with respect to the historical time period in which they grew up. The term "generation" refers to a cohort (group) of individuals born during the same period in history whose attitudes, values, and habits have been shaped by events that took place in the world during their formative years of development. People growing up in different generations are likely to develop different attitudes and beliefs because of the different historical events they experienced during their upbringing.

Box 4.2 contains a brief summary of different generations, the key historical events they experienced, and the personal characteristics commonly associated with each generational group (Lancaster, Stillman, & Williams, 2002).

Box 4.2

Generational Diversity: A Snapshot Summary

- The Traditional Generation (a.k.a. "Silent Generation") (born 1922–1945). This generation was influenced by events such as the Great Depression and World Wars I and II. Characteristics associated with people growing up at this time include loyalty, patriotism, respect for authority, and conservatism.

- The Baby Boomer Generation (born 1946–1964). This generation was influenced by events such as the Vietnam War, Watergate, and the civil rights movement. Characteristics associated with people growing up at this time include idealism, emphasis on self-fulfillment, and concern for social justice and equal rights.

- Generation X (born 1965–1980). This generation was influenced by Sesame Street, the creation of MTV, AIDS, and soaring divorce rates. They were the first "latchkey children"—youngsters who used their own key to let themselves into their home after school—because their mother (or single mother) was working outside the home. Characteristics associated with people growing up at this time include self-reliance, resourcefulness, and ability to adapt to change.

- Generation Y (a.k.a. "Millennials") (born 1981–2002). This generation was influenced by the September 11, 2001, terrorist attack on the United States, the shooting of students at Columbine High School, and the collapse of the Enron Corporation. Characteristics associated with people growing up at this time include a preference for working and playing in groups, familiarity with technology, and willingness to engage in volunteer service in their community (the "civic generation"). This is also the most ethnically diverse generation, which may explain why they're more open to diversity than previous generations and are more likely to view diversity positively.

> You guys [in the media] have to get used to it. This is a new day and age, and for my generation that's a very common word. It's like saying 'bro.' That's how we address our friends. That's how we talk."
> —Matt Barnes, 33-year-old, biracial professional basketball player, explaining to reporters after being fined for using the word "niggas" in a tweet to some of his African American teammates

- Generation Z (a.k.a. "The iGeneration") (born 1994–present). This generation includes the latter half of Generation Y. They grew up during the wars in Afghanistan and Iraq, terrorism, the global recession and climate change. Consequently, they have less trust in political systems and industrial corporations than previous generations. During their formative years, the world wide web was in place, so they're quite comfortable with technology and rely heavily on the Internet, Wikipedia, Google, Twitter, MySpace, Facebook, Instant Messaging, image boards, and YouTube. They expect immediate gratification through technology and accept the lack of privacy associated with social networking. For these reasons, they're also referred to as the "digital generation."

Look back at the characteristics associated with your generation. Which of these characteristics accurately reflect your personal characteristics and those of your closest friends? Which do not?

Sexual Diversity: Gay, Lesbian, Bisexual, and Transgender (GLBT)

Humans experience and express sexuality in diverse ways. "Sexual diversity" refers to differences in human *sexual orientation*—the gender (male or female) an individual is physically attracted to, and *sexual identity*—the gender an individual identifies with or considers himself or herself or to be. The spectrum of sexual diversity includes:

Heterosexuals—males who are sexually attracted to females, and females who are sexually attracted to males

Gays—males who are sexually attracted to males

Lesbians—females who are sexually attracted to females

Bisexuals—individuals who are sexually attracted to males and females

Transgender—individuals who do not identify with the gender they were assigned at birth, or don't feel they belong to a single gender (e.g., transsexuals, transvestites, and bigender)

College campuses across the country are increasing their support for GLBT (gay, lesbian, bisexual, transgendered) students, creating centers and services to facilitate their acceptance and adjustment. These centers and services play an important role in combating homophobia and related forms of sexual prejudice on campus, while promoting awareness and tolerance of all forms of sexual diversity. By accepting individuals who span the spectrum of sexual diversity, we acknowledge and appreciate the reality that heterosexuality isn't the one-and-only form of human sexual expression (Dessel, Woodford, Warren, 2012). This growing acknowledgment is reflected in the Supreme Court's historic decision to legalize same-sex marriage nationwide (Dolan & Romney, 2015).

The Benefits of Experiencing Diversity

Thus far, this chapter has focused on *what* diversity is; we now turn to *why* diversity is worth experiencing. National surveys show that by the end of their first year in college, almost two-thirds of students report "stronger" or "much stronger" knowledge of people from different races and cultures than they had when they first began college, and the majority of them became more open to diverse cultures, viewpoints and values (HERI, 2013; HERI, 2014). Students who develop more openness to and knowledge of diversity are likely to experience the following benefits.

It is difficult to see the picture when you are inside the frame."
—An old saying (author unknown)

Diversity Increases Self-Awareness and Self-Knowledge

Interacting with people from diverse backgrounds increases self-knowledge and self-awareness by enabling you to compare your life experiences with others whose experiences may differ sharply from your own. When you step outside yourself to contrast your experiences with others from different backgrounds, you move beyond ethnocentrism and gain a *comparative perspective*—a reference point that positions you to see how your particular cultural background has shaped the person you are today.

A comparative perspective also enables us to learn how our cultural background has advantaged or disadvantaged us. For instance, learning about cross-cultural differences in education makes us aware of the limited opportunities people in other countries have to attend college and how advantaged we are in America—where a college education is available to everyone, regardless of their race, gender, age, or prior academic history.

Note

The more you learn from people who are different than yourself, the more you learn about yourself.

Diversity Deepens Learning

Research consistently shows that we learn more from people who differ from us than we do from people similar to us (Pascarella, 2001; Pascarella & Terenzini, 2005). Learning about different cultures and interacting with people from diverse cultural groups provides our brain with more varied routes or pathways through which to connect (learn) new ideas. Experiencing diversity "stretches" the brain beyond its normal "comfort zone," requiring it to work harder to assimilate something unfamiliar. When we encounter the unfamiliar, the brain has to engage in extra effort to understand it by comparing and contrasting it to something we already know (Acredolo & O'Connor, 1991; Nagda, Gurin, & Johnson, 2005). This added expenditure of mental energy results in the brain forming neurological connections that are deeper and more durable (Willis, 2006). Simply stated, humans learn more from diversity than they do from similarity or familiarity. In contrast, when we restrict the diversity of people with whom we interact (out of habit or prejudice), we limit the breadth and depth of our learning.

Diversity Promotes Critical Thinking

Studies show that students who experience high levels of exposure to various forms of diversity while in college—such as participating in multicultural courses and campus events and interacting with peers from different ethnic backgrounds—report the greatest gains in:

- thinking *complexly*—ability to think about all parts and sides of an issue (Association of American Colleges & Universities, 2004; Gurin, 1999),
- *reflective* thinking—ability to think deeply about personal and global issues (Kitchener, Wood, & Jensen, 2000), and
- *critical* thinking—ability to evaluate the validity of their own reasoning and the reasoning of others (Gorski, 2009; Pascarella, et al., 2001).

These findings are likely explained by the fact that when we're exposed to perspectives that differ from our own, we experience "cognitive dissonance"—a state of cognitive (mental) disequilibrium or imbalance that "forces" our mind to consider multiple perspectives simultaneously; this makes our thinking less simplistic, more complex, and more comprehensive (Brookfield, 1987; Gorski, 2009).

Diversity Stimulates Creative Thinking

Cross-cultural knowledge and experiences enhance personal creativity (Leung, et al., 2008; Maddux & Galinsky, 2009). When we have diverse perspectives at our disposal, we have

When the only tool you have is a hammer, you tend to see every problem as a nail."
—Abraham Maslow, humanistic psychologist, best known for his self-actualization theory of human motivation

What I look for in musicians is generosity. There is so much to learn from each other and about each other's culture. Great creativity begins with tolerance."
—Yo-Yo Ma, French-born, Chinese-American virtuoso cellist, composer, and winner of multiple Grammy Awards

more opportunities to shift perspectives and discover "multiple partial solutions" to problems (Kelly, 1994). Furthermore, ideas acquired from diverse people and cultures can "cross-fertilize," giving birth to new ideas for tackling old problems (Harris, 2010). Research shows that when ideas are generated freely and exchanged openly in groups comprised of people from diverse backgrounds, powerful "cross-stimulation" effects can occur, whereby ideas from one group member trigger new ideas among other group members (Brown, Dane, & Durham, 1998). Research also indicates that seeking out diverse alternatives, perspectives, and viewpoints enhances our ability to reach personal goals (Stoltz, 2014).

Note

By drawing on ideas generated by people from diverse backgrounds and bouncing your ideas off them, divergent or expansive thinking is stimulated; this leads to synergy (multiplication of ideas) and serendipity (unexpected discoveries).

In contrast, when different cultural perspectives are neither sought nor valued, the variety of lenses available to us for viewing problems is reduced, which, in turn, reduces our capacity to think creatively. Ideas are less likely to diverge (go in different directions); instead, they're more likely to converge and merge into the same cultural channel—the one shared by the homogeneous group of people doing the thinking.

Diversity Enhances Career Preparation and Career Success

Whatever line of work you decide to pursue, you're likely to find yourself working with employers, coworkers, customers, and clients from diverse cultural backgrounds. America's workforce is now more diverse than at any other time in history and will grow ever more diverse throughout the 21st century; by 2050, the proportion of American workers from minority ethnic and racial groups will jump to 55% (U.S. Census Bureau, 2008).

National surveys reveal that policymakers, business leaders, and employers seek college graduates who are more than just "aware" of or "tolerant" of diversity. They want graduates who have actual *experience* with diversity (Education Commission of the States, 1995) and are able to collaborate with diverse coworkers, clients, and customers (Association of American Colleges & Universities, 2002; Hart Research Associates, 2013). Over 90% of employers agree that all students should have experiences in college that teach them how to solve problems with people whose views differ from their own (Hart Research Associates, 2013).

The current "global economy" also requires skills relating to international diversity. Today's work world is characterized by economic interdependence among nations, international trading (imports/exports), multinational corporations, international travel, and almost instantaneous worldwide communication—due to rapid advances in the world wide web (Dryden & Vos, 1999; Friedman, 2005). Even smaller companies and corporations have become increasingly international in nature (Brooks, 2009). As a result, employers in all sectors of the economy now seek job candidates who possess the following skills and attributes: sensitivity to human differences, ability to understand and relate to people from different cultural backgrounds, international knowledge, and ability to communicate in a second language (Fixman, 1990; National Association of Colleges & Employers, 2014; Office of Research, 1994; Hart Research Associates, 2013).

As a result of these domestic and international trends, *intercultural competence* has become an essential skill for success in the 21st century (Thompson & Cuseo, 2014). Intercultural competence may be defined as the ability to appreciate and learn from human differences and to interact effectively with people from diverse cultural backgrounds. It includes "knowledge of cultures and cultural practices (one's own and others), complex cognitive skills for decision making in intercultural contexts, social skills to function effectively in diverse groups, and personal attributes that include flexibility and openness to new ideas" (Wabash National Study of Liberal Arts Education, 2007).

When all men think alike, no one thinks very much."
—Walter Lippmann, distinguished journalist and originator of the term "stereotype"

The benefits that accrue to college students who are exposed to racial and ethnic diversity during their education carry over in the work environment. The improved ability to think critically, to understand issues from different points of view, and to collaborate harmoniously with co-workers from a range of cultural backgrounds all enhance a graduate's ability to contribute to his or her company's growth and productivity."
—Business/Higher Education Forum

Technology and advanced communications have transformed the world into a global community, with business colleagues and competitors as likely to live in India as in Indianapolis. In this environment, people need a deeper understanding of the thinking, motivations, and actions of different cultures, countries and regions."
—The Partnership for 21st Century Skills

What intercultural skills do you think you already possess?

What intercultural skills do you think you need to develop?

Note

The wealth of diversity on college campuses today represents an unprecedented educational opportunity. You may never again be a member of a community with so many people from such a wide variety of backgrounds. Seize this opportunity to strengthen your education and career preparation.

Overcoming Barriers to Diversity

Before we can capitalize on the benefits of diversity, we need to overcome obstacles that have long impeded our ability to appreciate and seek out diversity. These major impediments are discussed below.

Ethnocentrism

A major advantage of culture is that it builds group solidarity, binding its members into a supportive, tight-knit community. Unfortunately, culture not only binds us, it can also blind us from taking different cultural perspectives. Since culture shapes thought and perception, people from the same ethnic (cultural) group run the risk of becoming *ethnocentric*—centered on their own culture to such a degree they view the world solely through their own cultural lens (frame of reference) and fail to consider or appreciate other cultural perspectives (Colombo, Cullen, & Lisle, 2013).

Optical illusions are a good example of how our particular cultural perspective can influence (and distort) our perceptions. Compare the lengths of the two lines in Figure 4.4. If you perceive the line on the right to be longer than the one on the left, your perception has been shaped by Western culture. People from Western cultures, such as Americans, perceive the line on the right to be longer. However, both lines are actually equal in length. (If you don't believe it, take out a ruler and measure them.) Interestingly, this perceptual error isn't made by people from non-Western cultures—whose living spaces and architectural structures are predominantly circular (e.g., huts or igloos)—in contrast to rectangular-shaped buildings with angled corners that typify Western cultures (Segall, Campbell, & Herskovits, 1966).

The optical illusion depicted in Figure 4.4 is just one of a number of illusions experienced by people in certain cultures, but not others (Shiraev & Levy, 2013). Cross-cultural differences in susceptibility to optical illusions illustrate

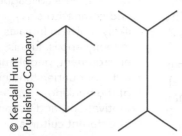

Figure 4.4
Optical Illusion

how strongly our cultural experiences can influence and sometimes misinform our perception of reality. People think they are seeing things objectively (as they actually are) but they're really seeing things subjectively—as viewed from their particular cultural perspective.

If our cultural experience can influence our perception of the physical world, it can certainly shape our perception of social events and political issues. Research in psychology indicates that the more exposure humans have to somebody or something, the more familiar it becomes and the more likely it will be perceived positively and judged favorably. The effect of familiarity is so prevalent and powerful that social psychologists have come to call it the "familiarity principle"—that is, what is familiar is perceived as better or more acceptable (Zajonc, 1968, 1970, 2001). Thus, we need to be mindful that the familiarity of our cultural experiences can bias us toward seeing our culture as normal or better. By remaining open to the viewpoints of people who perceive the world from different cultural vantage points, we minimize our cultural blind spots, expand our range of perception, and position ourselves to perceive the world with greater clarity and cultural sensitivity.

© James Michael Doresey/Shutterstock.com

People whose cultural experiences involve living and working in circular structures would not be fooled by the optical illusion in Figure 4.4.

Stereotyping

"Stereotype" derives from two different roots: *stereo*—to look at in a fixed way—and *type*—to categorize or group together, as in the word "typical." Thus, to stereotype is to view individuals of the same type (group) in the same (fixed) way.

Stereotyping overlooks or disregards individuality; all people sharing the same group characteristic (e.g., race or gender) are viewed as having the same personal characteristics—as in the expression: "You know how they are; they're all alike." Stereotypes can also involve *bias*—literally meaning "slant"—a slant that can tilt toward the positive or the negative. Positive bias results in favorable stereotypes (e.g., "Asians are great in science and math"); negative bias leads to unfavorable stereotypes (e.g., "Asians are nerds who do nothing but study"). Here are some other examples of negative stereotypes:

- Muslims are religious terrorists.
- Whites can't jump (or dance).
- Blacks are lazy.
- Irish are alcoholics.
- Gay men are feminine; lesbian women are masculine.
- Jews are cheap.
- Women are weak.

While few people would agree with these crass stereotypes, overgeneralizations are often made about members of certain groups. Such negative overgeneralizations malign the group's reputation, rob group members of their individuality, and can weaken their self-esteem and self-confidence (as illustrated by the following experience).

When I was six years old, I was told by a six-year-old girl from a different racial group that all people of my race could not swim. Since I couldn't swim at that time and she could, I assumed she was correct. I asked a boy, who was a member of the same racial group as the girl, whether her statement was true. He responded emphatically: "Yes, it's true!" Since I was from an area where few other African Americans were around to counteract this belief about my racial group, I continued to buy into this stereotype until I finally took swimming lessons as an adult. After many lessons, I am now a lousy swimmer because I didn't even attempt to swim until I was an adult. Moral of this story: Group stereotypes can limit the confidence and potential of individual members of the stereotyped group.

—Aaron Thompson

Whether you are male or female, don't let gender stereotypes limit your career options.

1. Have you ever been stereotyped based on your appearance or group membership? If so, what was the stereotype and how did it make you feel?

2. Have you ever unintentionally perceived or treated a person in terms of a group stereotype rather than as an individual? What assumptions did you make about that person? Was that person aware of, or affected by, your stereotyping?

Prejudice

If all members of a stereotyped group are judged and evaluated in a negative way, the result is *prejudice*. The word "prejudice" literally means to "pre-judge." Typically, the pre-judgment is negative and involves *stigmatizing*—ascribing inferior or unfavorable traits to people who belong to the same group. Thus, prejudice may be defined as a negative stereotype held about a group of people that's formed before the facts are known.

People who hold a group prejudice typically avoid contact with members of that group. This enables the prejudice to continue unchallenged because there's little opportunity for the prejudiced person to have a positive experience with members of the stigmatized group that could contradict or disprove the prejudice. Thus, a vicious cycle is established in which the prejudiced person continues to avoid contact with individuals from the stigmatized group; this, in turn, continues to maintain and reinforce the prejudice.

Once prejudice has been formed, it often remains intact and resistant to change through the psychological process of *selective perception*—the tendency for biased (prejudiced) people to see what they *expect* to see and fail to see what contradicts their bias (Hugenberg & Bodenhausen, 2003). Have you ever noticed how fans rooting for their favorite sports team tend to focus on and "see" the calls of referees that go against their own team, but don't seem to react (or even notice) the calls that go against the opposing team? This is a classic example of selective perception. In effect, selective perception transforms the old adage, "seeing is believing," into "believing is seeing." This can lead prejudiced people to focus their attention on information that's consistent with their pre-judgment, causing them to "see" what supports or reinforces it and fail to see information that contradicts it.

Making matters worse, selective perception is often accompanied by *selective memory*—the tendency to remember information that's consistent with one's prejudicial belief and to forget information that's inconsistent with it or contradicts it (Judd, Ryan, & Parke, 1991). The mental processes of selective perception and selective memory often work together and often work *unconsciously*. As a result, prejudiced people may not even be aware they're using these biased mental processes or realize how these processes are keeping their prejudice permanently intact (Baron, Byrne, & Brauscombe, 2008).

> "See that man over there?
> Yes. Well, I hate him.
> But you don't know him.
> That's why I hate him."
> —Gordon Allport, influential social psychologist and author of The Nature of Prejudice

> We see what is behind our eyes."
> —Chinese proverb

Have you witnessed selective perception or selective memory—people seeing or recalling what they believe is true (due to bias), rather than what's actually true? What happened and why do you think it happened?

Discrimination

Literally translated, the term *discrimination* means "division" or "separation." Whereas prejudice involves a belief, attitude or opinion, discrimination involves an *act* or *behavior.* Technically, discrimination can be either positive or negative. A discriminating eater may only eat healthy foods, which is a positive quality. However, discrimination is most often associated with a harmful act that results in a prejudiced person treating another individual, or group of individuals, in an unfair manner. Thus, it could be said that discrimination is prejudice put into action. For instance, to fire or not hire people on the basis of their race, gender, or sexual orientation is an act of discrimination.

Box 4.3 below contains a summary of the major forms of discrimination, prejudice, and stereotypes that have plagued humanity. As you read through the following list, place a check mark next to any item that you, a friend, or family member has experienced.

Box 4.3

Stereotypes, Prejudices, and Forms of Discrimination: A Snapshot Summary

- Ethnocentrism: viewing one's own culture or ethnic group as "central" or "normal," while viewing different cultures as "deficient" or "inferior."

  Example: Viewing another culture as "abnormal" or "uncivilized" because its members eat animals our culture views as unacceptable to eat, although we eat animals their culture views as unacceptable to eat.

- Stereotyping: viewing all (or virtually all) members of the same group in the same way—as having the same personal qualities or characteristics.

  Example: "If you're Italian, you must be in the Mafia, or have a family member who is."

- Prejudice: negative prejudgment about another group of people.

  Example: Women can't be effective leaders because they're too emotional.

- Discrimination: unequal and unfair treatment of a person or group of people—prejudice put into action.

Example: Paying women less than men for performing the same job, even though they have the same level of education and job qualifications.

- Segregation: intentional decision made by a group to separate itself (socially or physically) from another group.

  Example: "White flight"—white people moving out of neighborhoods when people of color move in.

- Racism: belief that one's racial group is superior to another group and expressing that belief in attitude (prejudice) or action (discrimination).

> "Let us all hope that the dark clouds of racial prejudice will soon pass away and . . . in some not too distant tomorrow the radiant stars of love and brotherhood will shine over our great nation."
> —Martin Luther King, Jr., Civil rights leader, humanitarian, and youngest recipient of the Nobel Peace Prize

Box 4.3 *(Continued)*

Example: Confiscating land from American Indians based on the unfounded belief that they are "uncivilized" or "savages."

- Institutional Racism: racial discrimination rooted in organizational policies and practices that disadvantage certain racial groups.

  Example: Race-based discrimination in mortgage lending, housing, and bank loans.

- Racial Profiling: investigating or arresting someone solely on the basis of the person's race, ethnicity, or national origin—without witnessing actual criminal behavior or possessing incriminating evidence.

  Example: Police making a traffic stop or conducting a personal search based solely on an individual's racial features.

- Slavery: forced labor in which people are considered to be property, held against their will, and deprived of the right to receive wages.

  Example: Enslavement of Blacks, which was legal in the United States until 1865.

- "Jim Crow" Laws: formal and informal laws created by whites to segregate Blacks after the abolition of slavery.

  Example: Laws in certain parts of the United States that once required Blacks to use separate bathrooms and be educated in separate schools.

- Apartheid: an institutionalized system of "legal racism" supported by a nation's government. (Apartheid derives from a word in the Afrikaan language, meaning "apartness.")

  Example: South Africa's national system of racial segregation and discrimination that was in place from 1948 to 1994.

> Never, never, and never again shall it be that this beautiful land will again experience the oppression of one by another."
> —Nelson Mandela, anti-apartheid revolutionary, first Black president of South Africa after apartheid, and winner of the Nobel Peace Prize

- Hate Crimes: criminal action motivated solely by prejudice toward the crime victim.

  Example: Acts of vandalism or assault aimed at members of a particular ethnic group or persons of a particular sexual orientation.

- Hate Groups: organizations whose primary purpose is to stimulate prejudice, discrimination, or aggression toward certain groups of people based on their ethnicity, race, religion, etc.

  Example: The Ku Klux Klan—an American terrorist group that perpetrates hatred toward all non-white races.

- Genocide: mass murdering of a particular ethnic or racial group.

  Example: The Holocaust, in which millions of Jews were systematically murdered during World War II. Other examples include the murdering of Cambodians under the Khmer Rouge regime, the murdering of Bosnian Muslims in the former country of Yugoslavia, and the slaughter of the Tutsi minority by the Hutu majority in Rwanda.

- Classism: prejudice or discrimination based on social class, particularly toward people of lower socioeconomic status.

  Example: Acknowledging the contributions made by politicians and wealthy industrialists to America, while ignoring the contributions of poor immigrants, farmers, slaves, and pioneer women.

- Religious Intolerance: denying the fundamental human right of people to hold religious beliefs, or to hold religious beliefs that differ from one's own.

  Example: An atheist who forces nonreligious (secular) beliefs on others, or a member of a religious group who believes that people who hold different religious beliefs are infidels or "sinners" whose souls will not be saved.

> Rivers, ponds, lakes and streams— they all have different names, but they all contain water. Just as religions do—they all contain truths."
> —Muhammad Ali, three-time world heavyweight boxing champion, member of the International Boxing Hall of Fame, and recipient of the Spirit of America Award as the most recognized American in the world

- Anti-Semitism: prejudice or discrimination toward Jews or people who practice the religion of Judaism.

  Example: Disliking Jews because they're the ones who "killed Christ."

- Xenophobia: fear or hatred of foreigners, outsiders, or strangers.

(continued)

Box 4.3 (Continued)

Example: Believing that immigrants should be banned from entering the country because they'll undermine our economy and increase our crime rate.

- Regional Bias: prejudice or discrimination based on the geographical region in which an individual is born and raised.
  Example: A northerner thinking that all southerners are racists.

- Jingoism: excessive interest and belief in the superiority of one's own nation—without acknowledging its mistakes or weaknesses—often accompanied by an aggressive foreign policy that neglects the needs of other nations or the common needs of all nations.
  Example: "Blind patriotism"—failure to see the shortcomings of one's own nation and viewing any questioning or criticism of one's own nation as being disloyal or "unpatriotic." (As in the slogan, "America: right or wrong" or "America: love it or leave it!")

> Above all nations is humanity."
> —Motto of the University of Hawaii

- Terrorism: intentional acts of violence committed against civilians that are motivated by political or religious prejudice.

Example: The September 11, 2001, attacks on the United States.

- Sexism: prejudice or discrimination based on sex or gender.
  Example: Believing that women should not pursue careers in fields traditionally filled only by men (e.g., engineering or politics) because they lack the innate qualities or natural skills to do so.

- Heterosexism: belief that heterosexuality is the only acceptable sexual orientation.
  Example: Believing that gays should not have the same legal rights and opportunities as heterosexuals.

- Homophobia: extreme fear or hatred of homosexuals.
  Example: Creating or contributing to anti-gay web-sites, or "gay bashing" (acts of violence toward gays).

- Ageism: prejudice or discrimination toward certain age groups, particularly toward the elderly.
  Example: Believing that all "old" people have dementia and shouldn't be allowed to drive or make important decisions.

- Ableism: prejudice or discrimination toward people who are disabled or handicapped (physically, mentally, or emotionally).
  Example: Intentionally avoiding social contact with people in wheelchairs.

REFLECTION

As you read through the above list, did you, a friend, or family member experience any of the form(s) of prejudice listed?

If yes, what happened and why do you think it happened?

Strategies for Overcoming Stereotypes and Prejudices

We may hold prejudices, stereotypes, or subtle biases that bubble beneath the surface of our conscious awareness. The following practices and strategies can help us become more aware of our unconscious biases and relate more effectively to individuals from diverse groups.

Consciously avoid preoccupation with physical appearances. Remember the old proverb: "It's what inside that counts." Judge others by the quality of their inner qualities, not by the familiarity of their outer features. Get beneath the superficial surface of appearances and relate to people not in terms of how they look but who they are and how they act.

Form impressions of others on a person-to-person basis, not on the basis of their group membership. This may seem like an obvious and easy thing to do, but research shows that humans have a natural tendency to perceive individuals from unfamiliar groups as being more alike (or all alike) than members of their own group (Taylor, Peplau, & Sears, 2006). Thus, we need to remain mindful of this tendency and make a conscious effort to perceive and treat individuals of diverse groups as unique human beings, not according to some general (stereotypical) rule of thumb.

Note

It's valuable to learn about different cultures and the common characteristics shared by members of the same culture; however, this shouldn't be done while ignoring individual differences. Don't assume that all individuals who share the same cultural background share the same personal characteristics.

(Review your results from the My MI Advantage Inventory. How might the recommendations you received about your interpersonal skills enable you to become more adept at connecting with people from cultural backgrounds that are different from your own?)

Strategies for Increasing Interpersonal Contact and Interaction with Members of Diverse Groups

Place yourself in situations and locations on campus where you will come in regular contact with individuals from diverse groups. Distancing ourselves from diversity ensures we'll never experience diversity and benefit from it. Research in social psychology shows that relationships are more likely to form among people who come in regular contact with

> I grew up in a very racist family. Even just a year ago, I could honestly say 'I hate Asians' with a straight face and mean it. My senior AP language teacher tried hard to teach me not to be judgmental. He got me to be open to others, so much so that my current boyfriend is half Chinese."
> —First-year college student

> Stop judging by mere appearances, and make a right judgment."
> —Bible, John 7:24

> You can't judge a book by the cover."
> —1962 hit song by Elias Bates, a.k.a. Bo Diddley (Note: a "bo diddley" is a one-stringed African guitar)

REFLECTION

Your comfort level while interacting with people from diverse groups is likely to depend on how much prior experience you've had with members of those groups. Rate the amount or variety of diversity you have experienced in the following settings:

1. The high school you attended	high	moderate	low
2. The college or university you now attend	high	moderate	low
3. The neighborhood in which you grew up	high	moderate	low
4. Places where you have been employed	high	moderate	low

Which setting had the most and the least diversity?

What do you think accounted for this difference?

one another (Latané, et al., 1995), and research on diversity reveals that when there's regular contact between members of different racial or ethnic groups, stereotyping is sharply reduced and intercultural friendships are more likely to develop (Pettigrew, 1997, 1998). You can create these conditions by making an intentional attempt to sit near diverse students in the classroom, library, or student café, and by joining them for class discussion groups or group projects.

Take advantage of social media to "chat" virtually with students from diverse groups on your own campus, or students on other campuses. Electronic communication can be a convenient and comfortable way to initially interact with members of diverse groups with whom you have had little prior experience. After interacting *online*, you're more likely to feel more comfortable about interacting *in person*.

Engage in co-curricular experiences involving diversity. Review your student handbook to find co-curricular programs, student activities, student clubs, or campus organizations that emphasize diversity awareness and appreciation. Studies indicate that participation in co-curricular experiences relating to diversity promotes critical thinking (Pascarella & Terenzini, 2005) and reduces unconscious prejudice (Blair, 2002).

Consider spending time at the multicultural center on your campus, or joining a campus club or organization that's devoted to diversity awareness (e.g., multicultural or international student club). Putting yourself in these situations will enable you to make regular contact with members of cultural groups other than your own; it also sends a clear message to members of these groups that you value their culture because you've taken the initiative to connect with them on "their turf."

If your campus sponsors multicultural or cross-cultural retreats, strongly consider participating in them. A retreat setting can provide a comfortable environment in which you can interact personally with diverse students without being distracted by your customary social circle and daily routine.

If possible, participate in a study abroad or travel study program that gives you the opportunity to live in another country and interact directly with its native citizens. In addition to coursework, you can gain international knowledge and a global perspective by participating in programs that enable you to actually *experience* a different country. You can do this for a full term or for a shorter time period (e.g., January, May, or summer term). To prepare for international experiences, take a course in the language, culture, or history of the nation to which you will be traveling.

Research on students who participate in study abroad programs indicates that these experiences promote greater appreciation of cross-cultural differences, greater interest in world affairs, and greater commitment to peace and international cooperation (Bok, 2006; Kaufmann, et al., 1992). Additional research shows that study abroad benefits students' personal development, including improved self-confidence, sense of independence, and ability to function in complex environments (Carlson, et al., 1990; IES Abroad News, 2002).

Incorporate diversity courses into your planned schedule of classes. Review your college catalog (bulletin) and identify courses that are designed to promote understanding or appreciation of diversity. These courses may focus on diverse cultures found within the United States (sometimes referred to as multicultural courses) or diverse cultures associated with different countries (sometimes referred to as international or cross-cultural courses).

In a national study of college students who experienced multicultural courses, it was discovered that students of all racial and ethnic groups made significant gains in learning and intellectual development (Smith, 1997; Smith, et al., 1997).

Taking courses focusing on international diversity can help you develop the global perspective needed for success in today's international economy and enhance the quality of your college transcript (Brooks, 2009; Cuseo, et al., 2013; National Association of Colleges & Employers, 2003).

Be on the lookout for diversity implications associated with topics you're reading about or discussing in class. Consider the multicultural and cross-cultural ramifications of material you're studying and use examples of diversity to support or illustrate your points. If you're allowed to choose a topic for a research project, select one that relates to diversity or has implications for diversity.

Seek out the views and opinions of classmates from diverse backgrounds. Discussions among students of different races and cultures can reduce prejudice and promote intercultural appreciation, but only if each member's cultural identity and perspective is sought out and valued by members of the discussion group (Baron, Byrne, & Brauscombe, 2008). During class discussions, you can demonstrate leadership by seeking out views and opinions of classmates from diverse backgrounds and ensuring that the ideas of people from minority groups are included and respected. Also, after class discussions, you can ask students from different backgrounds if there was any point made or position taken in class that they would have strongly questioned or challenged.

If there is little or no diversity among students in class, encourage your classmates to look at topics from diverse perspectives. For instance, you might ask: "If there were international students here, what might they be adding to our discussion?" or, "If members of certain minority groups were here, would they be offering a different viewpoint?"

If you are given the opportunity to form your own discussion groups and group project teams, join or create groups composed of students from diverse backgrounds. You can gain greater exposure to diverse perspectives by intentionally joining or forming learning groups with students who differ in terms of gender, age, race, or ethnicity. Including diversity in your discussion groups not only creates social variety, it also enhances the quality of your group's work by allowing members to gain access to and learn from multiple perspectives. For instance, in learning groups comprised of students that are diverse with respect to age, older students will bring a broad range of life experiences that younger students can draw upon and learn from, while younger students can provide a more contemporary and idealistic perspective to the group's discussions. Gender diversity is also likely to infuse group discussions with different learning styles and approaches to understanding issues. Studies show that males are more likely to be "separate knowers"—they tend to "detach" themselves from the concept or issue being discussed so they can analyze it. In contrast, females are more likely to be "connected knowers"—they tend to relate personally to concepts and connect them with their own experiences and the experiences of others. For example, when interpreting a poem, males are more likely to ask: "What techniques can I use to analyze it?" In contrast, females would be more likely to ask: "What is the poet trying to say to me?" (Belenky, et al., 1986). It's also been found that females are more likely to work collaboratively during group discussions and collect the ideas of other members; in contrast, males are more likely to adopt a competitive approach and debate the ideas of others (Magolda, 1992). Both of these styles of learning are valuable and you can capitalize on these different styles by forming gender-diverse discussion groups.

Form collaborative learning teams with students from diverse backgrounds. A learning *team* is more than a discussion group that tosses around ideas; it moves beyond discussion to *collaboration*—its members "co-labor" (work together) to reach the same goal. Research from kindergarten through college indicates that when students collaborate in teams, their academic performance and interpersonal skills are strengthened (Cuseo, 1996). Also, when individuals from different racial groups work collaboratively toward the same goal, racial prejudice is reduced and interracial friendships are more likely to be formed (Allport, 1954; Amir, 1976; Brown, et al., 2003; Dovidio, Eller, & Hewstone, 2011). These positive developments may be explained, in part, by the fact that when members of diverse groups come together on the same team, nobody is a member of an "out" group ("them"); instead, everybody belongs to the same "in" group ("us") (Pratto, et al., 2000; Sidanius, et al., 2000).

In an analysis of multiple studies involving more than 90,000 people from 25 different countries, it was found that when interaction between members of diverse groups took place under the conditions described in Box 4.4, prejudice was significantly reduced (Pettigrew & Tropp, 2000) and the greatest gains in learning took place (Johnson, Johnson, & Smith, 1998; Slavin, 1995).

Box 4.4

Tips for Teamwork: Creating Diverse and Effective Learning Teams

1. Intentionally form learning teams with students who have different cultural backgrounds and life experiences. Teaming up only with friends or classmates whose backgrounds and experiences are similar to yours can actually impair your team's performance because teammates can get off track and onto topics that have nothing to do with the learning task (e.g., what they did last weekend or what they're planning to do next weekend).

2. Before jumping into group work, take some time to interact informally with your teammates. When team members have some social "warm up" time (e.g., time to learn each other's names and learn something about each other), they feel more comfortable expressing their ideas and are more likely to develop a stronger sense of team identity. This feeling of group solidarity can create a foundation of trust among group members, enabling them to work together as a team, particularly if they come from diverse (and unfamiliar) cultural backgrounds.

   The context in which a group interacts can influence the openness and harmony of their interaction. Group members are more likely to interact openly and collaboratively when they work in a friendly, informal environment that's conducive to relationship building. A living room or a lounge area provides a warmer and friendlier team-learning atmosphere than a sterile classroom.

3. Have teammates work together to complete a single work product. One jointly created product serves to highlight the team's collaborative effort and collective achievement (e.g., a completed sheet of answers to questions, or a comprehensive list of ideas). Creating a common final product helps keep individuals thinking in terms of "we" (not "me") and keeps the team moving in the same direction toward the same goal.

4. Group members should work interdependently—they should depend on each other to reach their common goal and each member should have equal opportunity to contribute to the team's final product. Each teammate should take responsibility for making an indispensable contribution to the team's end product, such as contributing: (a) a different piece of *information* (e.g., a specific chapter from the textbook or a particular section of class notes), (b) a particular form of *thinking* to the learning task (e.g., analysis, synthesis, or application), or (c) a different *perspective* (e.g., national, international, or global). Said in another way, each group member should assume personal responsibility for a piece that's needed to complete the whole puzzle.

   Similar to a sports team, each member of a learning team should have a specific role to play. For instance, each teammate could perform one of the following roles:

   - manager—whose role is to assure that the team stays on track and keeps moving toward its goal;
   - moderator—whose role is to ensure that all teammates have equal opportunity to contribute;
   - summarizer—whose role is to monitor the team's progress, identifying what has been accomplished and what still needs to be done;
   - recorder—whose role is to keep a written record of the team's ideas.

5. After concluding work in diverse learning teams, take time to reflect on the experience. The final step in any learning process, whether it be learning from a lecture or learning from a group discussion, is to step back from the process and thoughtfully review it. Deep learning requires not only effortful action but also thoughtful reflection (Bligh, 2000; Roediger, Dudai, & Fitzpatrick, 2007). You can reflect on your experiences with diverse learning groups by asking yourself questions that prompt you to process the ideas shared by members of your group and the impact those ideas had on you. For instance, ask yourself (and your teammates) the following questions:

   - What major similarities in viewpoints did all group members share? (What were the common themes?)
   - What major differences of opinion were expressed by diverse members of our group? (What were the variations on the themes?)
   - Were there particular topics or issues raised during the discussion that provoked intense reactions or emotional responses from certain members of our group?
   - Did the group discussion lead any individuals to change their mind about an idea or position they originally held?

   When contact among people from diverse groups takes place under the five conditions described in this box, group work is transformed into *teamwork* and promotes higher levels of thinking and deeper appreciation of diversity. A win–win scenario is created: Learning and thinking are strengthened while bias and prejudice are weakened (Allport, 1979; Amir, 1969; Aronson, Wilson, & Akert, 2013; Cook, 1984; Sherif, et al., 1961).

Have you had an experience with a member of an unfamiliar racial or cultural group that caused you to change your attitude or viewpoint toward that group?

Take a stand against prejudice or discrimination by constructively disagreeing with students who make stereotypical statements and prejudicial remarks. By saying nothing, you may avoid conflict, but your silence may be perceived by others to mean that you agree with the person who made the prejudicial remark. Studies show that when members of the same group observe another member of their own group making prejudicial comments, prejudice tends to increase among all group members—probably due to peer pressure of group conformity (Stangor, Sechrist, & Jost, 2001). In contrast, if a person's prejudicial remark is challenged by a member of one's own group, particularly a fellow member who is liked and respected, that person's prejudice decreases along with similar prejudices held by other members of the group (Baron, Byrne, & Brauscombe, 2008). Thus, by taking a leadership role and challenging peers who make prejudicial remarks, you're likely to reduce that person's prejudice as well as the prejudice of others who hear the remark. In addition, you help create a campus climate in which students experience greater satisfaction with their college experience and are more likely to complete their college degree. Studies show that a campus climate which is hostile toward students from minority groups lowers students' level of college satisfaction and college completion rates of both minority and majority students (Cabrera, et al., 1999; Eimers & Pike, 1997; Nora & Cabrera, 1996).

Note

By actively opposing prejudice on campus, you demonstrate diversity leadership and moral character. You become a role model whose actions send a clear message that valuing diversity is not only the smart thing to do, it's the right thing to do.

REFLECTION

If you heard another student telling an insulting racial or gender joke, do you think you would do anything about it? Why?

Chapter Summary and Highlights

Diversity refers to the variety of groups that comprise humanity (the human species). Humans differ from one another in multiple ways, including physical features, religious beliefs, mental and physical abilities, national origins, social backgrounds, gender, and sexual orientation. Diversity involves the important political issue of securing equal rights and social justice for all people; however, it's also an important *educational* issue—an integral element of the college experience that enriches learning, personal development, and career preparation.

When a group of people share the same traditions and customs, it creates a culture that serves to bind people into a supportive, tight-knit community. However, culture can also lead its members to view the world solely through their own cultural lens (known as ethnocentrism), which can blind them to other cultural perspectives. Ethnocentrism can contribute to stereotyping—viewing individual members of another cultural group in the same (fixed) way, in which they're seen as having similar personal characteristics.

Stereotyping can result in prejudice—a biased prejudgment about another person or group of people that's formed before the facts are known. Stereotyping and prejudice often go hand in hand because if the stereotype is negative, members of the stereotyped group are then judged negatively. Discrimination takes prejudice one step further by converting the negative prejudgment into behavior that results in unfair treatment of others. Thus, discrimination is prejudice put into action.

Once stereotyping and prejudice are overcome, we are positioned to experience diversity and reap its multiple benefits—which include sharper self-awareness, deeper learning, higher-level thinking, and better career preparation.

The increasing diversity of students on campus, combined with the wealth of diversity-related educational experiences found in the college curriculum and co-curriculum, presents you with an unprecedented opportunity to infuse diversity into your college experience. Seize this opportunity and capitalize on the power of diversity to increase the quality of your college education and your prospects for success in the 21st century.

Learning More through the World Wide Web:

Internet-Based Resources

For additional information on diversity, see the following websites:

Stereotyping:
ReducingStereotypeThreat.org at www.reducingstereotypethreat.org

Prejudice and Discrimination:
Southern Poverty Law Center at www.splcenter.org/

Human Rights:
Amnesty International at www.amnesty.org/en/discrimination
Center for Economic & Social Justice at www.cesj.org

Sexism in the Media:
"Killing Us Softly" at www.youtube.com/watch?v=PTlmho_RovY

LGBT Acceptance and Support:
"It Gets Better Project," at www.itgetsbetter.org

Quote Reflections

Review the sidebar quotes contained in this chapter and select two that were especially meaningful or inspirational to you.

For each quote, provide a three- to five-sentence explanation why you chose it.

Reality Bite

Hate Crime: A Racially Motivated Murder

Jasper County, Texas, has a population of approximately 31,000 people. In this county, 80% of the people are White, 18% are Black, and 2% are of other races. The county's poverty rate is considerably higher than the national average, and its average household income is significantly lower. In 1998, the mayor, the president of the Chamber of Commerce, and two councilmen were Black. From the outside, Jasper appeared to be a town with racial harmony, and its Black and White leaders were quick to state that there was no racial tension in Jasper.

However, one day, James Byrd Jr.—a 49-year-old African American man—was walking home along a road one evening and was offered a ride by three White males. Rather than taking Byrd home, Lawrence Brewer (age 31), John King (age 23), and Shawn Berry (age 23), three men linked to White-supremacist groups, took Byrd to an isolated area and began beating him. They then dropped his pants to his ankles, painted his face black, chained Byrd to their truck, and dragged him for approximately three miles. The truck was driven in a zigzag fashion to inflict maximum pain on the victim. Byrd was decapitated after his body collided with a culvert in a ditch alongside the road. His skin, arms, genitalia, and other body parts were strewn along the road, while his torso was found dumped in front of a Black cemetery. Medical examiners testified that Byrd was alive for much of the dragging incident.

When they were brought to trial, the bodies of Brewer and King were covered with racist tattoos; they were eventually sentenced to death. As a result of the murder, Byrd's family created the James Byrd Foundation for Racial Healing. A wrought iron fence that separated Black and White graves for more than 150 years in Jasper Cemetery was removed in a special unity service. Members of the racist Ku Klux Klan have since visited the gravesite of Byrd several times, leaving racist stickers and other marks that angered the Jasper community and Byrd's family.

Source: *Louisiana Weekly* (February 3, 2003).

Reflection Questions

1. What factors do you think were responsible for this incident?

2. Could this incident have been prevented? If yes, how? If no, why not?

3. How likely do you think an incident like this could take place in your hometown or near your college campus?

4. If this event happened to take place in your hometown, how do you think members of your community would react?

Gaining Awareness of Your Group Identities

We are members of multiple groups at the same time and our membership in these overlapping groups can influence our personal development and identity. In the following figure, consider the shaded center circle to be yourself and the six unshaded circles to be six different groups you belong to and have influenced your development.

Fill in the unshaded circles with the names of groups to which you think you belong that have had the most influence on your personal development and identity. You can use the diversity spectrum (p. 234) to help you identify different groups to which you may be a member. Don't feel you have to fill in all six circles. What's more important is to identify those groups that you think have had a significant influence on your personal development or identity.

Reflection Questions

1. Which one of your groups has had the greatest influence on your personal development or identity? Why?

2. Have you ever felt limited or disadvantaged by being a member of any group(s) to which you belong? Why?

3. Have you ever felt advantaged or privileged by your membership in any group(s)? Why?

Intercultural Interview

1. Identify a person on your campus who is a member of an ethnic or racial group that you've had little previous contact. Ask that person for an interview, and during the interview, include the following questions:
   - What does "diversity" mean to you?
   - What prior experiences have affected your current viewpoints or attitudes about diversity?
   - What would you say have been the major influences and turning points in your life?
   - Who would you cite as your positive role models, heroes, or sources of inspiration?
   - What societal contributions made by your ethnic or racial group would you like others to be aware of and acknowledge?
   - What do you hope will never again be said about your ethnic or racial group?

2. If you were the interviewee instead of the interviewer, how would you have answered the above questions?

3. What do you think accounts for the differences (and similarities) between your answers to the above questions and those provided by the person you interviewed?

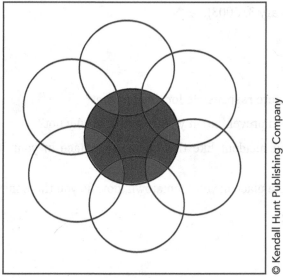

Hidden Bias Test**

Go to www.tolerance.org/activity/test-yourself-hidden-bias and take one or more of the hidden bias tests on this website. These tests assess subtle bias with respect to gender, age, ethnic minority groups, religious denominations, sexual orientations, disabilities, and body weight.

After completing the test, answer the following questions:

1. Did the results reveal any bias(es) you weren't unaware of?

2. Did you think the assessment results were accurate or valid?

3. What do you think best accounts for or explains your results?

4. If your closest family member and best friend took the test, how do you think their results would compare with yours?

_____

_____

_____

_____

_____

_____

_____

_____

_____

_____

_____

_____

_____

_____

_____

_____

What Majors Best Complement My Values and Personality?

Learning Objectives

- Identify three values that are most important to you by participating in the values activity.

- Discover the four aspects of your personality using the MBTI framework.

- Explain how your MBTI personality affects your career interests and the process of choosing a major.

*Using Values to Make Important Life Decisions

Values are what we think is important and what we feel is right and good. Our values tell the world who we are. They help us to determine which goals are more valuable than others and to spend time on what is most important. Our values make us different and unique individuals. We often take pride in our values by displaying them on bumper stickers, tee shirts, and tattoos.

Values come from many sources, including our parents, friends, the media, our religious background, our culture, society, and the historical time in which we live. Knowing our values helps to make good decisions about work and life. For example, consider a situation in which a person is offered a high-paying job that involves a high degree of responsibility and stress. If the person values challenge and excitement and views stress as a motivator, the chances are that it would be a good decision to take the job. If the person values peace of mind and has a difficult time coping with stress, it might be better to forgo the higher income and maintain quality of life. Making decisions consistent with our values is one of the keys to happiness and success.

Researchers studied values in 70 different countries around the world and found 10 values rated as important around the world.[10] As you read the list, think about your own personal values.

The 10 Most Important Values around the World

- **Achievement**: personal success
- **Benevolence**: concern about the welfare of others
- **Conformity**: acting within social norms
- **Hedonism**: personal gratification and pleasure
- **Power**: status and prestige
- **Security**: safety, harmony, law, and order
- **Self-direction**: independent thought and action
- **Stimulation**: excitement, novelty, and challenge
- **Tradition**: respect for cultural or religious customs
- **Universalism**: understanding and appreciating all people and nature

Values Checklist

Assessing Your Personal Values

Use the following checklist to begin to think about what values are important to you.
Place a checkmark next to any value that is important to you. There are no right or wrong answers. If you think of other values that are important to you, add them to the bottom of the list.

_____ Having financial security	_____ Having good family relationships
_____ Making a contribution to humankind	_____ Preserving the environment
_____ Being a good parent	_____ Having the respect of others
_____ Being honest	_____ Becoming famous
_____ Acquiring wealth	_____ Happiness
_____ Being a wise person	_____ Freedom and independence
_____ Becoming an educated person	_____ Common sense
_____ Believing in a higher power (God)	_____ Having pride in my culture
_____ Preserving civil rights	_____ Doing community service
_____ Never being bored	_____ Achieving my goals in life
_____ Enjoying life and having fun	_____ Having adventures
_____ Making something out of my life	_____ Having leisure time
_____ Being an ethical person	_____ Having good health
_____ Feeling safe and secure	_____ Being loyal
_____ Having a good marriage	_____ Having a sense of accomplishment
_____ Having good friends	_____ Participating in church activities
_____ Having social status	_____ Being physically fit
_____ Being patriotic	_____ Helping others
_____ Having power	_____ Being a good person
_____ Having good morals	_____ Having time to myself
_____ Being creative	_____ Loving and being loved
_____ Having control over my life	_____ Being physically attractive
_____ Growing and developing	_____ Achieving something important
_____ Feeling competent	_____ Accepting who I am
_____ Feeling relaxed	_____ Appreciating natural beauty
_____ Having prestige	_____ Using my artistic talents
_____ Improving society	_____ Feeling good about myself
_____ Having good mental health	_____ Making a difference
_____ Being a good athlete	_____ Other: _____
_____ Enjoying the present moment	_____ Other: _____
_____ Maintaining peace of mind	_____ Other: _____

REFLECTION

What is your most important value? Why is it important to you?

Values

Test what you have learned by selecting the correct answers to the following questions.

1. Values are

   a. what we find interesting.
   b. what we find important.
   c. what we find entertaining.

2. Abraham Maslow described values as a

   a. circle.
   b. pyramid.
   c. square.

3. According to Maslow, our most basic needs are

   a. social.
   b. biological.
   c. intellectual.

4. According to Maslow, we are all aiming for

   a. independence.
   b. wealth.
   c. self-actualization.

5. Knowing what we value helps us to make good

   a. wages.
   b. decisions.
   c. expenditures.

REFLECTION

Write down your most important value. Write an intention statement about how you plan to act on this value. For example, my most important value is to maintain my good health. I intend to act on this value by eating right and exercising.

To assure your success in college, it is important to choose the major that is best for you. If you choose a major and career that match your personality, interests, aptitudes, and values, you will enjoy your studies and excel in your work. It was Picasso who said that you know you enjoy your work when you do not notice the time passing by. If you can become interested in your work and studies, you are on your way to developing passion and joy in your life. If you can get up each morning and enjoy the work that you do (at least on most days), you will surely have one of the keys to happiness.

Choose a Major That Matches Your Gifts and Talents

The first step in choosing the major that is right for you is to understand your personality type. Psychologists have developed useful theories of personality that can help you understand how personality type relates to the choice of major and career. The personality theory used in this textbook is derived from the work of Swiss psychologist Carl Jung (1875–1961). Jung believed that we are born with a predisposition for certain personality preferences and that healthy development is based on the lifelong nurturing of inborn preferences rather than trying to change a person to become something different. Each personality type has gifts and talents that can be nurtured over a lifetime.

> "To be what we are, and to become what we are capable of becoming, is the only end of life."
> Robert Louis Stevenson

While assessments are not exact predictors of your future major and career, they provide useful information that will get you started on the path of career exploration and finding the college major that is best suited to you. Knowledge of your personality and the personalities of others is not only valuable in understanding yourself, but also in appreciating how others are different. This understanding of self and others will empower you to communicate and work effectively with others. Complete the AchieveWORKS Personality assessment that is included with this textbook before you begin this chapter. (See the inside front cover for further information.)

© Andril Kondiuk/Shutterstock.com

Understanding Personality Types

Just as no two fingerprints or snowflakes are exactly alike, each person is a different and unique individual. Even with this uniqueness, however, we can make some general statements about personality. When we make generalizations, we are talking about averages. These averages can provide useful information about ourselves and other people, but it is important to remember that no individual is exactly described by the average. As you read through the following descriptions of personality types, keep in mind that we are talking about generalizations or beginning points for discussion and thoughtful analysis.

As you read through your personality description from the AchieveWORKS Personality assessment and the information in this text, **focus on your personal strengths and talents**. Building on these personal strengths has several important benefits. It increases self-esteem and self-confidence, which contribute to your success and enjoyment of life. Building on your strengths provides the energy and motivation required to put in the effort needed to accomplish any worthwhile task. The assessment also identifies some of your possible weaknesses or "blind spots." Just be aware of these blind spots so that they do not interfere with your success. Being aware of your blind spots can even be used to your advantage. For example, some personality types thrive by working with people. A career that involves much public contact is a good match for this personality type, whereas choosing a career where public contact is limited can lead to job dissatisfaction. Knowing about your personality type can help you make the right decisions to maximize your potential.

Personality type has four dimensions:

1. Extraversion or Introversion

2. Sensing or Intuition

3. Thinking or Feeling

4. Judging or Perceiving

These dimensions of personality will be defined and examined in more depth in the sections that follow.

Extraversion or Introversion

The dimension of extraversion or introversion defines how we interact with the world and how our energy flows. In the general school population, 75 percent of students are usually extraverts and 25 percent are introverts.

> *Extraverts (E) focus their energy on the world outside themselves. They enjoy interaction with others and get to know a lot of different people. They enjoy and are usually good at communication. They are energized by social interaction and prefer being active. These types are often described as talkative and social.*

> *Introverts (I) focus their energy on the world inside of themselves. They enjoy spending time alone to think about the world in order to understand it. Introverts prefer more limited social contacts, choosing smaller groups or one-on-one relationships. These types are often described as quiet or reserved.*

We all use the introvert and extravert modes while functioning in our daily lives. Whether a person is an extravert or an introvert is a matter of preference, like being left- or right-handed. We can use our nondominant hand, but it is not as comfortable as using our dominant hand. We are usually more skillful in using the dominant hand. For example, introverts can learn to function well in social situations, but later may need some peace and quiet to recharge. On the other hand, social contact energizes the extravert.

One personality type is not better than the other: it is just different. Being an extravert is not better than being an introvert. Each type has unique gifts and talents that can be used in different occupations. An extravert might enjoy working in an occupation with lots of public contact, such as being a receptionist or handling public relations. An introvert might enjoy being an accountant or writer. However, as with all of the personality dimensions, a person may have traits of both types.

Introverts and Extraverts

The list below describes some qualities of introverts and extraverts. **For each pair of items**, quickly choose the phrase that describes you best and highlight or place a checkmark next to it. Remember that one type is not better than another. You may also find that you are a combination type and act like an introvert in some situations and an extravert in others. Each type has gifts and talents that can be used in choosing the best major and career for you. To get an estimate of your preference, notice which column has the most checkmarks.

Introvert (I)	Extravert (E)
_____ Energized by having quiet time alone	_____ Energized by social interaction
_____ Tend to think first and talk later	_____ Tend to talk first and think later
_____ Tend to think things through quietly	_____ Tend to think out loud
_____ Tend to respond slowly, after thinking	_____ Tend to respond quickly, before thinking
_____ Avoid being the center of attention	_____ Like to be the center of attention
_____ Difficult to get to know, private	_____ Easy to get to know, outgoing
_____ Have a few close friends	_____ Have many friends, know lots of people
_____ Prefer quiet for concentration	_____ Can read or talk with background noise
_____ Listen more than talk	_____ Talk more than listen
_____ View telephone calls as a distraction	_____ View telephone calls as a welcome break
_____ Talk to a few people at parties	_____ Talk to many different people at parties
_____ Share special occasions with one or a few people	_____ Share special occasions with large groups
_____ Prefer to study alone	_____ Prefer to study with others in a group
_____ Prefer the library to be quiet	_____ Talk with others in the library
_____ Described as quiet or reserved	_____ Described as talkative or friendly
_____ Work systematically	_____ Work through trial and error

Here are some qualities that describe the ideal work environment. Again, as you **read through each pair of items**, place a checkmark next to the work environment that you prefer.

Introvert (I)	Extravert (E)
_____ Work alone or with individuals	_____ Much public contact
_____ Quiet for concentration	_____ High-energy environment
_____ Communication one-on-one	_____ Present ideas to a group
_____ Work in small groups	_____ Work as part of a team
_____ Focus on one project until complete	_____ Variety and action
_____ Work without interruption	_____ Talk to others
_____ **Total** (from both charts above)	_____ **Total** (from both charts above)

Do these results agree with your personality assessment on the AchieveWORKS Personality assessment? If your results are the same, this is a good indication that your results are useful and accurate. Are there some differences with the results obtained from your personality assessment? If your results are different, this provides an opportunity for further reflection about your personality type. Here are a couple of reasons why your results may be different.

1. You may be a combination type with varying degrees of preference for each type.

2. You may have chosen your personality type on the AchieveWORKS Personality assessment based on what you think is best rather than what you truly are. Students sometimes do this because of the myth that there are good and bad personality types. It is important to remember that each personality type has strengths and weaknesses. By identifying strengths, you can build on them by choosing the right major and career. By being aware of weaknesses, you can come up with strategies to compensate for them to be successful.

Look at the total number of checkmarks for extravert and introvert on the two above charts. Do you lean toward being an introvert or an extravert? Remember that one type is not better than the other and each has unique gifts and talents. On the chart below, place an X on the line to indicate how much you prefer introversion or extraversion. If you selected most of the introvert traits, place your X somewhere on the left side. If you selected most of the extravert traits, place your X somewhere on the right side. If you are equally introverted and extraverted, place your X in the middle.

Introvert _____|_____ Extravert

Do you generally prefer introversion or extraversion? In the box below, write **I** for introversion or **E** for extraversion. If there is a tie between **E** and **I**, write **I**.

Notice that it is possible to be a combination type. At times you might prefer to act like an introvert, and at other times you might prefer to act like an extravert. It is beneficial to be able to balance these traits. However, for combination types, it is more difficult to select specific occupations that match this type

REFLECTION

Look at the results from AchieveWORKS Personality assessment and your own self-assessment above. Are you an introvert or an extravert or a combination of these two types? Can you give examples of how it affects your social life, school, or work? Write a paragraph about this preference.

Sensing or Intuition

The dimension of sensing or intuition describes how we take in information. In the general school population, 70 percent of students are usually sensing types and 30 percent are intuitive types.

Sensing (S) persons prefer to use the senses to take in information (what they see, hear, taste, touch, smell). They focus on "what is" and trust information that is concrete and observable. They learn through experience.

Intuitive (N) persons rely on instincts and focus on "what could be." While we all use our five senses to perceive the world, intuitive people are interested in relationships, possibilities, meanings, and implications. They value inspiration and trust their "sixth sense" or hunches. (Intuitive is designated as N so it is not confused with I for Introvert.)

We all use both of these modes in our daily lives, but we usually have a preference for one mode or the other. Again, there is no best preference. Each type has special skills that can be applied to the job market. For example, you would probably want your tax preparer to be a sensing type who focuses on concrete information and fills out your tax form correctly. An inventor or artist would probably be an intuitive type.

ACTIVITY

Sensing and Intuitive

Here are some qualities of sensing and intuitive persons. As you **read through each pair of items**, quickly highlight or place a checkmark next to the item that usually describes yourself.

Sensing (S)	INtuitive (N)
_____ Trust what is certain and concrete	_____ Trust inspiration and inference
_____ Prefer specific answers to questions	_____ Prefer general answers that leave room for interpretation
_____ Like new ideas if they have practical applications (if you can use them)	_____ Like new ideas for their own sake (you don't need a practical use for them)
_____ Value realism and common sense	_____ Value imagination and innovation
_____ Think about things one at a time and step by step	_____ Think about many ideas at once as they come to you
_____ Like to improve and use skills learned before	_____ Like to learn new skills and get bored using the same skills
_____ More focused on the present	_____ More focused on the future
_____ Concentrate on what you are doing	_____ Wonder what is next
_____ Do something	_____ Think about doing something
_____ See tangible results	_____ Focus on possibilities
_____ If it isn't broken, don't fix it	_____ There is always a better way to do it

Sensing (S)	INtuitive (N)
_____ Prefer working with facts and figures	_____ Prefer working with ideas and theories
_____ Focus on reality	_____ Use fantasy
_____ Seeing is believing	_____ Anything is possible
_____ Tend to be specific and literal (say what you mean)	_____ Tend to be general and figurative (use comparisons and analogies)
_____ See what is here and now	_____ See the big picture

Here are some qualities that describe the ideal work environment. Again, as you **read through each pair of items**, place a checkmark next to the work environment that you prefer.

Sensing (S)	INtuitive (N)
_____ Use and practice skills	_____ Learn new skills
_____ Work with known facts	_____ Explore new ideas and approaches
_____ See measurable results	_____ Work with theories
_____ Focus on practical benefits	_____ Use imagination and be original
_____ Learn through experience	_____ Freedom to follow your inspiration
_____ Pleasant environment	_____ Challenging environment
_____ Use standard procedures	_____ Invent new products and procedures
_____ Work step-by-step	_____ Work in bursts of energy
_____ Do accurate work	_____ Find creative solutions
_____ **Total** (from both charts above)	_____ **Total** (from both charts above)

Look at the two charts above and see whether you tend to be more sensing or intuitive. One preference is not better than another: it is just different. On the chart below, place an X on the line to indicate your preference for sensing or intuitive. Again, notice that it is possible to be a combination type with both sensing and intuitive preferences.

Sensing _____|_____Intuitive

Do you generally prefer sensing or intuition? In the box below, write **S** for sensing or **N** for intuitive. If there is a tie between **S** and **N**, write **N**.

[ ]

REFLECTION

Look at the results from AchieveWORKS Personality assessment and your own self-assessment above. Are you a sensing, intuitive, or combination type? Can you give examples of how it affects your social life, school, or work? Write a paragraph about this preference.

Thinking or Feeling

The dimension of thinking or feeling defines how we prefer to make decisions. In the general school population, 60 percent of males are thinking types and 40 percent are feeling types. For females, 60 percent are feeling types and 40 percent are thinking types.

Thinking (T) individuals make decisions based on logic. They are objective and analytical. They look at all the evidence and reach an impersonal conclusion. They are concerned with what they think is right.

Feeling (F) individuals make decisions based on what is important to them and matches their personal values. They are concerned about what they feel is right.

We all use logic and have feelings and emotions that play a part in decision making. However, the thinking person prefers to make decisions based on logic, and the feeling person prefers to make decisions according to what is important to self and others. This is one category in which men and women often differ. Most women are feeling types, and most men are logical types. When men and women are arguing, you might hear the following:

Man: "I think that . . ."

Woman: "I feel that . . ."

By understanding these differences, it is possible to improve communication and understanding. Be careful with generalizations, since 40 percent of men and women would not fit this pattern.

When thinking about careers, a thinking type would make a good judge or computer programmer. A feeling type would probably make a good social worker or kindergarten teacher.

ACTIVITY

Thinking and Feeling

The following chart shows some qualities of thinking and feeling types. As you **read through each pair of items**, quickly highlight or place a checkmark next to the items that usually describe yourself.

Thinking (T)	Feeling (F)
_____ Apply impersonal analysis to problems	_____ Consider the effect on others
_____ Value logic and justice	_____ Value empathy and harmony
_____ Fairness is important	_____ There are exceptions to every rule
_____ Truth is more important than tact	_____ Tact is more important than truth
_____ Motivated by achievement and accomplishment	_____ Motivated by being appreciated by others
_____ Feelings are valid if they are logical	_____ Feelings are valid whether they make sense or not
_____ Good decisions are logical	_____ Good decisions take others' feelings into account

Thinking (T)

_____ Described as cool, calm, and objective

_____ Love can be analyzed

_____ Firm-minded

_____ More important to be right

_____ Remember numbers and figures

_____ Prefer clarity

_____ Find flaws and critique

_____ Prefer firmness

Feeling (F)

_____ Described as caring and emotional

_____ Love cannot be analyzed

_____ Gentle-hearted

_____ More important to be liked

_____ Remember faces and names

_____ Prefer harmony

_____ Look for the good and compliment

_____ Prefer persuasion

Here are some qualities that describe the ideal work environment. As you **read through each pair of items**, place a checkmark next to the items that usually describe the work environment that you prefer.

Thinking (T)

_____ Maintain business environment

_____ Work with people I respect

_____ Be treated fairly

_____ Fair evaluations

_____ Solve problems

_____ Challenging work

_____ Use logic and analysis

_____ **Total** (from both charts above)

Feeling (F)

_____ Maintain close personal relationships

_____ Work in a friendly, relaxed environment

_____ Be able to express personal values

_____ Appreciation for good work

_____ Make a personal contribution

_____ Harmonious work situation

_____ Help others

_____ **Total** (from both charts above)

While we all use thinking and feeling, what is your preferred type? Look at the charts above and notice whether you are more the thinking or feeling type. One is not better than the other. On the chart below, place an X on the line to indicate how much you prefer thinking or feeling.

Thinking _____|_____ Feeling

Do you generally prefer thinking or feeling? In the box below, write **T** for thinking or **F** for feeling. If there is a tie between **T** and **F**, write **F**.

☐

REFLECTION

Look at the results from AchieveWORKS Personality assessment and your own self-assessment above. Are you a thinking, feeling, or combination type? Can you give examples of how it affects your social life, school, or work? Write a paragraph about this preference.

Judging or Perceiving

The dimension of judging or perceiving refers to how we deal with the external world. In other words, do we prefer the world to be structured or unstructured? In the general school population, the percentage of each of these types is approximately equal.

*Judging (J) types like to live in a structured, orderly, and planned way. They are happy when their lives are structured and matters are settled. They like to have control over their lives. **Judging does not mean to judge others**. Think of this type as being orderly and organized.*

*Perceptive (P) types like to live in a spontaneous and flexible way. They are happy when their lives are open to possibilities. They try to understand life rather than control it. **Think of this type as spontaneous and flexible**.*

Since these types have very opposite ways of looking at the world, there is a great deal of potential for conflict between them unless there is an appreciation for the gifts and talents of both. In any situation, we can benefit from people who represent these very different points of view. For example, in a business situation, the judging type would be good at managing the money, while the perceptive type would be good at helping the business to adapt to a changing marketplace. It is good to be open to all the possibilities and to be flexible, as well as to have some structure and organization.

ACTIVITY

Judging and Perceptive

As you **read through each pair of items**, quickly highlight or place a checkmark next to the items that generally describe yourself.

Judging (J)	Perceptive (P)
_____ Happy when the decisions are made and finished	_____ Happy when the options are left open; something better may come along
_____ Work first, play later	_____ Play first, do the work later
_____ It is important to be on time	_____ Time is relative
_____ Time flies	_____ Time is elastic
_____ Feel comfortable with routine	_____ Dislike routine
_____ Generally keep things in order	_____ Prefer creative disorder
_____ Set goals and work toward them	_____ Change goals as new opportunities arise
_____ Emphasize completing the task	_____ Emphasize how the task is done
_____ Like to finish projects	_____ Like to start projects
_____ Meet deadlines	_____ What deadline?
_____ Like to know what I am getting into	_____ Like new possibilities and situations
_____ Relax when things are organized	_____ Relax when necessary
_____ Follow a routine	_____ Explore the unknown
_____ Focused	_____ Easily distracted
_____ Work steadily	_____ Work in spurts of energy

Here are some qualities that describe the ideal work environment. Again, as you **read through each pair of items**, place a checkmark next to the work environment that you prefer.

Judging (J)		Perceptive (P)	
_____	Follow a schedule	_____	Be spontaneous
_____	Clear directions	_____	Minimal rules and structure
_____	Organized work	_____	Flexibility
_____	Logical order	_____	Many changes
_____	Control my job	_____	Respond to emergencies
_____	Stability and security	_____	Take risks and be adventurous
_____	Work on one project until done	_____	Juggle many projects
_____	Steady work	_____	Variety and action
_____	Satisfying work	_____	Fun and excitement
_____	Like having high responsibility	_____	Like having interesting work
_____	Accomplish goals on time	_____	Work at my own pace
_____	Clear and concrete assignments	_____	Minimal supervision
_____	**Total** (from both charts above)	_____	**Total** (from both charts above)

Look at the charts above and notice whether you are more the judging type (orderly and organized) or the perceptive type (spontaneous and flexible). We need the qualities of both types to be successful and deal with the rapid changes in today's world. On the chart below, place an X on the line to indicate how much you prefer judging or perceiving.

Judging _____|_____ Perceptive

Do you generally have judging or perceptive traits? In the box below, write **J** for judging or **P** for perceptive. If there is a tie between **J** and **P**, write **P**.

REFLECTION

Look at the results from AchieveWORKS Personality assessment and your own self-assessment above. Are you a thinking, feeling, or combination type? Can you give examples of how it affects your social life, school, or work? Write a paragraph about this preference.

"Knowing thyself is the height of wisdom."
Socrates

Summarize Your Results

Look at your results above and summarize them on this composite chart. Notice that we are all unique, according to where the Xs fall on the scale.

Extravert (E) _____|_____ Introvert (I)

Sensing (S) _____|_____ Intuitive (N)

Thinking (T) _____|_____ Feeling (F)

Judging (J) _____|_____ Perceptive (P)

Write the letters representing each of your preferences: _____

The above letters represent your estimated personality type based on your understanding and knowledge of self. It is a good idea to confirm that this type is correct for you by completing the online AchieveWORKS Personality assessment.

© Gustavo Frazao/Shutterstock.com

Personality Types

Test what you have learned by selecting the correct answer to the following questions.

1. A person who is energized by social interaction is a/an:

   a. introvert
   b. extravert
   c. feeling type

2. A person who is quiet and reserved is a/an:

   a. introvert
   b. extravert
   c. perceptive type

3. A person who relies on experience and trusts information that is concrete and observable is a/an:

   a. judging type
   b. sensing type
   c. perceptive type

4. A person who focuses on "what could be" is a/an:

   a. perceptive type
   b. thinking type
   c. intuitive type

5. A person who makes decisions based on logic is a/an:

   a. thinker
   b. perceiver
   c. sensor

6. A person who makes decisions based on personal values is a/an:

   a. feeling type
   b. thinking type
   c. judging type

7. The perceptive type:

   a. has extrasensory perception
   b. likes to live life in a spontaneous and flexible way
   c. always considers feelings before making a decision

8. The judging type likes to:

   a. judge others
   b. use logic
   c. live in a structured and orderly way

9. Personality assessments are an exact predictor of your best major and career.

   a. true
   b. false

10. Some personality types are better than others.

    a. true
    b. false

Personality and Career Choice

While it is not possible to predict exactly your career and college major by knowing your personality type, it can help provide opportunities for exploration. The AchieveWORKS personality assessment links your personality type with suggested matching careers in the O*Net career database continually updated by the U.S. Department of Labor. You can find additional information at the College Success 1 website: http://www.collegesuccess1.com/careers.html. This page includes a description of each type, general occupations to consider, specific job titles, and suggested college majors.

© iQoncept/Shutterstock.com

Personality and Preferred Work Environment

Knowing your personality type will help you to understand your preferred work environment and provide some insights into selecting the major and career that you would enjoy. Selecting the work environment that matches your personal preferences helps you to be energized on the job and to minimize stress. Understanding other types will help you to work effectively with co-workers. As you read this section, think about your ideal work environment and how others are different.

Extraverts are career generalists who use their skills in a variety of ways. They like variety and action in a work environment that provides the opportunity for social interaction. Extraverts communicate well and meet people easily. They like to talk while working and are interested in other people and what they are doing. They enjoy variety on the job and like to perform their work in different settings. They learn new tasks by talking with others and trying out new ideas. Extraverts are energized by working as part of a team, leading others in achieving goals, and having opportunities to communicate with others.

Introverts are career specialists who develop in-depth skills. The introvert likes quiet for concentration and likes to focus on a work task until it is completed. They need time to think before taking action. This type often chooses to work alone or with one other person and prefers written communication such as emails to oral communication or presentations. They learn new tasks by reading and reflecting and using mental practice. Introverts are energized when they can work in a quiet environment with few interruptions. They are stressed when they have to work in a noisy environment and do not have time alone to concentrate on a project.

The **sensing** type is realistic and practical and likes to develop standard ways of doing the job and following a routine. They are observant and interested in facts and finding the truth. They keep accurate track of details, make lists, and are good at doing precise work. This type learns from personal experience and the experience of others. They use their experience to move up the job ladder. Sensing types are energized when they are doing practical work with tangible outcomes where they are required to organize facts and details, use common sense, and focus on one project at a time. They are stressed when they have to deal with frequent or unexpected change.

The **intuitive** type likes to work on challenging and complex problems where they can follow their inspirations to find creative solutions. They like change and finding new ways of doing work. This type focuses on the whole picture rather than the details. The intuitive type is an initiator, promoter, and inventor of ideas. They enjoy learning a new skill more than using it. They often change careers to follow their creative inspirations. Intuitive types are energized by working in an environment where they can use creative insight, imagination, originality, and individual initiative. They are stressed when they have to deal with too many details or have little opportunity for creativity.

The **thinking** type likes to use logical analysis in making decisions. They are objective and rational and treat others fairly. They want logical reasons before accepting any new ideas. They follow policy and are often firm-minded and critical, especially when dealing with illogic in others. They easily learn facts, theories, and principles. They are interested in careers with money, prestige, or influence. Thinking types are energized when they are respected for their expertise and recognized for a job well done. They enjoy working with others who are competent and efficient. They become stressed when they work with people they consider to be illogical, unfair, incompetent, or overly emotional.

© cristovao/Shutterstock.com

The **feeling** type likes harmony and the support of co-workers. They are personal, enjoy warm relationships, and relate well to most people. Feeling types know their personal values and apply them consistently. They enjoy doing work that provides a service to people and often do work that requires them to understand and analyze their own emotions and those of others. They prefer a friendly work environment and like to learn with others. They enjoy careers in which they can make a contribution to humanity. Feeling types are energized by working in a friendly, congenial, and supportive work environment. They are stressed when there is conflict in the work environment, especially when working with controlling or demanding people.

The **judging** type likes a work environment that is structured, settled, and organized. They prefer work assignments that are clear and definite. The judging type makes lists and plans to get the job done on time. They make quick decisions and like to have the work finished. They are good at doing purposeful and exacting work. They prefer to learn only the essentials that are necessary to do the job. This type carefully plans their career path. Judging types are energized by working in a predictable and orderly environment with clear responsibilities and deadlines. They become stressed when the work environment becomes disorganized or unpredictable.

<aside>
"True greatness is starting where you are, using what you have, and doing what you can."

Arthur Ashe
</aside>

The **perceptive** type likes to be spontaneous and go with the flow. They are comfortable in handling the unplanned or unexpected in the work environment. They prefer to be flexible in their work and feel restricted by structures and schedules. They are good at handling work which requires change and adaptation. They are tolerant and have a "live and let live" attitude toward others. Decisions are often postponed because this type wants to know all there is to know and explore all the options before making a decision. This type is often a career changer who takes advantage of new job openings and opportunities for change. Perceptive types are energized when the work environment is flexible and they can relax and control their own time. They are stressed when they have to meet deadlines or work under excessive rules and regulations.

More on Personality Type
Personality and Decision Making

Your personality type affects how you think and how you make decisions. Knowing your decision-making style will help you make good decisions about your career and personal life as well as work with others in creative problem solving. Each

© Stephen Coburn/Shutterstock.com

personality type views the decision-making process in a different way. Ideally, a variety of types would be involved in making a decision so that the strengths of each type could be utilized. As you read through the following descriptions, think about your personality type and how you make decisions as well as how others are different.

The **introvert** thinks up ideas and reflects on the problem before acting. The **extravert** acts as the communicator in the decision-making process. Once the decision is made, they take action and implement the decision. The **intuitive** type develops theories and uses intuition to come up with ingenious solutions to the problem. The **sensing** type applies personal experience to the decision-making process and focuses on solutions that are practical and realistic.

The thinking and feeling dimensions of personality are the most important factors in determining how a decision is made. Of course, people use both thinking and feeling in the decision-making process, but tend to prefer or trust either thinking or feeling. Those who prefer **thinking** use cause-and-effect reasoning and solve problems with logic. They use objective and impersonal criteria and include all the consequences of alternative solutions in the decision-making process. They are interested in finding out what is true and what is false. They use laws and principles to treat everyone fairly. Once a decision is made, they are firm-minded, since the decision was based on logic. This type is often critical of those who do not use logic in the decision-making process. The **feeling** type considers human values and motives in the decision-making process (whether they are logical or not) and values harmony and maintaining good relationships. They consider carefully how much they care about each of the alternatives and how they will affect other people. They are interested in making a decision that is agreeable to all parties. Feeling types are tactful and skillful in dealing with people.

It is often asked if thinking types have feelings. They do have feelings, but use them as a criterion to be factored into the decision-making process. Thinking types are more comfortable when feelings are controlled and often think that feeling types are too emotional. Thinking types may have difficulties when they apply logic in a situation where a feeling response is needed, such as in dealing with a spouse. Thinking types need to know that people are important in making decisions. Feeling types need to know that behavior will have logical consequences and that they may need to keep emotions more controlled to work effectively with thinking types.

Judging and **perceptive** types have opposite decision-making strategies. The judging type is very methodical and cautious in making decisions. Once they have gone through the decision-making steps, they like to make decisions quickly so that they can have closure and finish the project. The perceptive type is an adventurer who wants to look at all the possibilities before making a decision. They are open-minded and curious and often resist closure to look at more options.

If a combination of types collaborates on a decision, it is more likely that the decision will be a good one that takes into account creative possibilities, practicality, logical consequences, and human values.

Personality and Time Management

How we manage our time is not just a result of personal habits: it is also a reflection of our personality type. Probably the dimension of personality type most connected to time management is the judging or perceptive trait. **Judging** types like to have things under control and live in a planned and orderly manner. **Perceptive** types prefer more spontaneity and flexibility. Understanding the differences between these two types will help you to better understand yourself and others.

Judging types are naturally good at time management. They often use schedules as a tool for time management and organization. Judging types plan their time and work steadily to accomplish goals. They are good at meeting deadlines and often put off relaxation, recreation, and fun. They relax after projects are completed. If they have too many projects, they find it difficult to find time for recreation. Since judging types like to have projects under control, there is a danger that projects will be completed too quickly and that quality will suffer. Judging types may need to slow down and take the time to do quality work. They may also need to make relaxation and recreation a priority.

Perceptive types are more open-ended and prefer to be spontaneous. They take time to relax, have fun, and participate in recreation. In working on a project, perceptive types want to brainstorm all the possibilities and are not too concerned about finishing projects. This type procrastinates when the time comes to make a final decision and finish a project. There is always more information to gather and more possibilities to explore. Perceptive types are easily distracted and may move from project to project. They may have several jobs going at once. These types need to try to focus on a few projects at a time in order to complete them. Perceptive types need to work on becoming more organized so that projects can be completed on time.

Research has shown that students who are judging types are more likely to have a higher grade point average in the first semester.[1] It has also been found that the greater the preference for intuition, introversion, and judgment, the better the grade point average.[2] Why is this true? Many college professors are intuitive types that use intuition and creative ideas. The college environment requires quiet time for reading and studying, which is one of the preferences of introverts. Academic environments require structure, organization, and completion of assignments. To be successful in an academic environment requires adaptation by some personality types. Extroverts need to spend more quiet time reading and studying. Sensing types need to gain an understanding of intuitive types. Perceptive types need to use organization to complete assignments on time.

© STILLFX/Shutterstock.com

Personality and Money

Does your personality type affect how you deal with money? Otto Kroeger and Janet Thuesen make some interesting observations about how different personality types deal with money.

- **Judging types (orderly and organized).** These types excel at financial planning and money management. They file their tax forms early and pay their bills on time.

- **Perceptive types (spontaneous and flexible).** These types adapt to change and are more creative. Perceivers, especially intuitive perceivers, tend to freak out as the April 15 tax deadline approaches and as bills become due.

- **Feeling types (make decisions based on feelings).** These types are not very money-conscious. They believe that money should be used to serve humanity. They are often attracted to low-paying jobs that serve others.[3]

In studying stockbrokers, these same authors note that ISTJs (introvert, sensing, thinking, and judging types) are the most conservative investors, earning a small but reliable return on investments. The ESTPs (extravert, sensing, thinking, perceptive types) and ENTPs (extravert, intuitive, thinking, perceptive types) take the biggest risks and earn the greatest returns.[4]

Personality and Learning Strategies

Knowing about your personality type can help you to choose learning strategies that work for you.

© Monkey Business Images/Shutterstock.com

- **Extraverts** enjoy interactions with others and like to get to know other people. They learn best by discussing what they have learned with others. Form a study group. Be careful that excess socialization does not distract you from getting your studying done.

- **Introverts** are more quiet and reserved. They enjoy spending time alone to think about what they are studying. Study in the library. Be careful about missing out on the opportunities to share ideas with others.

- **Sensing** types focus on the senses (what they can see, hear, taste, touch, and smell.) These types are good at mastering the facts and details. Improve learning by first focusing on the big picture or broad outline and then the details will be easier to remember.

- **Intuitive** types focus on the big picture and may miss the details. Ask yourself, "What is the main point?" To improve learning, begin by looking at the big picture or broader outline and then organize the facts and details under the main ideas so you can recall them.

- **Thinking** types are good at logic. Make a personal connection with the material by asking yourself, "What do I think of these ideas?" Discuss or debate your ideas with others while remembering to respect their ideas.

- **Feeling** types are motivated by finding personal meaning in their studies. Ask yourself, "How is this material related to my life and what is important to me?" Look for a supportive environment or study group.

- **Judging** types are good at organizing the material to be learned and working steadily to accomplish their goals. Organize the material to be learned into manageable chunks to aid in recall.

- **Perceptive** types are spontaneous, flexible, adaptable, and open to new information. Pay attention to organizing your work and meeting deadlines to improve success in college and on the job. Be careful not to overextend yourself by working on too many projects at once.

Understanding Your Professor's Personality

© Alexander Raths/Shutterstock.com

Different personality types have different expectations of teachers.

- Extraverts want faculty who encourage class discussion.
- Introverts want faculty who give clear lectures.
- Sensing types want faculty who give clear and specific assignments.
- Intuitive types want faculty who encourage independent thinking.
- Thinking types want faculty who make logical presentations.
- Feeling types want faculty who establish personal rapport with students.
- Judging types want faculty to be organized.
- Perceptive types want faculty to be entertaining and inspiring.

College students and faculty often have different personality types. In summary,

College faculty tend to be	College students tend to be
Introverted	Extraverted
Intuitive	Sensing
Judging	Perceptive

Of course, the above is not always true, but there is a good probability that you will have college professors who are very different from you. What can you do if you and your professor have different personality types? First, try to understand the professor's personality. This has been called "psyching out the professor." You can usually tell the professor's personality type on the first day of class by examining class materials and observing his or her manner of presentation. If you understand the professor's personality type, you will know what to expect. Next, try to appreciate what the professor has to offer. You may need to adapt your expectations to be successful. For example, if you are an introvert, make an effort to participate in class discussions. If you are a perceptive type, be careful to meet the due dates of your assignments.

Personality and Career Choice

While it is not possible to predict exactly your career and college major by knowing your personality type, it can be helpful in providing opportunities for exploration. Here are some general descriptions of personality types and preferred careers. Included are general occupational fields, frequently chosen occupations, and suggested majors. These suggestions about career selections are based on the general characteristics of each type and research that correlates personality type with choice of a satisfying career.[5] Read the descriptions, careers and majors that match your personality type and then continue your career exploration with the online database in the Do What You Are personality assessment included with your textbook.

ISTJ

ISTJs are responsible, loyal, stable, practical, down-to-earth, hardworking, and reliable. They can be depended upon to follow through with tasks. They value tradition, family, and security. They are natural leaders who prefer to work alone, but can adapt to working with teams if needed. They like to be independent and have time to think things through. They are able to remember and use concrete facts and information. They make decisions by applying logic and rational thinking. They appreciate structured and orderly environments and deliver products and services in an efficient and orderly way.

© 2014, iQoncept. Used under license with Shutterstock, Inc.

General occupations to consider

business	education	health care
service	technical	military
law and law enforcement	engineering	management

Specific job titles

business executive	lawyer	electronic technician
administrator	judge	computer occupations
manager	police officer	dentist
real estate agent	detective	pharmacist
accountant	corrections officer	primary care physician
bank employee	teacher (math, trade, technical)	nursing administrator
stockbroker		respiratory therapist
auditor	educational administrator	physical therapist
hairdresser	coach	optometrist
cosmetologist	engineer	chemist
legal secretary	electrician	military officer or enlistee

College majors

business	engineering	chemistry
education	computers	biology
mathematics	health occupations	vocational training
law		

From Explorer's Guide: Starting Your College Journey with a Sense of Purpose, **Third Edition**
by Bill Millard.

ISTP

ISTPs are independent, practical, and easygoing. They prefer to work individually and frequently like to work outdoors. These types like working with objects and often are good at working with their hands and mastering tools. They are interested in how and why things work and are able to apply technical knowledge to solving practical problems. Their logical thinking makes them good troubleshooters and problem solvers. They enjoy variety, new experiences, and taking risks. They prefer environments with little structure and have a talent for managing crises. The ISTP is happy with occupations that involve challenge, change, and variety.

General occupations to consider

sales	technical	business and finance
service	health care	vocational training
corrections		

Specific job titles

sales manager	engineer	office manager
insurance agent	electronics technician	small business manager
cook	software developer	banker
firefighter	computer programmer	economist
pilot	radiologic technician	legal secretary
race car driver	exercise physiologist	paralegal
police officer	coach	computer repair
corrections officer	athlete	airline mechanic
judge	dental assistant/hygienist	carpenter
attorney	physician	construction worker
intelligence agent	optometrist	farmer
detective	physical therapist	military officer or enlistee

College majors

business	computers	health occupations
vocational training	biology	physical education
law		

ISFJ

ISFJs are quiet, friendly, responsible, hardworking, productive, devoted, accurate, thorough, and careful. They value security, stability, and harmony. They like to focus on one person or project at a time. ISFJs prefer to work with individuals and are very skillful in understanding people and their needs. They often provide service to others in a very structured way. They are careful observers, remember facts, and work on projects requiring accuracy and attention to detail. They have a sense of space and function that leads to artistic endeavors such as interior decorating or landscaping. ISFJs are most comfortable working in environments that are orderly, structured, and traditional. While they often work quietly behind the scenes, they like their contributions to be recognized and appreciated.

General occupations to consider

health care	education	artistic
social service	business	religious occupations
corrections	technical	vocational training

Specific job titles

nurse	social worker	counselor
physician	social services	secretary
medical technologist	administrator	cashier
dental hygienist	child care worker	accountant
health education	speech pathologist	personnel administrator
practitioner	librarian	credit counselor
dietician	curator	business manager
physical therapist	genealogist	paralegal
nursing educator	corrections worker	computer occupations
health administrator	probation officer	engineer
medical secretary	teacher (preschool,	interior decorator
dentist	grades 1–12)	home economist
medical assistant	guidance counselor	religious educator
optometrist	educational administrator	clergy
occupational therapist		

College majors

health occupations	education	graphics
biology	business	religious studies
psychology	engineering	vocational training
sociology	art	

ISFP

ISFPs are quiet, reserved, trusting, loyal, committed, sensitive, kind, creative, and artistic. They have an appreciation for life and value serenity and aesthetic beauty. These types are individualistic and generally have no desire to lead or follow; they prefer to work independently. They have a keen awareness of their environment and often have a special bond with children and animals. ISFPs are service-oriented and like to help others. They like to be original and unconventional. They dislike rules and structure and need space and freedom to do things in their own way.

General occupations to consider

artists	technical	business
health care	service	vocational training

Specific job titles

artist	recreation services	forester
designer	physical therapist	botanist
fashion designer	radiologic technician	geologist
jeweler	medical assistant	mechanic
gardener	dental assistant/hygienist	marine biologist
potter	veterinary assistant	teacher (science, art)
painter	veterinarian	police officer
dancer	animal groomer/trainer	beautician
landscape designer	dietician	merchandise planner
carpenter	optician/optometrist	stock clerk
electrician	exercise physiologist	store keeper
engineer	occupational therapist	counselor
chef	art therapist	social worker
nurse	pharmacy technician	legal secretary
counselor	respiratory therapist	paralegal

College majors

art	forestry	psychology
health occupations	geology	counseling
engineering	education	social work
physical education	business	vocational training
biology		

INFJ

INFJs are idealistic, complex, compassionate, authentic, creative, and visionary. They have strong value systems and search for meaning and purpose to life. Because of their strong value systems, INFJs are natural leaders or at least follow those with similar ideas. They intuitively understand people and ideas and come up with new ideas to provide service to others. These types like to organize their time and be in control of their work.

General occupations to consider

counseling	religious occupations	health care
education	creative occupations	social services
science	arts	business

Specific job titles

career counselor	director of religious	dental hygienist
psychologist	education	speech pathologist
teacher (high school or	fine artist	nursing educator
college English, art,	playwright	medical secretary
music, social sciences,	novelist	pharmacist
drama, foreign	poet	occupational therapist
languages, health)	designer	human resources
librarian	architect	manager
home economist	art director	marketer
social worker	health care administrator	employee assistance
clergy	physician	program
	biologist	merchandise planner
		environmental lawyer

College majors

psychology	drama	architecture
counseling	foreign languages	biology
education	English	business
art	health occupations	law
music	social work	science

INFP

INFPs are loyal, devoted, sensitive, creative, inspirational, flexible, easygoing, complex, and authentic. They are original and individualistic and prefer to work alone or with other caring and supportive individuals. These types are service-oriented and interested in personal growth. They develop deep relationships because they understand people and are genuinely interested in them. They dislike dealing with details and routine work. They prefer a flexible working environment with a minimum of rules and regulations.

General occupations to consider

creative arts	counseling	health care
education	religious occupations	organizational development

Specific job titles

artist	photographer	dietician
designer	carpenter	psychiatrist
writer	teacher (art, drama, music, English, foreign languages)	physical therapist
journalist		occupational therapist
entertainer		speech pathologist
architect	psychologist	laboratory technologist
actor	counselor	public health nurse
editor	social worker	dental hygienist
reporter	librarian	physician
journalist	clergy	human resources
musician	religious educator	specialist
graphic designer	missionary	social scientist
art director	church worker	consultant

College majors

art	foreign languages	medicine
music	architecture	health occupations
graphic design	education	social work
journalism	religious studies	counseling
English	psychology	business

INTJ

INTJs are reserved, detached, analytical, logical, rational, original, independent, creative, ingenious, innovative, and resourceful. They prefer to work alone and work best alone. They can work with others if their ideas and competence are respected. They value knowledge and efficiency. They enjoy creative and intellectual challenges and understand complex theories. They create order and structure. They prefer to work with autonomy and control over their work. They dislike factual and routine kinds of work.

General occupations to consider

business and finance	education	law
technical occupations	health care and medicine	creative occupations
science	architecture	engineering

Specific job titles

management consultant	astronomer	dentist
human resources planner	computer programmer	biomedical engineer
economist	biomedical researcher	attorney
international banker	software developer	manager
financial planner	network integration specialist	judge
investment banker		electrical engineer
scientist	teacher (university)	writer
scientific researcher	school principal	journalist
chemist	mathematician	artist
biologist	psychiatrist	inventor

computer systems analyst	psychologist	architect
electronic technician	neurologist	actor
design engineer	physician	musician
architect		

College majors

business	physics	journalism
finance	education	art
chemistry	mathematics	architecture
biology	medicine	drama
computers	psychology	music
engineering	law	vocational training
astronomy	English	

INTP

INTPs are logical, analytical, independent, original, creative, and insightful. They are often brilliant and ingenious. They work best alone and need quiet time to concentrate. They focus their attention on ideas and are frequently detached from other people. They love theory and abstract ideas and value knowledge and competency. INTPs are creative thinkers who are not too interested in practical application. They dislike detail and routine and need freedom to develop, analyze, and critique new ideas. These types maintain high standards in their work.

General occupations to consider

planning and development	technical	academic
	professional	creative occupations
health care		

Specific job titles

computer software designer	pharmacist	historian
	engineer	philosopher
computer programmer	electrician	college teacher
research and development	dentist	researcher
systems analyst	veterinarian	logician
financial planner	lawyer	photographer
investment banker	economist	creative writer
physicist	psychologist	artist
plastic surgeon	architect	actor
psychiatrist	psychiatrist	entertainer
chemist	mathematician	musician
biologist	archaeologist	inventor
pharmaceutical researcher		

College majors

computers	philosophy	mathematics
business	music	archaeology
physics	art	history
chemistry	drama	English
biology	engineering	drama
astronomy	psychology	music
medicine	architecture	vocational training

ESTP

ESTPs have great people skills and are action-oriented, fun, flexible, adaptable, and resourceful. They enjoy new experiences and dealing with people. They remember facts easily and have excellent powers of observation that they use to analyze other people. They are good problem solvers and can react quickly in an emergency. They like adventure and risk and are alert to new opportunities. They start new projects but do not necessarily follow through to completion. They prefer environments without too many rules and restrictions.

General occupations to consider

sales	entertainment	technical
service	sports	trade
active careers	health care	business
finance		

Specific job titles

marketing professional	insurance agent	dentist
firefighter	sportscaster	carpenter
police officer	news reporter	farmer
corrections officer	journalist	construction worker
paramedic	tour agent	electrician
detective	dancer	teacher (trade, industrial,
pilot	bartender	technical)
investigator	auctioneer	chef
real estate agent	professional athlete or	engineer
exercise physiologist	coach	surveyor
flight attendant	fitness instructor	radiologic technician
sports merchandise sales	recreation leader	entrepreneur
stockbroker	optometrist	land developer
financial planner	pharmacist	retail sales
investor	critical care nurse	car sales

College majors

business	vocational training	English
physical education	education	journalism
health occupations		

ESTJ

ESTJs are loyal, hardworking, dependable, thorough, practical, realistic, and energetic. They value security and tradition. Because they enjoy working with people and are orderly and organized, these types like to take charge and be the leader. This personality type is often found in administrative and management positions. ESTJs work systematically and efficiently to get the job done. These types are fair, logical, and consistent. They prefer a stable and predictable environment filled with action and a variety of people.

General occupations to consider

managerial	service	professional
sales	technical	military leaders
business	agriculture	

Specific job titles

retail store manager
fire department manager
small business manager
restaurant manager
financial or bank officer
school principal
sales manager
top-level manager in city/
   county/state
   government
management consultant
corporate executive

military officer or enlistee
office manager
purchasing agent
police officer
factory supervisor
corrections
insurance agent
detective
judge
accountant
nursing administrator
mechanical engineer

physician
chemical engineer
auditor
coach
public relations worker
cook
personnel or labor
   relations worker
teacher (trade, industrial,
   technical)
mortgage banker

College majors

business
business management
accounting
finance

small business
   management
engineering
agriculture

law
education
vocational training

ESFP

ESFPs are practical, realistic, independent, fun, social, spontaneous, and flexible. They have great people skills and enjoy working in environments that are friendly, relaxed, and varied. They know how to have a good time and make an environment fun for others. ESFPs have a strong sense of aesthetics and are sometimes artistic and creative. They often have a special bond with people or animals. They dislike structure and routine. These types can handle many activities or projects at once.

General occupations to consider

education
social service
food preparation

health care
entertainment
child care

business and sales
service

Specific job titles

child care worker
teacher (preschool,
   elementary school,
   foreign languages,
   mathematics)
athletic coach
counselor
library assistant
police officer
public health nurse
respiratory therapist
physical therapist
physician
emergency medical
   technician
dental hygienist
chef

medical assistant
critical care nurse
dentist
dental assistant
exercise physiologist
dog obedience trainer
veterinary assistant
travel or tour agent
recreation leader or
   amusement site worker
photographer
designer
film producer
musician
performer
actor

promoter
special events coordinator
editor or reporter
retail merchandiser
fund raiser
receptionist
real estate agent
insurance agent
sporting equipment sales
retail sales
retail management
waiter or waitress
cashier
cosmetologist
hairdresser
religious worker

College majors

education	health occupations	journalism
psychology	art	drama
foreign languages	design	music
mathematics	photography	business
physical education	English	vocational training
culinary arts	child development	

ESFJ

ESFJs are friendly, organized, hardworking, productive, conscientious, loyal, dependable, and practical. These types value harmony, stability, and security. They enjoy interacting with people and receive satisfaction from giving to others. ESFJs enjoy working in a cooperative environment in which people get along well with each other. They create order, structure, and schedules and can be depended on to complete the task at hand. They prefer to organize and control their work.

General occupations to consider

health care	social service	business
education	counseling	human resources
child care		

Specific job titles

medical or dental assistant	coach	sales representative
nurse	administrator of	hairdresser
radiologic technician	elementary	cosmetologist
dental hygienist	or secondary school	restaurant worker
speech pathologist	administrator of student	recreation or amusement
occupational therapist	personnel	site worker
dentist	child care provider	receptionist
optometrist	home economist	office manager
dietician	social worker	cashier
pharmacist	administrator of social	bank employee
physician	services	bookkeeper
physical therapist	police officer	accountant
health education	counselor	sales
practitioner	community welfare	insurance agent
medical secretary	worker	credit counselor
teacher (grades 1–12,	religious educator	merchandise planner
foreign languages,	clergy	
reading)		

College majors

health occupations	education	religious studies
biology	psychology	business
foreign languages	counseling	vocational training
English	sociology	child development

ENFP

ENFPs are friendly, creative, energetic, enthusiastic, innovative, adventurous, and fun. They have great people skills and enjoy providing service to others. They are intuitive and perceptive about people. ENFPs are good at anything that interests them and can enter a variety of fields. These types dislike routine and detailed tasks and may have difficulty following through and completing tasks. They enjoy occupations in which they can be creative and interact with people. They like a friendly and relaxed environment in which they are free to follow their inspiration and participate in adventures.

General occupations to consider

creative occupations	counseling	social service
marketing	health care	entrepreneurial business
education	religious services	arts
environmental science		

Specific job titles

journalist	public relations	physical therapist
musician	counselor	consultant
actor	clergy	inventor
entertainer	psychologist	sales
fine artist	teacher (health, special	human resources
playwright	education, English, art,	manager
newscaster	drama, music)	conference planner
reporter	social worker	employment development
interior decorator	dental hygienist	specialist
cartoonist	nurse	restaurateur
graphic designer	dietician	merchandise planner
marketing	holistic health practitioner	environmental attorney
advertising	environmentalist	lawyer

College majors

journalism	business (advertising,	religious studies
English	marketing, public	health occupations
drama	relations)	law
art	counseling	vocational training
graphic design	psychology	

ENFJ

ENFJs are friendly, sociable, empathetic, loyal, creative, imaginative, and responsible. They have great people skills and are interested in working with people and providing service to them. They are good at building harmony and cooperation and respect other people's opinions. These types can find creative solutions to problems. They are natural leaders who can make good decisions. They prefer an environment that is organized and structured and enjoy working as part of a team with other creative and caring people.

General occupations to consider

religious occupations	counseling	health care
creative occupations	education	business
communications	human services	administration

Specific job titles

director of religious education
minister
clergy
public relations
marketing
writer
librarian
journalist
fine artist
designer
actor
musician or composer
fundraiser
recreational director
TV producer

newscaster
politician
editor
crisis counselor
school counselor
vocational or career counselor
psychologist
alcohol and drug counselor
teacher (health, art, drama, English, foreign languages)
child care worker
college humanities professor

social worker
home economist
nutritionist
speech pathologist
occupational therapist
physical therapist
optometrist
dental hygienist
family practice physician
psychiatrist
nursing educator
pharmacist
human resources trainer
travel agent
small business executive
sales manager

College majors

religious studies
business (public relations, marketing)
art
graphic design
drama

music
journalism
English
foreign languages
humanities
psychology

counseling
sociology
health occupations
business
vocational training

ENTP

ENTPs are creative, ingenious, flexible, diverse, energetic, fun, motivating, logical, and outspoken. They have excellent people skills and are natural leaders, although they dislike controlling other people. They value knowledge and competence. They are lively and energetic and make good debaters and motivational speakers. They are logical and rational thinkers who can grasp complex ideas and theories. They dislike environments that are structured and rigid. These types prefer environments that allow them to engage in creative problem solving and the creation of new ideas.

General occupations to consider

creative occupations
politics
engineering

law
business
science

health care
architecture
education

Specific job titles

photographer
marketing professional
journalist
actor
writer
musician or composer
editor
reporter
advertising director
radio/TV talk show host
producer

politician
political manager
political analyst
social scientist
psychiatrist
psychologist
engineer
construction laborer
research worker
electrician
lawyer

computer professional
corrections officer
sales manager
speech pathologist
health education practitioner
respiratory therapist
dental assistant
medical assistant
critical care nurse
counselor

art director

judge

human resources planner

new business developer

corporate executive

educator

architect

College majors

art

music

political science

photography

business (advertising,

psychology

journalism

marketing,

health occupations

drama

management,

computers

English

human resources)

vocational training

engineering

architecture

education

science

ENTJ

ENTJs are independent, original, visionary, logical, organized, ambitious, competitive, hardworking, and direct. They are natural leaders and organizers who identify problems and create solutions for organizations. ENTJs are often in management positions. They are good planners and accomplish goals in a timely manner. These types are logical thinkers who enjoy a structured work environment where they have opportunity for advancement. They enjoy a challenging, competitive, and exciting environment in which accomplishments are recognized.

General occupations to consider

business

management

science

finance

health care

law

Specific job titles

executive

manager in city/county/

accountant

manager

state government

auditor

supervisor

management trainer

financial manager

personnel manager

school principal

real estate agent

sales manager

bank officer

lawyer, judge

marketing manager

computer systems analyst

consultant

human resources planner

computer professional

engineer

corporate executive

credit investigator

corrections, probation

college administrator

mortgage broker

officer

health administrator

stockbroker

psychologist

small business owner

investment banker

physician

retail store manager

economist

College majors

business management

computers

engineering

finance

law

psychology

economics

medicine

vocational training

†Developing Your 30-second Elevator Pitch

You never get a second chance to make a first impression.

If you've ever searched for a job, you have probably been asked the question "Tell me about yourself." Most people fumble around with their reply and often begin sharing inappropriate personal or irrelevant information.

> **Think about how you have in the past answered this question, write a few reflections statements below.**

This is often the first question asked when conducting information interviews or networking. Your answer to this question is key to making a solid first impression and engaging the other person in a professional dialogue about who you are as a professional.

Situations That Lead to Someone Saying "Tell me about yourself"
• Conference networking with other participants
• Informational interview with working professionals
• Formal interview with potential employer
• Email communication with employers, recruiters, networking contacts, etc.
• Casual meeting, lunch, or other information situation with someone new

Your answer can both engage the other in further dialogue to gain their interest in learning more about you, and lead to a more strategic conversation that can catapult you forward in your job search.

This is commonly referred to as an "Elevator Pitch" or a 30-second verbal resume. Why? The length of your reply should be no longer than the time it takes when you meet a person in the elevator and the elevator arrives at their floor. That's not a lot of time to make an impression! Typically, this is 15–30 seconds. That is why we refer to it as your 30-second pitch or 30-second verbal resume. However, many people are able to share powerful pitches in 15 seconds or less. Regardless, you don't want to exceed 30 seconds as going beyond that time frame, you would most likely lose the other person's attention.

Depending on your situation, your reply will vary, but the elements of your response will be similar in most situations. In order to develop an engaging and powerful reply, you need to understand the situation you are in and why the other person is asking the question in the first place.

Your goal with your reply is to create opportunity by setting the tone, engaging the other person in a dialogue, and sometimes moving the situation to action or next steps.

Tips for Your Elevator Pitch
1. Use only your first name and pronounce it slowly. Most people will not remember last names.
2. Shake their hand firmly when introducing yourself and look them in the eye.
3. Practice. Practice. Practice. You must know all of the elements so you can comfortably adapt them to your situation.
4. Practice asking thoughtful questions to continue the dialogue.

What to include

- Your name.
- General information about where you are coming from.
- Your career focus and years of experience.
- Type of employment you are seeking.
- What you have done in your career.
- What you would like to ask this person.

. . . all to be communicated in 30 seconds!

Sample Pitch
Hello. I am Amy. I recently relocated to DC (or am an engineering student at *name of university or college*) and am seeking information about the DC job market. I have several months of experience through an intense internship with a local engineering firm. I am interested in civil engineering employment, but I don't know the local market. Do you know anyone who is a civil engineer or do you know someone who works with such professionals?

Good questions	Do NOT say:
• Do you know any economists or people who work with economists? • Would you be willing to meet with me for a half-hour sometime next week? • Do you know anybody who knows something about my career field? • Do you know anyone in my career field? • Do you know anybody at the university?	• Can you help me? • Can you find me a job? • Do you know where I can access information about this company? • Do you know of any jobs in this field? • Do you know of any positions at the university? • Where can I find jobs in this field?

Do	Don't
• Be specific • Use your first name only and say your name S-L-O-W-L-Y • Use a company name for a previous employer if it is well-known in the United States	• Give general information • Make a statement at the end—always keep the dialogue open—usually with a question • Ask for a job, position, or employment opportunity!!!

Interests, Values, & Personality Matrix

This activity is intended to help students think concretely about how interests, values, and personality influence major and career choice. You will read the name, interests, values, and personality type of each hypothetical student one by one. The class will then be asked to brainstorm what careers this person could pursue and what majors they may choose in order to get them to their desired position. After this discussion, ask what careers and majors could potentially leave this student unsatisfied. Make sure to have students explain the rationale they are using to come to their decisions. Depending on how much time is available for this activity, discussions about what the student would need to work on or pitfalls to avoid could also be explored (e.g. Susana may need to find a business partner that is more structured and good with numbers if she is going to start her own dance studio). At the end of the activity, you may want to ask each student to make their own matrix and work with a partner to brainstorm for one another. Feel free to add or make changes to this list.

NAME	INTERESTS	VALUES	PERSONALITY TYPE
Susanna	Music, Art, Dance	Autonomy; Being her own boss	Extrovert, Perceiving
Danny	History, Animals	Helping others; Helping Society	Sensing
Hakim	Math	Public recognition; Prestige	Introvert, Judging
Gloria	Working with children	Her family; being friends with co-workers	Feeling, Perceving
Patrick	Computers, Software	Financial security	Introvert, Sensing
Raj	Psychology	Working with people; Moral fulfillment	Extrovert, Intuition
Katia	Medicine, Public Health	Fast-paced environment, Variety	Sensing, Judging
Rachel	Law, Politics	Competition; Working under Pressure	Extrovert, Thinker
Felipe	Anatomy, Fitness	Work/Life balance, Working in a small organization	Intuition, Thinker

Exercise 1. Work Values

Name _____ Occupation #2_____

Work values are qualities about a job that are most significant and meaningful to you. Without them, the job would not be satisfying. Identify ten work values that are important to you and rank them from 1 to 10, 1 being most important.

_____ Great salary
_____ Recognition from others
_____ Security
_____ Fun
_____ Autonomy
_____ Variety
_____ Excitement
_____ Lots of leisure time
_____ Leadership role
_____ Helping others
_____ Prestige
_____ Creativity
_____ Improving society
_____ Influencing others
_____ Continuity
_____ Professional position

_____ Flexible work schedule
_____ Working outside
_____ Having an office
_____ Congenial workplace
_____ Competition
_____ Travel
_____ Affiliation
_____ Decision making
_____ Supervising others
_____ Work flexibility
_____ Public contact
_____ Working alone

Other
_____ a. _____
_____ b. _____
_____ c. _____

1. What are your top three work values?

2. Describe why each of these values is important to you.

How Can I Set Attainable and Realistic Goals for My Future?

Learning Objectives

- Share Innovation Challenge Pitches, give each other feedback, and discuss what was learned from this assignment.

- Use the steps of Planful Decision Making in career decision making.

- Outline three ways to become more motivated and progress toward your goals

- Develop three concrete and practical goals, using SMART guidelines—one personal, one academic, and one career.

- List three behaviors you will change when setting goals and making decisions regarding choosing a major.

‖Making Good Decisions

© 2014, Anastasia vish. Used under license with Shutterstock, Inc.

Knowing how to make a good decision about your career and important life events is very important to your future, as this short poem by J. Wooden sums up:

There is a choice you have to make, In everything you do

And you must always keep in mind, The choice you make, makes you. [1]

Sometimes people end up in a career because they simply seized an opportunity for employment. A good job becomes available and they happen to be in the right place at the right time. Sometimes people end up in a career because it is familiar to them, because it is a job held by a member of the family or a friend in the community. Sometimes people end up in a career because of economic necessity. The job pays well and they need the money. These careers are the result of chance circumstances. Sometimes they turn out well, and sometimes they turn out miserably.

Whether you are male or female, married or single, you will spend a great deal of your life working. By doing some careful thinking and planning about your career, you can improve your chances of success and happiness. Use the following steps to do some careful decision making about your career. Although you are the person who needs to make the decision about a career, you can get help from your college career center or your college counselor or advisor.

Steps in Making a Career Decision

1. **Begin with self-assessment.**
   - What is your personality type?
   - What are your interests?
   - What are your talents, gifts, and strengths?
   - What is your learning style?
   - What are your values?
   - What lifestyle do you prefer?

2. **Explore your options.**
   - What careers match your personal characteristics?

3. **Research your career options.**
   - Read the job description.
   - Investigate the career outlook.
   - What is the salary?
   - What training and education is required?
   - Speak with an advisor, counselor, or person involved in the career that interests you.
   - Choose a career or general career area that matches your personal characteristics.

4. **Plan your education to match your career goal.**
   - Try out courses in your area of interest.
   - Start your general education if you need more time to decide on a major.
   - Try an internship or part-time job in your area of interest.

5. **Make a commitment to take action and follow through with your plan.**

6. **Evaluate.**
   - Do you like the courses you are taking?
   - Are you doing well in the courses?
   - Continue research if necessary.

7. **Refine your plan.**
   - Make your plan more specific to aim for a particular career.
   - Select the college major that is best for you.

8. **Change your plan if it is not working.**
   - Go back to the self-assessment step.

The Decision-Making Process

- **Dependent decisions.** Different kinds of decisions are appropriate in different situations. When you make a dependent decision, you depend on someone else to make the decision for you. The dependent decision was probably the first kind of decision that you ever made. When your parents told you what to do as a child, you were making a dependent decision. As an adult, you make a dependent decision when your doctor tells you what medication to take for an illness or when your stockbroker tells you what stock you should purchase. Dependent decisions are easy to make and require little thought. Making a dependent decision saves time and energy.

  The dependent decision, however, has some disadvantages. You may not like the outcome of the decision. The medication that your doctor prescribes may have unpleasant side effects. The stock that you purchased may go down in value. When students ask a counselor to recommend a major or a career, they are making a dependent decision. When the decision does not work, they blame the counselor. Even if the dependent decision does have good results, you may become dependent on others to continue making decisions for you. Dependent decisions do work in certain situations, but they do not give you as much control over your own life.

- **Intuitive decisions.** Intuitive decisions are based on intuition or a gut feeling about what is the best course of action. Intuitive decisions can be made quickly and are useful in dealing with emergencies. If I see a car heading on a collision path toward me, I have to swerve quickly to the right or left. I do not have time to ask someone else what to do or think much about the alternatives. Another example of an intuitive decision is in gambling. If I am trying to decide whether to bet a dollar on red or black, I rely on my gut feeling to make a choice. Intuitive decisions may work out or they may not. You could make a mistake and swerve the wrong way as the car approaches or you could lose your money in gambling.

- **Planful decisions.** For important decisions, it is advantageous to use what is called a planful decision. The planful decision is made after carefully weighing the consequences and the pros and cons of the different alternatives. The planful decision-making strategy is particularly useful for such decisions as:
  - What will be my major?
  - What career should I choose?
  - Whom should I marry?

> "Find a job you like and add five days to every week".
>
> H. Jackson Browne

The steps in a planful decision-making process:

1. **State the problem.** When we become aware of a problem, the first step is to state the problem in the simplest way possible. Just stating the problem will help you to clarify the issues.

2. **Consider your values.** What is important to you? What are your hopes and dreams? By keeping your values in mind, you are more likely to make a decision that will make you happy.

3. **What are your talents?** What special skills do you have? How can you make a decision that utilizes these skills?

4. **Gather information.** What information can you find that would be helpful in solving the problem? Look for ideas. Ask other people. Do some research. Gathering information can give you insight into alternatives or possible solutions to the problem.

5. **Generate alternatives.** Based on the information you have gathered, identify some possible solutions to the problem.

6. **Evaluate the pros and cons of each alternative.** List the alternatives and think about the pros and cons of each one. In thinking about the pros and cons, consider your values and talents as well as your future goals.

7. **Select the best alternative.** Choose the alternative that is the best match for your values and helps you to achieve your goals.

8. **Take action.** You put your decision into practice when you take some action on it. Get started!

What Are My Lifetime Goals?

You have now completed the assessment part of the course and have a greater awareness of your personal strengths, vocational interests, values, and multiple intelligences. Use this knowledge to begin thinking about some goals for the future.

Setting goals helps you to establish what is important and provides direction for your life. Goals help you to focus your energy on what you want to accomplish. Goals are a promise to yourself to improve your life. Setting goals can help you turn your dreams into reality. Steven Scott in his book, *A Millionaire's Notebook,* lays out five steps in this process:

1. Dream or visualize.

2. Convert the dream into goals.

3. Convert your goals into tasks.

4. Convert your task into steps.

5. Take your first step and then the next.[2]

As you begin to think about your personal goals in life, make your goals specific and concrete. Rather than saying, "I want to be rich," make your goal something that you can break into specific steps. You might want to start learning about money management or begin a savings plan. Rather than setting a goal for happiness, think about what brings you happiness. If you want to live a long and healthy life, think about the health habits that will help you to accomplish your goal. You will need to break your goals down into specific tasks to be able to accomplish them.

Here are some criteria for successful goal setting:

1. **Is it achievable?** Do I have the skills, abilities, and resources to accomplish this goal? If not, am I willing to spend the time to develop the skills, abilities, and resources needed to achieve this goal?

2. **Is it realistic?** Do I believe I can achieve it? Am I positive and optimistic about this goal?

3. **Is it specific and measurable?** Can it be counted or observed? The most common goal mentioned by students is happiness in life. What is happiness, and how will you know when you have achieved it? Is happiness a career you enjoy, owning your own home, or a travel destination?

4. **Do you want to do it?** Is this a goal you are choosing because it gives you personal satisfaction rather than meeting a requirement or an expectation of someone else?

5. **Are you motivated to achieve it?** What are your rewards for achieving it?

6. **Does the goal match your values?** Is it important to you?

7. **What steps do you need to take to begin?** Am I willing to take action to start working on it?

8. **When will you finish this goal?** Set a date to accomplish your goal.

> "A goal is a dream with a deadline."
>
> Napoleon Hill

REFLECTION

Write a paragraph about your lifetime goals. Use any of these questions to guide your thinking:

What is your career goal? If you do not know what your career goal is, describe your preferred work environment. Would your ideal career require a college degree?

What are your family goals? Are you interested in marriage and family? What would be your important family values?

What are your social goals (friends, community, and recreation)?

When you are older and look back on your life, what are the three most important life goals that you would want to make sure to accomplish?

†**Do you know people who:**

- Have careers that suffer today because they failed to plan adequately yesterday?
- Are so focused on future goals that they neglect the present?
- Set objectives and then just expect them to happen?
- Have lives that have been made inflexible by overly detailed plans?

Plan without realistically taking future conditions into consideration? If so, you know people who do not effectively use goal setting and planning to take charge of their careers and lives.

The Future in Perspective

Futurists maintain that through collective actions, everyone participates in creating the future.

In his book, **The Innovators: How a Group of Inventors, Hackers, Geniuses, and Geeks Created the Digital Revolution, Walter Isaacson** recounts an interaction between a corporate planning director at Xerox and Alan Kay. Pendery kept asking Kay and others for an assessment of "trends" that foretold what the future might hold for the company. During one maddening session, Kay, whose thoughts often seemed tailored to go directly from his tongue to wikiquotes, shot back a line that was to become Xerox PARC's creed: "The best way to predict the future is to invent it."[1]

The story of the Digital Revolution as recounted by Isaacson shows how the digital world we take for granted was created by many people, going back not just decades but centuries. "But the main lesson to draw from the birth of computers," recounts Isaacson, is that innovation is usually a group effort, involving collaboration between visionaries and engineers, and that creativity comes from drawing on many sources. Only in storybooks do inventions come like a thunderbolt, or a light bulb popping out of the head of a lone individual in a basement or garage.

The BEST WAY to predict the future IS TO INVENT IT

Ozerina Anna/Shutterstock.com

Influencing Your Career Future

Just as collective actions shaped the Digital Revolution, and in many ways the future of work, your individual actions shape your personal destiny. The term *self-fulfilling prophecy* describes this phenomenon of individual expectations influencing future results. For example, if you approach a job interview fully prepared and expecting to perform well, you are likely to succeed. In contrast, if you expect to perform poorly ("I never do well in face-to-face contacts" or "I always choke under pressure"), you are likely to fail.

Having chosen a career, you may be tempted to make minimal plans, sit back, and "let it happen." Unfortunately, what usually happens with this approach is failure. Like everyone else, you will probably experience some setbacks as you pursue a career. Lacking shorter-range goals and specific career plans, you may find these setbacks overwhelming and doubt that you can succeed. Feeling out of control, you might then reinforce your pessimism by expecting further setbacks instead of looking for other options and opportunities. Not surprisingly, a cycle of victimization develops, and few career choices are attained.

On the other hand, with comprehensive, short-range goals and plans, it is easy to view setbacks in a large perspective. You can recognize other, often better, alternatives that were not obvious before. Of course, no one can absolutely predict the future. Yet developing and following objectives and plans do give you far more control, direction, and motivation. In this way, your own self-fulfilling prophecy will be success.

www.subtropica/Shutterstock.com

Career Goals/Objectives

Career goals provide you with purpose and direction for your career and life. People without goals experience more conflict and uncertainty because they just react to whatever happens instead of trying to infuse their lives with meaning. These people are likely to have far more days when they have no compelling reason for even getting out of bed. In contrast, people with carefully chosen, clearly defined goals know what they want out of their lives and careers.

Another function of clearly defined goals is that they enable people to channel their energy into meaningful activity and may even create more energy in the pursuit of life goals. The following example illustrates this point.

Designing and Building Your Future Career and Life

Denise was a conscientious and efficient administrative assistant whose true passion was hiking and backpacking in wilderness areas. Feeling unchallenged and tied down in her office setting, she decided to attend college as a way to initiate a career

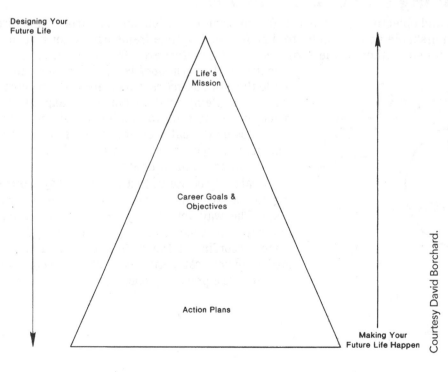

Courtesy David Borchard.

change. Unmotivated and discouraged by her lack of clear direction, she dropped out her first semester. She was unable to see how her love of the outdoors had any relationship to a possible new career direction. Through the assistance of a career counselor, however, she saw that conserving natural resources for the enjoyment of everyone was the motivating force in her life.

With renewed purpose, Denise reentered college, majored in geology, and made the Dean's List in her first semester back. She joined the Appalachian Trail Conservancy in its mission to maintain sections of the Appalachian Trail. Currently, she is collaborating with an architect friend on the development of a design for an energy-efficient home utilizing solar and geothermal power. Having a clearly defined career objective has enabled Denise to channel her energies toward results that amaze even her.

In effect, having clearly defined goals brings the future into the present. Instead of procrastinating, you can take appropriate present action because you are clear about what direction you want to go. Accordingly, you can also see what actions will move you in your chosen direction and what will not.

In this way, goals enable you to take charge of your life. Rather than just sitting back and letting things happen to you, you can use goals as catalysts for action. People who just let things happen to them are actually at the mercy of circumstances. They use up their energy fighting, denying, or rationalizing unpleasant realities.

As you create goals and act upon them, you influence your future. In other words, your mental images and attitudes about the future largely determine the shape of your future. No one can totally control the future because of unknown circumstances over which there is little control. Goal-oriented people, however, tend to be far more successful at getting what they want rather than simply taking what they can get.

Defining Your Goals/Objectives

Goals and objectives are specific, future-oriented statements of purpose and direction accomplishable within a definite time frame. The time frame can be long, medium, or short range. Although the terms *goal* and *objective* are often used interchangeably,

sometimes the term *goal* is used for long-range aims while the word *objective* is used for related short-range intentions. Being well within our grasp, short-range objectives enable us to establish and reach tangible outcomes on the path toward our long-range goals. As we complete our objectives, we are then in a position to set and accomplish new ones.

Goals may be stated in a variety of ways corresponding to the strength of your commitment to complete them. The way you state your goals clearly indicates that how determined you are to achieve your desired outcome. According to David Ellis, there is a hierarchy of goal-statement categories, each successively more powerful than the preceding one.[2]

Least Powerful	Category 1—Statements of Possibility
	"I probably will . . ." or
	"I might be able to . . ."
	Category 2—Statements of Desire
	"I want to . . ." or
	"I'd really like to . . ."
	Category 3—Statements of Intent
	"I'll try to . . ." or
	"I'll do the best I can to . . ."
	Category 4—Statements of Promise
	"I will . . ." or
Most Powerful	"I'm committed to . . ."

Courtesy David Borchard

David Ellis's Hierarchy of Goal-Statement Categories.[3]

Notice that with each higher category, the language gets increasingly stronger and the likelihood that the goal will be completed gets more believable. In people's daily interactions, the strongest language (category 4) is reserved for activities requiring the highest level of commitment, such as marriage vows or promissory notes. In a court of law where the truthfulness of witnesses can mean the difference between life and death of an accused person, the most powerful language is used when swearing in witnesses: "I promise to tell the truth, the whole truth, and nothing but the truth."

Pay attention to the language you use when you state your own goals. If you state a goal in the language of category 2 (desire), "I want to get a better job," examine your willingness to make a stronger commitment to reaching that goal. Then restate your goal in the language of category 3 (intent) or category 4 (promise), "I'll do my best to get a better job" or "I will get a better job."

Review the Hierarchy of Goal-Statement Categories. Reflect on the words you commonly use and how you state your goals. What category do you use the most?

Are there situations where it is okay to represent your goals in category 1 or 2?

When it comes to your future, what would it take for you to be able to present your goals using category 4 languages?

A goal is a dream taken seriously.

It has been said before in this book that dreams are good but they need action. Goals are important but can be too short sighted and rigid. Consider this statement by John C. Maxwell, "I've studied successful people for almost forty years. I've known hundreds of high-profile people who achieved big dreams. And I've achieved a few dreams of my own. What I've discovered is that a lot of people have misconceptions about dreams. . . . Here is my definition of a dream that can be put to the test and pass: a dream is an inspiring picture of the future that energizes your mind, will, and emotions, empowering you to do everything you can to achieve it."

John C. Maxwell, Put Your Dream to the Test: 10 Questions to Help You See It and Seize It[4]

Think of the components. First it contains an inspiring picture of the future. It is something that can be visualized. It energizes your mind meaning that it gets the attention of your intellect. You think about it and consider all aspects of the dream. It also energizes your will meaning that it is going to take some effort. You will have positive emotion around it as it energizes your emotions. Finally, it will empower you to action. It is going to be something that you will be willing to take action to achieve.

The dream of being in good physical condition is not going to happen if you sit around eating chips watching movies. You will never realize that your dream of owning a car that really cools if you spend every dime you make on things that catch your attention in the moment instead of saving your money. Without the willingness to do something about it your dream it will just be that—a dream.

Watching a group of college football players get ready for a scrimmage game, a faculty member was impressed with their dedication. It occurred to the faculty member, who himself had endured the rigors of academic preparation, how disciplined these young men were in pursuit of their own dreams. Their daily work outs that often left little free time, their disciplined eating and body training, the memorization of plays, their focus on their own personal performance alongside their ability to integrate those skills with the other players on the field, all impressed their professor. For him, it was a picture of the goal setting principles that he often taught in his classes. Being "all-in" to achieve the end result, these players kept their eye not only on the team goal of winning but also on their own personal long-range career goals, which for many included playing in the NFL.

PAUSE

Consider your own dreams. Is there anything you want that meets the Maxwell definition of a dream or is seen by others in your disciplined pursuit?

If so, explain it here. If not, use the space to consider what that dream could be and elaborate on what it would take to make it happen.

Clarifying What You Want in a Career

Knowing what you really want in a career is necessary before you can develop believable career goals. Clarifying your wants, however, may not be so easy. Wants are often confused with "shoulds" that are beliefs about what you ought to do, be, or have. "Shoulds" usually are influenced strongly by the thinking of others. Your parents, social institutions, the media, public opinion, or current popular values try to convince you of what you should do, have, or be. At your place of worship, you may be reminded of your duty to contribute your time and money to the support of the congregation. Marketers bombard you with overt and subtle secular "should" messages: "remove unsightly hair," "think differently," "eat fresh," "just do it." "Should" messages from a variety of sources serve as nagging reminders of what we are "supposed" to do.

"Wants," on the other hand, are expressions of what you really desire to have, do, or be. They reflect those things that attract your interest or enthusiasm, those things that grow from your wishes, dreams, aspirations, and fantasies. They reflect the inner you—the real you.

"Shoulds" can prevent you from being in touch with your true "wants." For this reason, it is important to clearly separate your "shoulds" from your "wants." Career goals created out of "shoulds" do not work because they are too much like New Year's resolutions—full of good intentions, but in the end, usually resisted. Career goals developed out of true "wants," however, enlist our full energy and provide a winning combination. Here is an example of how to transform a "should" into a "want":

- I *should* lose weight.
- I *want* to maintain my weight at a neat and trim 130 pounds.

Comprehensive Career Goals and Objectives

Establishing reachable long-range career goals is crucial for providing future direction and perspective. But a long-range goal is less useful in clarifying what step you should take next. Long-range goals extend at least 10 years into the future. It would be nearly impossible to sit down today and produce a detailed plan for the next 10 years that would help you attain these goals. Even if you had the patience and perspective to do this, your plan would be foolishly rigid. Your own life will change, and the working world will present new opportunities. Accordingly, your plans and long-range goals will change.

For this reason, the easiest and most productive approach is to devise medium-range and short-range career objectives based on your long-range goals. A medium-range objective generally covers one to five years. As these medium-range objectives are reached, you can devise new ones to direct your progress toward the related long-range goal. Sometimes, you will want to change these medium-range objectives when they no longer are suitable. Short-range objectives cover up to one year. You will frequently revise short-range objectives.

The advantages of medium- and short-range objectives are numerous. First of all, they are totally flexible. As changes and opportunities occur, these short-range objectives can easily be revised. Also, you don't have to wait 10 or more years to attain them. Successfully achieving short-range objectives keeps you motivated. If you feel discouraged because you have not yet found a suitable career choice, setting short-term objectives will provide direction for your continuing exploration. Finally, short-range objectives are specific enough to provide guidelines for making step-by-step plans. Without these plans, your future becomes a question mark—or worse.

Developing Goals

1. *Long-Range Goals:* These goals establish the general career direction you want to achieve over the long run or at least 10 years into the future. Occasionally, you will find better alternatives and change your long-range goals.

2. *Medium-Range Objectives:* These are the career objectives you want to achieve in the next one to five years, so they are more specific. As these objectives are reached, you will establish others to progress toward related long-range goals. Medium-range objectives are frequently revised and sometimes changed completely as new options appear.

3. *Short-Range Objectives:* These are career objectives you want to achieve in one year or less, so they are very specific. These objectives are frequently revised or changed completely as new options appear.

By beginning with your long-range goals, you can work backwards. You may find that as you progress in your career, your goals will change. If you decided to go on a vacation without a destination, you would be somewhere. But if you decided that you wanted to go on vacation to San Luis Obispo and from there tour the Central Coast of California and you were starting from New York City, you would find a few APPS and chart your course. Deciding to take a plane, train, automobile, or walk would impact your trip. If you decide to drive, you may decide to sightsee along the way. During your sightseeing, you may decide that you want to spend more time in this area and decide not to complete your journey to California. Many careers start off headed in one direction but for some reason wind up at another place. This doesn't mean the initial decision was bad, it simply means that another option was presented along the way that perhaps was not previously considered or was rejected at the time.

Review the goal definitions and examples in the section "Developing Goals." Look these over carefully before devising your own short-range objective statements.

Mission statements are the ideal outcomes you seek in your life.
Career goals and objectives are the realistic outcomes you seek in your career.
Action plans are the specific actions required to achieve your objectives.

Notice that your mission is your ideal or ultimate outcome, while your objectives and goals define what you can accomplish realistically within a specified time frame. Plans lay out the steps required to get what you want.

What do I want ideally?	MISSION
What can I accomplish realistically?	GOALS AND OBJECTIVES
How can I accomplish it?	PLANS

William was a high school misfit. His parents took him out of public school and placed him in a private school, where William did his best to prove that his parents had made a mistake. The culmination of his efforts came when he failed a class his senior year and was unable to graduate with his class.

After completing summer school to obtain his high school diploma, William jumped from one job to another, either leaving when he got bored or getting fired. He attempted to enlist in the Marine Corps but was unable to pass the physical. Angry and discouraged, William hit bottom when he was apprehended for reckless driving and placed in his parent's custody.

Given an ultimatum by his parents to "shape up" or suffer the consequences, William reluctantly agreed to try the local community college. He took just two classes for his first semester, a career planning class and an art class (art was the only subject William had enjoyed in high school). Finding an environment where his creative interests and talents were recognized and encouraged, William began to believe in himself. Through the career planning process he discovered that what he really wanted to do was express himself creatively, especially through photography.

Prior to the start of his second semester, William changed from an undeclared major to a visual arts major. Filled with enthusiasm and having educational and career direction for the first time in his life, William

Tom Tom/Shutterstock.com

took a full academic load in his second semester, narrowly missing the Dean's List. One of his photographic collages was chosen for the student art show, and he received a second-place ribbon.

This summer, William is working as a photographer's assistant. In his free time, he wanders the countryside taking pictures. He is learning how to obtain the special effects he wants. The best prints will be placed in a portfolio when he transfers to the art institute in one year.

Through realistic goal setting and effective action planning, William has found direction and focus for his career journey.

Final Notes on Goals, Objectives, and Plans

Setting goals and objectives and devising action plans are skills that can be developed. Both are also ongoing processes. Many people are reluctant to set goals and objectives or make the supporting plans because they fear they will then be committed to them no matter what. Others are afraid of even positive change or afraid of failing to meet the objectives that they have set. All of these emotional reactions are perfectly understandable and normal. However, consider that the only purpose of goals, objectives, and plans is to provide productive direction and motivation, along with the time to accommodate change. Therefore, they should never be turned into nonproductive, rigid commitments, or burdens.

Since people and the working world change, goals, objectives, and plans should change whenever it is in your best interest. You will need to make these minor or major changes as you learn about new options or challenges in your career. In other words, career planning is a lifelong process. The more you practice these skills, the more effective you will become in taking charge of your career and your life.

Summary

By developing a view of the future, you can build the kind of future you really want to have. No one can predict your fate exactly. However, the taking-charge method of career/life planning does allow you far more control and influence over your prospects. The career/life planning process includes clarifying what you want in your future career and life, setting prioritized goals to get what you want, and translating these into realistic objectives and planned actions.

As your personal needs and aspirations change and the working world changes, you will repeat parts of this process with increasing skill and confidence. Thus, career/life decision-making becomes a life-long process, leading you to as much fulfillment as you seek.

Endnotes

1. Walter Isaacson, *The innovators: how a group of hackers, geniuses, and geeks created the digital revolution* (New York: Simon & Schuster Paperbacks, 2015).

2. David Ellis, *Here & Now Instructor's Newsletter*, November 1986: 1, 4. This newsletter can be obtained by contacting College Survival, Inc., 2650 Jackson Boulevard, Rapid City, South Dakota 57702.

3. Ibid.

4. John C. Maxwell, *Put your dream to the test: 10 questions to help you see it and seize it* (Nashville: Thomas Nelson, Inc., 2011).

Other sources related to this APP:

Edward S. Cornish, *Planting Seeds for the Future* (Stamford, CT: Champion International Corp., 2000). Copies can be obtained by writing to Champion International Corporation, Department 5360, 1 Landmark Square, Stamford, Connecticut 06921.

Intensive Course in the Crystal Life/Work Planning Process, John C. Crystal Center, Inc., 894 Plandome Road, Manhasset, New York 11030.

James D. McHolland, *Human Potential Seminar Basic Guidebook* (Evanston, Illinois: National Center for Human Potential Seminars & Services, 1976). The publisher's address is 2527 Hastings Avenue, Evanston, Illinois 60201

STEP 1
Identifying What You Want in Your Career

1. Before identifying what you do want in your career, it is important to know what you don't want or want to avoid. List below those things you have currently in your life, career, and/or job that you do not want.

    _____

    _____

    _____

2. Some elements of your current life, career, and/or job give you energy and pleasure. List below these current elements in your life, career, and/or job that you do want to retain.

    _____

    _____

    _____

3. Now that you have more clarity about your skills, interests, and values and have made a tentative or definite career choice, what else is important for you to have in your career? List below the things you truly want in your future career and/or job that you don't have now.

    _____

    _____

    _____

4. From numbers 2 and 3 above, develop a list of your top 10 career wants. Eliminate those that are really "shoulds" from your list or restate them as "wants." Now prioritize your list of 10, assigning "1" to the most important and "10" to the least important.

    My Top Ten Wants

    1. _____

    2. _____

    3. _____

    4. _____

    5. _____

    6. _____

    7. _____

    8. _____

    9. _____

    10. _____

5. Take the top five career wants from your prioritized list of 10, and restate each one as a specific career goal or objective.

Examples:

   a. I want to work with people who are highly committed to the customers/clients they serve.
   b. I want to obtain recognition from others for the work that I do.
   c. I want to make enough money to maintain the lifestyle I currently enjoy.
   d. I want a job that is within walking distance of my residence.
   e. I want a career that will enable me to use and develop my foreign language skills.

Five Career Goals

1. _____

2. _____

3. _____

4. _____

5. _____

STEP 2

Remember, career goal and objective statements follow certain guidelines to define effectively the direction you want your future to take. True career goals and objectives are:

1. *Achievable.* Achievable outcomes can be completed given the physical and mental limitations of the people setting the objectives.

2. *Believable.* People need to feel confident that they can complete the goal or objective—that it is within the realm of possibility for them.

3. *Specifically Stated.* True objectives are stated in concrete terms.

4. *Presented Without Alternative.* True objectives are clearly stated without any either/or clauses.

5. *Compatible with Your Values.* True statements of goals reflect the values that you profess.

Review Definitions and Examples

Look these over carefully before devising your own short-range objective statements. Remember these important points:

1. *Long-Range Goals:* These goals establish the general career direction you want to achieve over the long run or at least 10 years into the future.

2. *Medium-Range Objectives:* These are the career objectives you want to achieve in the next one to five years, so they are more specific.

3. *Short-Range Objectives:* These are career objectives you want to achieve in one year or less, so they are very specific.

Long-Range Goals

Vague	More Effective
I want to work with people I like.	I will work with people who are caring, creative, and intelligent.

Medium-Range Objectives

Vague	More Precise
I want to get a good education.	Within five years, I will have obtained a B.A. degree in psychology.

Short-Range Objectives

Vague Precise	
I will finish my A.A. degree.	Within one year, I will have completed my A.A. degree in respiratory therapy.

STEP 3
Revise Your Statements of Career Objectives

Check over your top five career objectives to see if they correspond to the guidelines just listed, then make any revisions that you feel are necessary. Perhaps your goal statements need to be more concrete, more clearly stated, or have a timeline added.

1. Career Objective: _____

_____

Revision: _____

_____

2. Career Objective: _____

_____

Revision: _____

_____

3. Career Objective: _____

_____

Revision: _____

_____

4. Career Objective: _____

_____

Revision: _____

_____

5. Career Objective: _____

    Revision: _____

    _____

STEP 4

Develop Comprehensive Statements of Career Goals

For this exercise, you will further revise your long-range statements of career goals. Using these long-range career goals as references, you will then establish related medium-range and short-range objectives. To illustrate, we will follow the example of Marlene. Initially, Marlene completed the following prioritized list of career-related life objectives:

1. I will be doing worthwhile, important work related to my math skills.
2. I will obtain professional recognition.
3. I will have opportunity for self-improvement.
4. I will have financial security.
5. I will be contributing to the solution of our inflation problems.

After Marlene's preliminary research with her work options, she decided to become an accountant. At that point, she was able to develop and refine her long-range career goals. Her revised goals are as follows:

1. I will work in a large public-service accounting firm, serving in a leadership position.
2. Within 10 years, I will receive recognition for my excellent work as a C.P.A.
3. I will work for an organization that encourages personal and professional growth by sponsoring workshops and funding continued education.
4. Within 12 years, I will be earning a salary equivalent to $60,000 in today's money.
5. I will be helping to solve our economic problems by teaching sound financial management and fiscal responsibility to my clients.

Marlene then developed the following medium-range and short-range objectives related to her top long-range career goals:

Long-Range Goal #1

I will work in a large public-service accounting firm, serving in a leadership position.

Medium-Range Objectives

1. Within one year, I will obtain my A.A. degree in accounting.
2. I will graduate with a B+ average.
3. While in college, I will research fully the types of accounting businesses I consider to be potential employers.

Short-Range Objectives

1. In one-and-a-half years, I will obtain an entry-level accounting position in a firm of my choice.
2. Within two years, I will have received my first salary raise.
3. Within three years, I will earn a major promotion.
4. Within five years, I will have earned my M.B.A. in accounting through part-time study.

Revise Your Goals

Revise your top five long-range career objectives so they are stated as precisely as possible at this point in your life. If you made a tentative career choice, your long-range career goals will be more vague. However, state them as precisely as you can, and concentrate on constructive short-range objectives to aid your career exploration. Fill in your top two long-range goals in the appropriate spaces.

After writing your long-range goals, write your related medium-range and short-range career objectives. Use Marlene's example as a guide.

Goal Planning:

Long-Range Goal #1
Medium-Range Objectives
Short-Range Objectives

Long-Range Goal #2
Medium-Range Objectives
Short-Range Objectives

STEP 5
Action Planning:
Review the differences among mission, goals, and plans.

What do I want ideally?	MISSION
What can I accomplish realistically?	GOALS AND OBJECTIVES
How can I accomplish it?	PLANS

Mission statements are the ideal outcomes you seek in your life.
Career goals and objectives are the realistic outcomes you seek in your career.
Action plans are the specific actions required to achieve your objectives.

Start the exercise by identifying your first significant step toward achieving your short-range objective and determining when you can complete that step. Use the following example as a guide as you develop your own action plans.

Example:
For long-range goal #1, Marlene's short-range objectives were as follows:
1. Within one year, I will obtain an A.A. degree in accounting.
2. I will graduate with a B+ average.
3. While in college, I will research fully the types of accounting businesses I consider potential employers.

From these objectives, Marlene developed the following action plans:

Steps to Take	Complete by
1. I will change my major from general studies to accounting.	May 15, 2018
2. I will talk with my academic advisor to see what courses I need to take.	June 1, 2018
3. I will investigate financial aid possibilities at the financial aid office, so I can afford to take four courses a semester.	June 1, 2018
4. I will enroll in two summer school courses.	June 15, 2018
5. I will increase my study time to 30 hours a week to improve my current grades.	July 1, 2018 to May 20, 2018
6. I will research public-service accounting firms in the area, looking at government directories, and consulting Dun and Bradstreet directories.	May 20, 2018
7. wThrough the college, I will arrange for an accounting internship with one of the firms I've identified in step 6.	Jan. 1, 2019

Directions:

1. Using Marlene's example as a guide, develop a list of action steps for the short-range objectives associated with your top two long-range goals.

2. As you review your cluster of short-range objectives for each long-range goal, think through all the related steps required to complete those objectives. List your steps on the following pages in logical sequence.

3. Indicate the approximate deadline for completing each of the steps you identify.

Action Steps for My First Short-Range Objective	Desired Completion Date

Action Steps for My Second Short-Range Objective	Desired Completion Date

Name _____   Date _____

SMART Goals Worksheet (Specific, Measurable, Achievable, Realistic, Timely)

Directions: Choose three goals: one personal, one academic, and one career related and complete the worksheet for each of those goals.

	1	2	3
Goal Statement			
What do I need to do to reach this goal? (Make sure this is detailed and specific)			
Where am I now?			
Obstacles in achieving this goal			
How I will address these obstacles			
Estimation of Accomplishment Date			

Presenter:

Presentation Strengths (two minimum):
Opportunities for Improvement (two minimum):
On a scale of 1 to 10 (1 = poor; 10 = Excellent)
The presenter was prepared:
The presenter was engaging:
Overall Score (1 – 10; 1 = poor; 10 = Excellent) _____

Presenter:

Presentation Strengths (two minimum):
Opportunities for Improvement (two minimum):
On a scale of 1 to 10 (1 = poor; 10 = Excellent)
The presenter was prepared:
The presenter was engaging:
Overall Score (1 – 10; 1 = poor; 10 = Excellent) _____

Presenter:

Presentation Strengths (two minimum):
Opportunities for Improvement (two minimum):
On a scale of 1 to 10 (1 = poor; 10 = Excellent)
The presenter was prepared:
The presenter was engaging:
Overall Score (1 – 10; 1 = poor; 10 = Excellent) _____

Presenter:

Presentation Strengths (two minimum):
Opportunities for Improvement (two minimum):
On a scale of 1 to 10 (1 = poor; 10 = Excellent)
The presenter was prepared:
The presenter was engaging:
Overall Score (1 – 10; 1 = poor; 10 = Excellent) _____

Presenter:

Presentation Strengths (two minimum):
Opportunities for Improvement (two minimum):
On a scale of 1 to 10 (1 = poor; 10 = Excellent)
The presenter was prepared:
The presenter was engaging:
Overall Score (1 – 10; 1 = poor; 10 = Excellent) _____

Presenter:

Presentation Strengths (two minimum):
Opportunities for Improvement (two minimum):
On a scale of 1 to 10 (1 = poor; 10 = Excellent)
The presenter was prepared:
The presenter was engaging:
Overall Score (1 – 10; 1 = poor; 10 = Excellent) _____

Presenter:

Presentation Strengths (two minimum):
Opportunities for Improvement (two minimum):
On a scale of 1 to 10 (1 = poor; 10 = Excellent)
The presenter was prepared:
The presenter was engaging:
Overall Score (1 – 10; 1 = poor; 10 = Excellent) _____

Presenter:

Presentation Strengths (two minimum):
Opportunities for Improvement (two minimum):
On a scale of 1 to 10 (1 = poor; 10 = Excellent)
The presenter was prepared:
The presenter was engaging:
Overall Score (1 – 10; 1 = poor; 10 = Excellent) _____

Presenter:

Presentation Strengths (two minimum):
Opportunities for Improvement (two minimum):
On a scale of 1 to 10 (1 = poor; 10 = Excellent)
The presenter was prepared:
The presenter was engaging:
Overall Score (1 – 10; 1 = poor; 10 = Excellent) _____

Presenter:

Presentation Strengths (two minimum):
Opportunities for Improvement (two minimum):
On a scale of 1 to 10 (1 = poor; 10 = Excellent)
The presenter was prepared:
The presenter was engaging:
Overall Score (1 – 10; 1 = poor; 10 = Excellent) _____

Presenter:

Presentation Strengths (two minimum):
Opportunities for Improvement (two minimum):
On a scale of 1 to 10 (1 = poor; 10 = Excellent)
The presenter was prepared:
The presenter was engaging:
Overall Score (1 – 10; 1 = poor; 10 = Excellent) ____

Presenter:

Presentation Strengths (two minimum):
Opportunities for Improvement (two minimum):
On a scale of 1 to 10 (1 = poor; 10 = Excellent)
The presenter was prepared:
The presenter was engaging:
Overall Score (1 – 10; 1 = poor; 10 = Excellent) ____

Presenter:

Presentation Strengths (two minimum):
Opportunities for Improvement (two minimum):
On a scale of 1 to 10 (1 = poor; 10 = Excellent)
The presenter was prepared:
The presenter was engaging:
Overall Score (1 – 10; 1 = poor; 10 = Excellent) ____

Presenter:

Presentation Strengths (two minimum):
Opportunities for Improvement (two minimum):
On a scale of 1 to 10 (1 = poor; 10 = Excellent)
The presenter was prepared:
The presenter was engaging:
Overall Score (1 – 10; 1 = poor; 10 = Excellent) ____

Presenter:

Presentation Strengths (two minimum):
Opportunities for Improvement (two minimum):
On a scale of 1 to 10 (1 = poor; 10 = Excellent)
The presenter was prepared:
The presenter was engaging:
Overall Score (1 – 10; 1 = poor; 10 = Excellent) ____

Presenter:

Presentation Strengths (two minimum):
Opportunities for Improvement (two minimum):
On a scale of 1 to 10 (1 = poor; 10 = Excellent)
The presenter was prepared:
The presenter was engaging:
Overall Score (1 – 10; 1 = poor; 10 = Excellent) ____

Rank the top three presentations: #1 _____ #2 _____ #3 _____

Provide a brief paragraph that details the reasoning behind your ranking.

What Have I Learned from UNI 150 and What Are My Next Steps?

Learning Objectives

- Learn and practice effective presentation skills.

- Integrate research and self-knowledge

- Evaluate fit of majors/careers being considered.

College students begin their college education with the dream of having a better future and achieving happiness in life. This chapter includes some tools for thinking positively about your future, analyzing what happiness means, and taking the steps to achieve happiness in your life.

Thinking Positively about Your Career

You have assessed your personal strengths, interests, and values and are on your way to choosing a major and career that will achieve your goals and make you happy in life. It is interesting to note that thoughts about work often determine whether it is just a job, a career, or a calling that makes life interesting and fulfilling. For example, consider the parable of the bricklayers:

> Three bricklayers are asked: "What are you doing?"
> The first says, "I am laying bricks."
> The second says, "I am building a church."
> The third says, "I am building the house of God."[1]

The first bricklayer has a job, the second one has a career, and the third one approaches his job with a sense of purpose and optimism; he has a calling. Depending on your thoughts, any career can be a job, a career, or a calling. You can find your calling by thinking about your purpose and how your job makes the world a better place. Although purposes are unique, you can analyze your beliefs about any job in this way and look for greater satisfaction in what you are doing. If your current work is not a calling, find ways to change or improve it to match your personal strengths and purpose. People who have found their calling are consistently happier than those who have a job or even a career.

© kentoh/Shutterstock.com

"Hope arouses, as nothing else can arouse, a passion for the possible."
Rev. William Coffin Jr.

"Three grand essentials to happiness in this life are something to do, something to love, and something to hope for."
Joseph Addison

"Learn from yesterday, hope for tomorrow. The important thing is to not to stop questioning."
Albert Einstein

Optimism, Hope, and Future-Mindedness

You can increase your chances of success by using three powerful tools: optimism, hope, and future-mindedness. These character traits lead to achievement in athletics, academics, careers, and even politics. They also have positive mental and physical effects. They reduce anxiety and depression as well as contributing to physical well-being. In addition, they aid in problem solving and searching out resources to solve problems. A simple definition of optimism is expecting good events to happen in the future and working to make them happen. Optimism leads to continued efforts to accomplish goals, whereas pessimism leads to giving up on accomplishing goals. A person who sets no goals for the future cannot be optimistic or hopeful.

Being hopeful is another way of thinking positively about the future. Hope is the expectation that tomorrow will be better than today.[2] When you face challenges, you learn from mistakes, expect a positive outcome, and work to overcome the challenge. It is the opposite of accepting failure, expecting the worst, and giving up. In this way hope is related to the growth mindset and perseverance, or grit. One research study showed for entering college freshmen, level of hope was a better predictor of college grades than standardized tests or high school grade point average.[3] Students who have a high level of hope set higher goals and work to attain them. If they are not successful, they think about what went wrong and learn from it, or change goals and move in a new direction with a renewed sense of hope for a positive future.

Future-mindedness is thinking about the future, expecting that desired events and outcomes will occur, and then acting in a way that makes the positive outcomes come true. It involves setting goals for the future and taking action to accomplish these goals as well as being confident in accomplishing these goals. Individuals with future-mindedness are conscientious and hardworking and can delay gratification. They make to-do lists and use schedules and day planners. Individuals who are future-minded would agree with these statements:[4]

- Despite challenges, I always remain hopeful about the future.
- I always look on the bright side.
- I believe that good will always triumph over evil.
- I expect the best.
- I have a clear picture in mind about what I want to happen in the future.
- I have a plan for what I want to be doing five years from now.
- If I get a bad grade or evaluation, I focus on the next opportunity and plan to do better.

Believe in Yourself

Anthony Robbins defines belief as "any guiding principle, dictum, faith, or passion that can provide meaning and direction in life . . . Beliefs are the compass and maps that guide us toward our goals and give us the surety to know we'll get there."[5] The beliefs that we have about ourselves determine how much of our potential we will use and how successful we will be in the future. If we have positive beliefs about ourselves, we will feel confident and accomplish our goals in life. Negative beliefs get in the way of our success. Robbins reminds us that we can change our beliefs and choose new ones if necessary.

> *"The birth of excellence begins with our awareness that our beliefs are a choice. We usually do not think of it that way, but belief can be a conscious choice. You can choose beliefs that limit you, or you can choose beliefs that support you. The trick is to choose the beliefs that are conducive to success and the results you want and to discard the ones that hold you back."[6]*

The Self-Fulfilling Prophecy

The first step in thinking positively is to examine your beliefs about yourself, your life, and the world around you. Personal beliefs are influenced by our environment, significant events that have happened in life, what we have learned in the past, and our picture of the future. Beliefs cause us to have certain expectations about the world and ourselves. These expectations are such a powerful influence on behavior that psychologists use the term "self-fulfilling prophecy" to describe what happens when our expectations come true.

For example, if I believe that I am not good in math (my expectation), I may not try to do the assignment or may avoid taking a math class (my behavior). As a result, I am not good in math. My expectations have been fulfilled. Expectations can also have a positive effect. If I believe that I am a good student, I will take steps to enroll in college and complete my assignments. I will then become a good student. The prophecy will again come true.

"Attitude is the librarian of our past, the speaker of our present and the prophet of our future."
John Maxwell

"¡Sí, se puede!" (Yes, you can!)
César Chávez

"If I believe I cannot do something, it makes me incapable of doing it. But when I believe I can, then I acquire the ability to do it, even if I did not have the ability in the beginning."
Mahatma Gandhi

To think positively, it is necessary to recognize your negative beliefs and turn them into positive beliefs. Some negative beliefs commonly heard from college students include the following:

I don't have the money for college.
English was never my best subject.
I was never any good at math.

When you hear yourself saying these negative thoughts, remember that these thoughts can become self-fulfilling prophecies. First of all, notice the thought. Then see if you can change the statement into a positive statement such as:

I can find the money for college.
English has been a challenge for me in the past, but I will do better this time.
I can learn to be good at math.

If you believe that you can find money for college, you can go to the financial aid office and the scholarship office to begin your search for money to attend school. You can look for a better job or improve your money management. If you believe that you will do better in English, you will keep up with your assignments and go to the tutoring center or ask the professor for help. If you believe that you can learn to be good at math, you will attend every math class and seek tutoring when you do not understand. Your positive thoughts will help you to be successful.

Positive Self-Talk and Affirmations

Self-talk refers to the silent inner voice in our heads. This voice is often negative, especially when we are frustrated or trying to learn something new. Have you ever had thoughts about yourself that are similar to these:

How could you be so stupid!
That was dumb!
You idiot!

ACTIVITY

What do you say to yourself when you are angry or frustrated? Write several examples of your negative self-talk.

Negative thoughts can actually be toxic to your body. They can cause biochemical changes that can lead to depression and negatively affect the immune system.[7] Negative self-talk causes anxiety and poor performance and is damaging to self-esteem. It can also lead to a negative self-fulfilling prophecy. Positive thoughts can help us build self-esteem, become confident in our abilities, and achieve our goals. These positive thoughts are called affirmations.

If we make the world with our thoughts, it is important to become aware of the thoughts about ourselves that are continuously running through our heads. Are your thoughts positive or negative? Negative thoughts lead to failure. What we hear over and over again shapes our beliefs. If you say over and over to yourself such things as, "I am stupid," "I am ugly," or "I am fat," you will start to believe these things and act in a way that supports your beliefs. Positive thoughts help to build success. If you say to yourself, "I'm a good person," "I'm doing my best," or "I'm doing fine," you will begin to believe these things about yourself and act in a way that supports these beliefs. Here are some guidelines for increasing your positive self-talk and making affirmations:

1. Monitor your thoughts about yourself and become aware of them. Are they positive or negative?

2. When you notice a negative thought about yourself, imagine creating a new video with a positive message.

3. Start the positive message with "I" and use the present tense. Using an "I" statement shows you are in charge. Using the present tense shows you are ready for action now.

4. Focus on the positive. Think about what you want to achieve and what you can do rather than what you do not want to do. For example, instead of saying, "I will not eat junk food," say, "I will eat a healthy diet."

5. Make your affirmation stronger by adding an emotion to it.

6. Form a mental picture of what it is that you want to achieve. See yourself doing it successfully.

7. You may need to say the positive thoughts over and over again until you believe them and they become a habit. You can also write them down and put them in a place where you will see them often.

> "The most common way people give up their power is by thinking they don't have any."
> Alice Walker

Here are some examples of negative self-talk and contrasting positive affirmations:

Negative: I'm always broke.

Affirmation: I feel really good when I manage my finances. See yourself taking steps to manage finances. For example, a budget or savings plan.

Negative: I'm too fat. It just runs in the family.

Affirmation: I feel good about myself when I exercise and eat a healthy diet. See yourself exercising and eating a healthy diet.

Negative: I can't do this. I must be stupid.

Affirmation: I can do this. I am capable. I feel a sense of accomplishment when I accomplish something challenging. See yourself making your best attempt and taking the first step to accomplish the project.

ACTIVITY

Select one example of negative self-talk that you wrote earlier. Use the examples above to turn your negative message into a positive one and write it here.

REFLECTION

Write five positive statements about your future.

Visualize Your Success

© Sergey Nivens/Shutterstock.com

Visualization is a powerful tool for using your brain to improve memory, deal with stress, and think positively. Coaches and athletes study sports psychology to learn how to use visualization along with physical practice to improve athletic performance. College students can use the same techniques to enhance college success.

If you are familiar with sports or are an athlete, you can probably think of times when your coach asked you to use visualization to improve your performance. In baseball, the coach reminds players to keep their eye on the ball and visualize hitting it. In swimming, the coach asks swimmers to visualize reaching their arms out to touch the edge of the pool at the end of the race. Pole-vaulters visualize clearing the pole and sometimes even go through the motions before making the jump. Using imagery lets you practice for future events and pre-experience achieving your goals. Athletes imagine winning the race or completing the perfect jump in figure skating. In this way they prepare mentally and physically and develop confidence in their abilities. It still takes practice to excel.

Just as the athlete visualizes and then performs, the college student can do the same. It is said that we create all things twice. First we make a mental picture, and then we create the physical reality by taking action. For example, if we are building a house, first we get the idea; then we begin to design the house we want. We start with a blueprint and then build the house. The blueprint determines what kind of house we construct. The same thing happens in any project we undertake. First we have a mental picture, and then we complete the project. Visualize what you would like to accomplish in your life as if you were creating a blueprint. Then take the steps to accomplish what you want.

As a college student, you might visualize yourself in your graduation robe walking across the stage to receive your diploma. You might visualize yourself in the exam room confidently taking the exam. You might see yourself on the job enjoying your future career. You can make a mental picture of what you would like your life to be and then work toward accomplishing your goal.

> "The future first exists in imagination, then planning, then reality."
> R.A. Wilson

Successful Beliefs

Stephen Covey's book *The 7 Habits of Highly Effective People* has been described as one of the most influential books of the 20th century.[8] In 2004, he released a new book called *The 8th Habit: From Effectiveness to Greatness.*[9] These habits are based on beliefs that lead to success.

1. **Be proactive.** Being proactive means accepting responsibility for your life. Covey uses the word "response-ability" for the ability to choose responses. The quality of your life is based on the decisions and responses that you make. Proactive people make things happen through responsibility and initiative. They do not blame circumstances or conditions for their behavior.

2. **Begin with the end in mind.** Know what is important and what you wish to accomplish in your life. To be able to do this, you will need to know your values and goals in life. You will need a clear vision of what you want your life to be and where you are headed.

3. **Put first things first.** Once you have established your goals and vision for the future, you will need to manage yourself to do what is important first. Set priorities so that you can accomplish the tasks that are important to you.

4. **Think win-win.** In human interactions, seek solutions that benefit everyone. Focus on cooperation rather than competition. If everyone feels good about the decision, there is cooperation and harmony. If one person wins and the other loses, the loser becomes angry and resentful and sabotages the outcome.

5. **First seek to understand, then to be understood.** Too often in our personal communications, we try to talk first and listen later. Often we don't really listen: we

use this time to think of our reply. It is best to listen and understand before speaking. Effective communication is one of the most important skills in life.

6. **Synergize.** A simple definition of synergy is that the whole is greater than the sum of its parts. If people can cooperate and have good communication, they can work together as a team to accomplish more than each individual could do separately. Synergy is also part of the creative process.

7. **Sharpen the saw.** Covey shares the story of a man who was trying to cut down a tree with a dull saw. As he struggled to cut the tree, someone suggested that he stop and sharpen the saw. The man said that he did not have time to sharpen the saw, so he continued to struggle. Covey suggests that we need to take time to stop and sharpen the saw. We need to stop working and invest some time in ourselves by staying healthy physically, mentally, spiritually, and socially. We need to take time for self-renewal.

8. **Find your voice, and inspire others to find theirs.** Believe that you can make a positive difference in the world and inspire others to do the same. Covey says that leaders "deal with people in a way that will communicate to them their worth and potential so clearly that they will come to see it in themselves." Accomplishing this ideal begins with developing one's own voice or "unique personal significance."[10]

> ### Successful Beliefs
>
> - Be proactive
> - Begin with the end in mind
> - Put first things first
> - Think win-win
> - First seek to understand, then to be understood
> - Synergize
> - Sharpen the saw
> - Find your voice, and inspire others to find theirs

REFLECTION

List five beliefs that will help you to be successful in the future.

QUIZ

Positive Thinking

Test what you have learned by selecting the correct answers to the following questions.

1. The self-fulfilling prophecy refers to

   a. the power of belief in determining your future.
   b. good fortune in the future.
   c. being able to foretell the future.

2. Positive self-talk results in

   a. lower self-esteem.
   b. overconfidence.
   c. higher self-esteem.

3. The statement "We create all things twice" refers to

   a. doing the task twice to make sure it is done right.
   b. creating and refining.
   c. first making a mental picture and then taking action.

4. A win-win solution means

   a. winning at any cost.
   b. seeking a solution that benefits everyone.
   c. focusing on competition.

5. The statement by Stephen Covey, "Sharpen the saw," refers to

   a. proper tool maintenance.
   b. studying hard to sharpen thinking skills.
   c. investing time to maintain physical and mental health.

Create Your Future

We are responsible for what happens in our lives. We make decisions and choices that create the future. Our behavior leads to success or failure. Too often we believe that we are victims of circumstance. When looking at our lives, we often look for others to blame for how our life is going:

- My grandparents did it to me. I inherited these genes.
- My parents did it to me. My childhood experiences shaped who I am.
- My teacher did it to me. He gave me a poor grade.
- My boss did it to me. She gave me a poor evaluation.
- The government did it to me. All my money goes to taxes.
- Society did it to me. I have no opportunity.

These factors are powerful influences in our lives, but we are still left with choices. Concentration camp survivor Viktor Frankl wrote a book, Man's Search for Meaning, in which he describes his experiences and how he survived his ordeal. His parents, brother, and wife died in the camps. He suffered starvation and torture. Through all of his sufferings and imprisonment, he still maintained that he was a free man because he could make choices.

We who lived in concentration camps can remember the men who walked through the huts comforting others, giving away their last piece of bread. They may have been few in number, but they offer sufficient proof that everything can be taken from a man but one thing: the last of the human freedoms—to choose one's attitude in any given set of circumstances, to choose one's own way. . . . Fundamentally, therefore, any man can, even under such circumstances, decide what shall become of him—mentally and spiritually. He may retain his human dignity even in a concentration camp.[3]

Viktor Frankl could not choose his circumstances at that time, but he did choose his attitude. He decided how he would respond to the situation. He realized that he still had the freedom to make choices. He used his memory and imagination to exercise his freedom. When times were the most difficult, he would imagine that he was in the classroom lecturing to his students about psychology.

He eventually did get out of the concentration camp and became a famous psychiatrist.

Hopefully none of you will ever have to experience the circumstances faced by Viktor Frankl, but we all face challenging situations. It is empowering to think that our behavior is more a function of our decisions rather than our circumstances. It is not productive to look around and find someone to blame for your problems. Psychologist Abraham Maslow says that instead of blaming we should see how we can make the best of the situation.

One can spend a lifetime assigning blame, finding a cause, "out there" for all the troubles that exist. Contrast this with the responsible attitude of confronting the situation, bad or good, and instead of asking, "What caused the trouble? Who was to blame?", asking, "How can I handle the present situation to make the best of it?"[4]

Author Stephen Covey suggests that we look at the word responsibility as "response-ability."[5] It is the ability to choose responses and make decisions about the future. When you are dealing with a problem, it is useful to ask yourself what decisions you made that led to the problem. How did you create the situation? If you created the problem, you can create a solution.

At times, you may ask, "How did I create this?", and find that the answer is that you did not create the situation. We certainly do not create earthquakes or hurricanes, for example. But we do create or at least contribute to many of the things that happen to us. Even if you did not create your circumstances, you can create your reaction to the situation. In the case of an earthquake, you can decide to panic or find the best course of action at the moment.

Stephen Covey believes that we can use our resourcefulness and initiative in dealing with most problems. When his children were growing up and they asked him how to solve a certain problem, he would say, "Use your R and I!". He meant resourcefulness and initiative. He notes that adults can use this R and I to get a good job.

But the people who end up with the good jobs are the proactive ones who are solutions to problems, not problems themselves, who seize the initiative to do whatever is necessary, consistent with correct principles, to get the job done.[6]

Use your resourcefulness and initiative to create the future that you want.

How can you create the future you want for yourself?

JOURNAL ENTRIES

Exploring Your Multiple Intelligences

Go to http://www.collegesuccess1.com/JournalEntries.htm for Word files of the Journal Entries.

Success over the Internet

Visit the College Success Website at http://www.collegesuccess1.com/

The *College Success Website* is continually updated with new topics and links to the material presented in this chapter. Topics include

- Multiple intelligences
- Emotional intelligence
- Goal setting

Contact your instructor if you have any problems in accessing the *College Success Website.**

_____

_____

_____

_____

_____

_____

_____

_____

_____

_____

_____

_____

_____

_____

_____

_____

_____

_____

Informational Interview Assignment

Students will interview someone in a career field of interest to them. **The interview must take place in person at the interviewee's place of employment. In addition, interviewees can NOT be family members or ASU faculty, staff or students. The individual must be employed outside of their home.** See the informational interview handout from career services for ways to find someone to interview and sample questions for the interviews.

There are a number of ways you can identify candidates for this assignment and start building your professional network!

- Handshake
- LinkedIn
- ASU Career Services
- Indeed.com
- Google

After interviewing the individual, answer the following questions with an in-depth and thoughtful essay (3-4 sentences per question). All papers are expected to be integrative essays done in paragraph format (4-5 sentences per paragraph, introduction, and conclusion). Essays should be **500 words** (word count should be included on the document). Follow appropriate formatting such as **double-spacing and 12-point font**. An interview with someone not eligible (see above criteria) will result in a deduction of points.

**To earn credit for this assignment, you must submit the individual's business card AND a picture of yourself at the interviewee's place of employment. If the individual does not have a business card, have the interviewee email the Instructor directly following the completion of your interview. Failure to turn in these two components will lead to the student earning no credit on this assignment!

One point extra credit for copying the Instructor on an email Thank You message to the person you interviewed.

At the top of the essay, list the interview information (see below):
Interview Information:
Name:
Occupation & Place of Employment:
Contact Information:

Reflection Questions to be answered in the essay:
- What was your impression of the career PRIOR to the interview? What assumptions did you have about that career?
- How did the interview go? (Reflect on comfort level, interaction in the interview, time allotted, etc.)
- What factual information did you learn about the career that was of particular interest or surprising to you (factual information about the specific career)?
- What personal information did you learn about the career that was of particular interest or surprising to you (personal information relates to personal satisfactions, disappointments, experience-based opinions of the interviewee)?
- How has your view of this career changed? What are your next steps for finding out additional information about the career path you would like to follow (this does not have to be in line with this career)?

UNI 150 Final Presentation Critique   Your Name: _____

Ensure that at least eight unique peers are included in the form below. Write two to three sentences below each sentence elaborating on your reasoning.

The most creative and original presentation was given by _____ because . . .

The most engaging presentation was given by _____ because . . .

The person who demonstrated the most growth over the past semester was _____ because . . .

The presentation that surprised me was _____ because . . .

The most prepared presenter was _____ because . . .

The person who created the most visually appealing presentation was _____ because . . .

The presentation that needed the most improvement was given by _____ because . . .

The presentation that was least engaging was given by _____ because . . .

The least prepared presenter was _____ because . . .

The presentation that was most authentic and genuine was given by _____ because . . .

The funniest presentation given today was by _____ because . . .

The presentation I will remember six months from now is _____ because . . .

The overall best presentation was given by _____ because . . .

If I were to rank the top three presentations, I would rank #1 _____

#2 _____ and #3 _____

Extra Credit – Event Verification

To earn extra credit by attending a sanctioned event (please speak with your instructor for a full list of sanctioned events), please complete the following verification form and include a photo of you from the event. You'll need to print this form and get it signed by one of the event coordinators.

Your Name:

Date of Event:

Event Title:

Event Location:

Event Description:

Your Reflection (at least 250 words):

Event Coordinator Signature: _____

Event Coordinator Name: _____

Event Coordinator Title & Contact Info: _____

Extra Credit – Event Verification

To earn extra credit by attending a sanctioned event (please speak with your instructor for a full list of sanctioned events), please complete the following verification form and include a photo of you from the event. You'll need to print this form and get it signed by one of the event coordinators.

Your Name:

Date of Event:

Event Title:

Event Location:

Event Description:

Your Reflection (at least 250 words):

Event Coordinator Signature: _____

Event Coordinator Name: _____

Event Coordinator Title & Contact Info: _____

Extra Credit – Event Verification

To earn extra credit by attending a sanctioned event (please speak with your instructor for a full list of sanctioned events), please complete the following verification form and include a photo of you from the event. You'll need to print this form and get it signed by one of the event coordinators.

Your Name: **Date of Event:**

Event Title: **Event Location:**

Event Description:

Your Reflection (at least 250 words):

Event Coordinator Signature: _____

Event Coordinator Name: _____

Event Coordinator Title & Contact Info: _____

Extra Credit – Event Verification

To earn extra credit by attending a sanctioned event (please speak with your instructor for a full list of sanctioned events), please complete the following verification form and include a photo of you from the event. You'll need to print this form and get it signed by one of the event coordinators.

Your Name:

Date of Event:

Event Title:

Event Location:

Event Description:

Your Reflection (at least 250 words):

Event Coordinator Signature: _____

Event Coordinator Name: _____

Event Coordinator Title & Contact Info: _____

Acredolo, C., & O'Connor, J. (1991). On the difficulty of detecting cognitive uncertainty. *Human Development, 34*, 204–223.

Allport, G. W. (1954). *The nature of prejudice.* Cambridge, MA: Addison-Wesley.

Allport, G. W. (1979). *The nature of prejudice* (3rd ed.). Reading, MA: Addison-Wesley.

Amir, Y. (1969). Contact hypothesis in ethnic relations. *Psychological Bulletin, 71*, 319–342.

Amir, Y. (1976). The role of intergroup contact in change of prejudice and ethnic relations. In P. A. Katz (Ed.), *Towards the elimination of racism* (pp. 245–308). New York: Pergamon Press.

Anderson, M., & Fienberg, S. (2000). Race and ethnicity and the controversy over the US Census. *Current Sociology, 48*(3), 87–110.

Aronson, E., Wilson, T. D., & Akert, R. M. (2013). *Social psychology* (8th ed.). Upper Saddle River, NJ: Pearson/Prentice Hall.

Association of American Colleges & Universities (AAC&U). (2002). *Greater expectations: A new vision for learning as a nation goes to college.* Washington, DC: Author.

Association of American Colleges & Universities (AAC&U). (2004). *Our students' best work.* Washington, DC: Author.

Baron, et. al. (2008). *Social psychology* (12th ed). Boston, MA: Allyn & Bacon.

Belenky, M. F., Clinchy, B., Goldberger, N. R., & Tarule, J. M. (1986). *Women's ways of knowing: The development of self, voice, and mind.* New York: Basic Books.

Blair, I. V. (2002). The malleability of automatic stereotypes and prejudice. *Personality and Social Psychology Review, 6*(3), 242–261.

Bligh, D. A. (2000). *What's the use of lectures?* San Francisco: Jossey Bass.

Bok, D. (2006). *Our underachieving colleges: A candid look at how much students learn and why they should be learning more.* Princeton, NJ: Princeton University Press.

Bridgeman, B. (2003). *Psychology and evolution: The origins of mind.* Thousand Oaks, CA: Sage Publications.

Bronfenbrenner, U. (Ed.). (2005). *Making human beings human: Bioecological perspectives on human development.* Thousand Oaks, CA: Sage.

Brookfield, S. D. (1987). *Developing critical thinkers.* San Francisco, CA: Jossey-Bass.

Brooks, I. (2009). *Organisational behaviour* (4th ed.). Englewood Cliffs, NJ: Prentice Hall.

Brown, T. D., Dane, F. C., & Durham, M. D. (1998). Perception of race and ethnicity. *Journal of Social Behavior and Personality, 13*(2), 295–306.

Brown, K. T., Brown, T. N., Jackson, J. S., Sellers, R. M., & Manuel, W. J. (2003). Teammates on and off the field? Contact with Black teammates and the racial attitudes of White student athletes. *Journal of Applied Social Psychology, 33*, 1379–1403.

Cabrera, A., Nora, A., Terenzini, P., Pascarella, E., & Hagedorn, L. S. (1999). Campus racial climate and the adjustment of students to college: A comparison between White students and African American students. *The Journal of Higher Education, 70*(2), 134–160.

Caplan, P. J., & Caplan, J. B. (2008). *Thinking critically about research on sex and gender* (3rd ed.). New York: HarperCollins College Publishers.

Carlson, et al. (1990). Individual differences in the behavioral effects of stressors attributable to lateralized differences in mesocortical dopamine systems. *Society for Neuroscience Abstracts, 16*, 233.

Ciancotto, J. (2005). *Hispanic and Latino same-sex couple households in the United States: A report from the 2000 Census.* New York: The National Gay and Lesbian Task Force Policy Institute and the National Latino/a Coalition for Justice.

Colombo, G., Cullen, R., & Lisle, B. (2013). *Rereading America: Cultural contexts for critical thinking and writing* (9th ed.). Boston, MA: Bedford Books of St. Martin's Press.

Cook, S. W. (1984). Cooperative interaction in multiethnic contexts. In N. Miller & M. B. Brewer (Eds.), *Groups in contact: The psychology of desegregation* (pp. 291–302). New York: Academic Press.

Cuseo, J. B. (1996). *Cooperative learning: A pedagogy for addressing contemporary challenges and critical issues in higher education.* Stillwater, OK: New Forums Press.

Cuseo, J. B., et al. (2013). *Thriving in community college & beyond: Strategies for academic success and personal development.* Dubuque, IA: Kendall Hunt Publishing Company.

DeNavas-Walt, C., Proctor, B. D., & Smith, J. C. (2013). *Income, poverty, and health insurance coverage in the United States, 2012.* U.S. Census Bureau, Current Population Reports, P60-245, Washington, DC: U.S. Government Printing Office.

Dessel, A. (2012). Effects of intergroup dialogue: Public school teachers and sexual orientation prejudice. *Small Group Research, 41*(5), 556–592.

Dolan, M., & Romney, L. (2015, June 27). "Law in California is now a right for all." *Los Angeles Times*, pp. A1, A8.

Donald, J. G. (2002). *Learning to think: Disciplinary perspectives.* San Francisco: Jossey-Bass.

Dovidio, J. F., Eller, A., & Hewstone, M. (2011). Improving intergroup relations through direct, extended and other forms of indirect contact. *Group Processes & Intergroup Relations, 14*, 147–160.

Dryden, G., & Vos, J. (1999). *The learning revolution: To change the way the world learns.* Torrance, CA and Auckland, New Zealand: The Learning Web.

Education Commission of the States. (1995). *Making quality count in undergraduate education.* Denver, CO: ECS Distribution Center.

Education Commission of the States. (1996). *Bridging the gap between neuroscience and education.* Denver, CO: Author.

Eimers, M. T., & Pike, G. R. (1997). Minority and nonminority adjustment to college: Differences or similarities. *Research in Higher Education, 38*(1), 77–97.

Erickson, B. L., Peters, C. B., & Strommer, D. W. (2006). *Teaching first-year college students.* San Francisco: Jossey-Bass.

Family Care Foundation. (2015). *If the world were a village of 100 people.* Retrieved from http://www.familycare.org/special-interest/if-the-world-were-a-village-of-100-people/.

Feagin, J. R., & Feagin, C. B. (2007). *Racial and ethnic relations* (8th ed.). Englewood Cliffs, NJ: Prentice Hall.

Fixman, C. S. (1990). The foreign language needs of U.S. based corporations. *Annals of the American Academy of Political and Social Science, 511*, 25–46.

Friedman, T. L. (2005). *The world is flat: A brief history of the twenty-first century: Revitalizing the civic mission of schools.* Alexandria, VA: Farrar, Strauss & Giroux.

Gorski, P. C. (1995–2009). *Key characteristics of a multicultural curriculum.* Critical Multicultural Pavilion: Multicultural Curriculum Reform (An EdChange Project). Retrieved from www.edchange.org/multicultural/curriculum/characteristics.html.

Gould, E. & Wething, H. (2013). Health care, the market and consumer choice. *Inquiry, 50*(1), 85–86.

Gurin, P. (1999). New research on the benefits of diversity in college and beyond: An empirical analysis. *Diversity Digest* (spring). Retrieved from http://www.diversityweb.org/Digest/Sp99/benefits.html.

Harris, A. (2010). Leading system transformation. *School Leadership and Management, 30* (July).

Hart Research Associates. (2013). *It takes more than a major: Employer priorities for college learning and student success*. Washington, DC: Author.

HERI (Higher Education Research Institute). (2013). *Your first college year survey 2012*. Los Angeles, CA: Cooperative Institutional Research Program, University of California-Los Angeles.

HERI (Higher Education Research Institute). (2014). *Your first college year survey 2014*. Los Angeles, CA: Cooperative Institutional Research Program, University of California-Los Angeles.

Hugenberg, K., & Bodenhausen, G. V. (2003). Facing prejudice: Implicit prejudice and the perception of facial threat. *Psychological Science, 14*, 640–643.

IES Abroad News. (2002). *Study abroad: A lifetime of benefits.* Retrieved from www.iesabroad .org/study-abroad/news/study-abroad-lifetime-benefits.

Jablonski, N. G., & Chaplin, G. (2002). Skin deep. *Scientific American, (October)*, 75–81.

Johnson, D., Johnson, R., & Smith, K. (1998). Cooperative learning returns to college: What evidence is there that it works? *Change, 30*, 26–35.

Judd, C. M., Ryan, C. S., & Parke, B. (1991). Accuracy in the judgment of in-group and out-group variability. *Journal of Personality and Social Psychology, 61*, 366–379.

Kaufmann, N. L., Martin, J. M., & Weaver, H. D. (1992). *Students abroad: Strangers at home: Education for a global society.* Yarmouth, ME: Intercultural Press.

Kelly, K. (1994). *Out of control: The new biology of machines, social systems, and the economic world.* Reading, MA: Addison-Wesley.

Kitchener, K., Wood, P., & Jensen, L. (2000, August). *Curricular, co-curricular, and institutional influence on real-world problem-solving.* Paper presented at the annual meeting of the American Psychological Association, Boston.

Kochlar, R., Fry, R., & Taylor, P. (2011). Wealth gaps rise to record highs between Whites, Blacks, Hispanics, twenty-to-one. *Pew Research Social and Demographics Trends* (July). Retrieved from http://www.pewsocialtrends.org/2011/07/26/wealth-gaps-rise-to-record-highs-between-whites-blacks-hispanics/

Lancaster, L., et al. (2002). *When generations collide: Who they are. Why they clash.* New York: HarperCollins.

Latané, B., Liu, J. H., Nowak, A., Bonevento, N., & Zheng, L. (1995). Distance matters: Physical space and social impact. *Personality and Social Psychology Bulletin, 21*, 795–805.

Leung, A. K., Maddux, W. W., Galinsky, A. D., & Chie-yue, C. (2008). Multicultural experience enhances creativity: The when and how. *American Psychologist, 63*(3), 169–181.

Lewis, M., Paul, G. W., & Fennig, C. D. (Eds.). (2014). *Ethnologue: Languages of the world* (17th ed.). Dallas, TX: SIL International. Online version: http://www.ethnologue.com.

Luhman, R. (2007). *The sociological outlook.* Lanham, MD: Rowman & Littlefield.

Maddux, W. W. & Galinsky, A. D. (2009). Cultural borders and mental barriers: the relationship between living abroad and creativity. *Journal of Personality and Social Psychology, 96*(5), 1047–1061.

Magolda, M. B. B. (1992). *Knowing and reasoning in college.* San Francisco, CA: Jossey-Bass.

Mendez, F., Krahn, T., Schrack, B., Krahn, A. M., Veeramah, K., Woerner, A., Fomine, F. L. M., Bradman, N., Thomas, M., Karafet, T., & Hammer, M. (2013). An African American paternal lineage adds an extremely ancient root to the human Y chromosome phylogenetic tree. *The American Journal of Human Genetics, 92*, 454–459.

Meredith, M. (2011). *Born in Africa: The quest for the origins of human life.* New York: Public Affairs.

Nagda, B. R., Gurin, P., & Johnson, S. M. (2005). Living, doing and thinking diversity: How does pre-college diversity experience affect first-year students' engagement with college diversity? In R. S. Feldman (Ed.), *Improving the first year of college: Research and practice* (pp. 73–110). Mahwah, NJ: Lawrence Erlbaum.

Nathan, R. (2005). *My freshman year: What a professor learned by becoming a student.* London: Penguin.

National Association of Colleges and Employers (NACE). (2003). *Job outlook 2003 survey.* Bethlehem, PA: Author.

National Association of Colleges & Employers. (2014). *Job Outlook 2014 survey.* Bethlehem, PA: Author.

National Center for Education Statistics. (2011). *Digest of education statistics, table 237. Total fall enrollment in degree-granting institutions, by level of student, sex, attendance status, and race/ethnicity: Selected years, 1976 through 2010.* Alexandria, VA: U.S. Department of Education. Retrieved from http://neces.ed/gov/programs/digest/d11/tables/dt11_237.asp.

National Survey of Women Voters. (1998). *Autumn overview report conducted by DYG Inc.* Retrieved from http:www.diversityweb.org/research_and_trends/research_evaluation_impact_/campus_community_connections/ national_poll.cfm.

Nhan, D. (2012). "Census: Minorities constitute 37 percent of U.S. population." *National Journal: The Next America—Demographics 2012.* Retrieved from http:www.nationaljournal.com/thenextamerica/demographics/census-minorities-constitute-37-percent-of-u-s-population-20120517.

Nora, A., & Cabrera, A. (1996). The role of perceptions of prejudice and discrimination on the adjustment of minority college students. *The Journal of Higher Education, 67*(2), 119–148.

Office of Research. (1994). *What employers expect of college graduates: International knowledge and second language skills.* Washington, DC: Office of Educational Research and Improvement, U.S. Department of Education.

Olson, L. (2007). What does "ready" mean? *Education Week, 40,* 7–12.

Pascarella, E. T. (2001, November/December). Cognitive growth in college: Surprising and reassuring findings from the National Study of Student Learning. *Change,* 21–27.

Pascarella, E. T., & Terenzini, P. T. (2005). *How college affects students: A third decade of research* (Vol. 2). San Francisco, CA: Jossey-Bass.

Pascarella, E., Palmer, B., Moye, M., & Pierson, C. (2001). Do diversity experiences influence the development of critical thinking? *Journal of College Student Development, 42*(3), 257–291.

Peoples, J., & Bailey, G. (2011). *Humanity: An introduction to cultural anthropology.* Belmont, CA: Wadsworth, Cengage Learning. Retrieved from http://www.aacu.org/leap/documents/2009-employersurvey.pdf.

Pettigrew, T. F. (1997). Generalized intergroup contact effects on prejudice. *Personality and Social Psychology Bulletin, 23,* 173–185.

Pettigrew, T. F. (1998). Intergroup contact theory. *Annual Review of Psychology, 49,* 65–85.

Pettigrew, T. F., & Tropp, L. R. (2000). Does intergroup contact reduce prejudice? Recent meta-analytic findings. In S. Oskamp (Ed.), *Reducing prejudice and discrimination* (pp. 93–114). Mahwah, NJ: Lawrence Erlbaum Associates.

Pinker, S. (2000). *The language instinct: The new science of language and mind.* New York: Perennial.

Pratto, F., Liu, J. H., Levin, S., Sidanius, J., Shih, M., Bachrach, H., & Hegarty, P. (2000). Social dominance orientation and the legitimization of inequality across cultures. *Journal of Cross-Cultural Psychology, 31,* 369–409.

Reid, G. B. R., & Hetherington, R. (2010). *The climate connection: Climate change and modern evolution.* Cambridge, UK: Cambridge University Press.

Roediger, H. L., Dudai, Y., & Fitzpatrick, S. M. (2007). *Science of memory: concepts.* New York, NY: Oxford University Press.

Shah, A. (2009). *Global issues: Poverty facts and stats.* Retrieved from http://www.globalissues.org/artoc;e/26/poverty-facts-and-stats.

Sherif, M., Harvey, D. J., White, B. J., Hood, W. R., & Sherif, C. W. (1961). *The Robbers' cave experiment*. Norman, OK: Institute of Group Relations.

Shiraev, E. D., & Levy, D. (2013). *Cross-cultural psychology: Critical thinking and contemporary applications* (5th ed.).Upper Saddle River, NJ: Pearson Education.

Sidanius, J., Levin, S., Liu, H., & Pratto, F. (2000). Social dominance orientation, anti-egalitarianism, and the political psychology of gender: An extension and cross-cultural replication. *European Journal of Social Psychology, 30*, 41–67.

Slavin, R. E. (1995). *Cooperative learning* (2nd ed.). Boston: Allyn & Bacon.

Smith, D. (1997). How diversity influences learning. *Liberal Education, 83*(2), 42–48.

Smith, D. G., Guy, L., Gerbrick, G. L., Figueroa, M. A., Watkins, G. H., Levitan, T., Moore, L. C., Merchant, P. A., Beliak, H. D., & Figueroa, B. (1997). *Diversity works: The emerging picture of how students benefit.* Washington, DC: Association of American Colleges and Universities.

Stangor, C., Sechrist, G. B., & Jost, J. T. (2001). Changing racial beliefs by providing consensus information. *Personality and Social Psychology Bulletin, 27*, 484–494.

Stoltz, P. G. (2014). *Grit: The new science of what it takes to persevere, flourish, succeed.* San Luis Obispo: Climb Strong Press.

Taylor, S. E., Peplau, L. A., & Sears, D. O. (2006). *Social psychology* (12th ed.). Upper Saddle River, NJ: Pearson/Prentice-Hall.

Thompson, A., & Cuseo, J. (2014). *Diversity and the college experience*. Dubuque, IA: Kendall Hunt.

U.S. Census Bureau. (2008). *Bureau of Labor Statistics*. Washington, DC: Author.

United States Census Bureau. (2013a, July 8). *About race.* Retrieved from http://www.census.gov/topics/population/race/about.html.

U.S. Census Bureau. (2013b). *Poverty.* Retrieved from https://www.census.gov/hhes/www/poverty/data/threshld/.

United States Census Bureau. (2015, March). *Projections of the size and composition of the U.S. population: 2014 to 2060.* Retrieved from http://www.census.gov/content/dam/Census/library/publications/2015/demo/p25-1143.pdf.

Wabash National Study of Liberal Arts Education. (2007). *Liberal arts outcomes.* Retrieved from http:www.liberalarts.wabash.edu/ study-overview/.

Wheelright, J. (2005, March). Human, study thyself. *Discover*, 39–45.

Willis, J. (2006). *Research-based strategies to ignite student learning: Insights from a neurologist and classroom teacher*. Alexandria, VA: ASCD.

Zajonc, R. B. (1968). Attitudinal effects of mere exposure. *Journal of Personality and Social Psychology, 9*, Monograph Supplement, No. 2, Part 2.

Zajonc, R. B. (1970). Brainwash: Familiarity breeds comfort. *Psychology Today*, (February), 32–35, 60–62.

Zajonc, R. B. (2001). Mere exposure: A gateway to the subliminal. *Current Directions in Psychological Science, 10*, 224–228.

INDEX